Nature Walks
in Northern Vermont
and the Champlain Valley

Elizabeth Bassett

APPALACHIAN MOUNTAIN CLUB BOOKS
BOSTON, MASSACHUSETTS

Cover Photograph: Larry Lefever from Grant Heilman
All photographs by the author unless otherwise noted
Cover Design: Elisabeth Leydon Brady
Book Design: Carol Bast Tyler

Distributed by The Globe Pequot Press, Inc., Old Saybrook, CT

Library of Congress Cataloging-in-Publication Data
Bassett, Elizabeth
Nature walks in northern Vermont and the
Champlain Valley / Elizabeth Bassett.
p. cm.
"An AMC nature walks book."
Includes bibliographical references (p.) and index.
ISBN 1-878239-58-9 (alk. paper)
1. Walking—Vermont–Guidebooks. 2.Walking—Champlain Valley—
Guidebooks. 3.Nature study—Vermont—Guidebooks. 4. Nature study—
Champlain Valley—Guidebooks. 5. Vermont—Guidebooks. 6. Champlain
Velley—Guidbooks. I. Title.
GV199.42.V4B39   1998
917-43'10445—dc21   98-3375
CIP

The paper used in this publication meets the minimum requirements of the
American National Standard for Information Sciences—Permanence of Paper
for Printed Library Materials, ANSI Z39.48–1984.∞

**Due to changes in conditions,
use of the information in this book
is at the sole risk of the user.**

Printed on recycled paper using soy-based inks.
Printed in the United States of America.

10 9 8 7 6 5 4 3 2 1   98 99 00 01 02 03

Contents

Map of Walk Locations viii
Acknowledgments x
Introduction xi
How to Use This Book xii
Quick Reference Chart: Walks and Highlights xvi

Northern Lake Champlain and the Islands 1
1. Missisquoi National Wildlife Refuge 1
Swanton

2. Burton Island State Park 8
St. Albans Bay

3. Knight Point State Park 14
North Hero

4. North Hero State Park 19
North Hero

5. Ed Weed Fish Culture Station .25
Grand Isle

Burlington and Central Lake Champlain 31
6. Old Mill Park 31
Jericho

7. Intervale 36
Burlington

8. Ethan Allen Homestead 42
Burlington

9. Winooski Nature Trail, Winooski One, and Salmon Hole . . .49
Winooski and Burlington

10. East Woods Natural Area 55
South Burlington

11. Mud Pond Conservation Land 60
Williston

12. Colchester Bog Natural Area .65
Colchester

13. Delta Park 71
Colchester

14. Sunny Hollow 76
Colchester

15. Colchester Pond 82
Colchester

Southern Chittenden County .88
16. Shelburne Farms 88
Shelburne

17. LaPlatte River Marsh Natural Area 94
Shelburne

18. Allen Hill 100
Shelburne

19. Williams Woods Natural Area 106
Charlotte

20. Pease Mountain Natural Area 111
Charlotte

21. Mt. Philo State Park 117
Charlotte

Southern Champlain Valley .123
22. Kingsland Bay State Park 123
Ferrisburg

23. Button Bay State Park 129
Ferrisburg

24. Dead Creek Wildlife Management Area 135
Addison

25. Snake Mountain Wildlife Management Area 141
Weybridge and Addison

26. Mount Independence Historical Site 147
Orwell

27. Shaw Mountain Natural Area .152
Benson

Central Green Mountains and Valleys 158
28. Green Mountain Audubon Nature Center 158
Huntington

29. Mad River Greenway 165
Waitsfield

30. Robert Frost Interpretive Trail 170
Ripton

31. Abbey Pond Trail 176
Ripton

32. Leicester Hollow and Chandler Ridge 181
Brandon

33. Texas Falls 187
Hancock

Montpelier Area 193
34. Rock of Ages Granite Quarry .193
Barre

35. Hubbard Park 198
Montpelier

36. North Branch Nature Center and North 204
    Branch River Park
Montpelier

Waterbury/Stowe Area 211
37. Tundra Trail, Mount Mansfield 211
Stowe

38. Sterling Falls Gorge Natural Area 217
Stowe

39. History Hike, Little River State Park 223
Waterbury

40. Stevenson Brook Nature Trail, Little River State Park 231
Waterbury

New York

41. Point au Roche State Park 236
Plattsburgh

42. Ausable Chasm 242
Ausable Chasm

43. Coon Mountain Preserve 248
Westport

Organizations: Useful Names and Addresses 253
Bibliography 257
About the Author 259
About the AMC 260
Index 263
Alphabetical Listing of Areas 268

*To my parents who showed me
how to love nature and her bounties.*

Map of Walk Locations

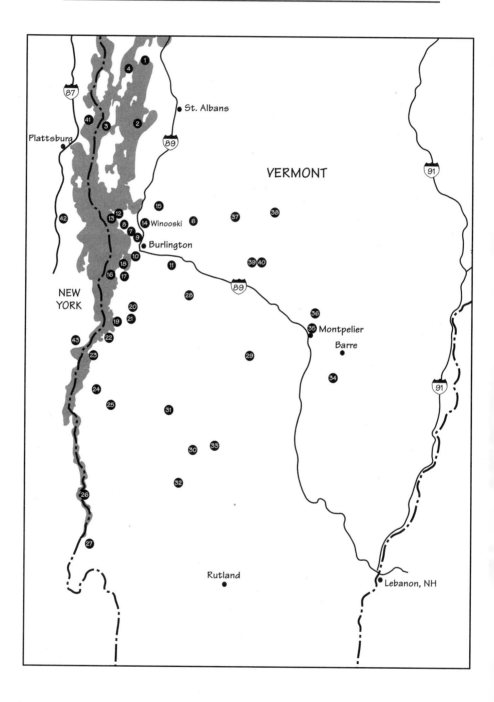

1. Missisquoi National Wildlife Refuge
2. Burton Island State Park
3. Knight Point State Park
4. North Hero State Park
5. Ed Weed Fish Culture Station
6. Old Mill Park
7. Intervale
8. Ethan Allen Homestead
9. Winooski Nature Trail, Winooski One, and Salmon Hole
10. East Woods Natural Area
11. Mud Pond Conseravtion Land
12. Colchester Bog Natural Area
13. Delta Park
14. Sunny Hollow
15. Colchester Pond
16. Shelburne Farms
17. LaPlatte River Marsh Natural Area
18. Allen Hill
19. Williams Woods Natural Area
20. Pease Mountain Natural Area
21. Mt. Philo State Park
22. Kingsland Bay State Park
23. Button Bay State Park
24. Dead Creek Wildlife Management Area
25. Snake Mountain Wildlife Management Area
26. Mount Independence Historical Site
27. Shaw Mountain Natural Area
28. Green Mountain Audubon Nature Center
29. Mad River Greenway
30. Robert Frost Interpretive Trail
31. Abbey Pond
32. Leicester Hollow and Chandler Ridge
33. Texas Falls
34. Rock of Ages Granite Quarry
35. Hubbard Park
36. North Branch Nature Center and North Branch River Park
37. Tundra Trail, Mount Mansfield
38. Sterling Falls Gorge Natural Area
39. History Hike, Little River State Park
40. Stevenson Brook Nature Trail, Little River State Park
41. Point au Roche State Park
42. Ausable Chasm
43. Coon Mountain Preserve

Acknowledgments

I'd like to thank the many dedicated and knowledgeable naturalists, conservationists, rangers, and caretakers who materialized from every quarter. Wisdom flowed at parks and preserves, in libraries, and from many organizations. This book is a testament to their generosity.

I am particularly grateful for the kindness of Norman Pellett, Walter Poleman, Rick Paradis, Maryke Gillis, Everett Marshall, Meg Smith, Jennifer Ely, Chuck Woessner, Gary Salmon, Jessica Dillner, Gar Anderson, Patricia Stone, Rick Bruce, Daphne Makinson, Steven Robbins, Mark LaBarr, Bill Howland, Chip Darmstadt, and Geoff Beyer. Thanks also to Elizabeth and Josie, owners of the Flying Pig Bookstore in Charlotte.

I am grateful to my editors, Gordon Hardy and Mark Russell, who held my hand (via e-mail) through the process.

Most of all, I must thank my husband, John, who cheerfully whipped up exotic risottos and vats of fresh corn chowder while I neglected the domestic scene, and Putnam and Victoria, our children, who often endured long waits for homework help. Thanks also to Lily, our chocolate Lab, who kept me company on many a walk.

Introduction

This beautiful, mostly rural part of the country can make us complacent. Sometimes we need to be reminded of our good fortune. This book contains forty-three such reminders as we explore rivers, streams, lakes, ponds, wetlands, bog, granite quarry, sand plain, gorge, chasm, Arctic tundra, sandy beach, flood-plain forest, Revolutionary War site, fossils, microphotographs of snowflakes, fish elevator, and fish hatchery.

Most of the walks are relatively short, focusing on the journey rather than the destination. Only a few are real hikes. While many trails lead to panoramic views or picturesque settings, the walks are about discovery. Take some time and curiosity and venture out.

A nature walk requires no special equipment. Sturdy shoes are adequate for most walks. Where hiking boots or waterproof boots are more appropriate, I have recommended them.

For longer walks it's a good idea to take an emergency kit. The contents should take care of most commonly encountered circumstances: compass; windbreaker or rain jacket; plastic bag containing waterproof matches, candle, first-aid kit, and toilet paper; seasonally, hat or earband and gloves or insect repellent; sunscreen; whistle; high-energy snacks; water; and binoculars. I carry a set of chemical hand warmers and a two-ounce emergency blanket the size of a deck of cards. Even in July, Vermont and northern New York can be cold places. Make sure also to bring appropriate maps.

Dress in layers for warmth and flexibility. Remember, cotton stays damp from sweat or rain. Long pants are good protection against poison ivy, brambles, or ticks. At the moment the serious tick-borne diseases of southern New England are rare in this region.

Rabies, however, has appeared in raccoons, foxes, and skunks. While rabid wildlife is rare, be mindful of the threat. Make sure your pet has a current rabies vaccination. If you see an animal acting strangely, give it wide berth and report it to the nearest game warden.

While Vermont is one of the safest states in the nation, it pays to be sensible. Remoteness has costs as well as benefits. If you walk alone make sure someone knows where you are and when you expect to return. Anyone can fall and get hurt. Dogs offer a measure of security. I have noted where dogs are not permitted or if they need to be leashed.

How to Use This Book

The ratings are for walks, not hikes. A difficult walk might include steep hills or sections of rocky footing, neither of which would challenge an experienced hiker. If a walk is rated easy, it is manageable by young children or an older walker. The time allowances are generous to encourage exploration.

Do bring the children. With their slow pace, curiosity, and proximity to the ground they often see things that adults miss. My children walked many of these trails when they were quite young.

The bibliography does not include an obvious category, common guidebooks to wildflowers, birds, and trees. There are several popular series and each has its advocates. I urge you to spend time in a bookstore looking at these books carefully. They use different systems, focus on different information, and assume different knowledge in the user. The choice is a personal one.

The Quick Reference Chart (p. xvi) identifies particular things you might hope to see on a walk. While every walk has plants, animals, and geology, the chart is meant to highlight features that are significant, abundant, or outstanding on a walk.

The distances to the trailhead were measured in one or both of our family cars, with and without snow tires. To my dismay, I got some disparate results. You will not get lost with these directions, but you may want to slow down before the intersections.

Nearly all of the walks are on public land, and most of them have no admission fee. Vermont state parks charge a modest fee, and there may be an admission fee at New York's Point au Roche State Park in the future. The Tundra Trail, atop Mount Mansfield, is free but both the Toll Road and the gondola are privately maintained and charge users. It is certainly possible, but outside the parameters of this book, to hike up Mount Mansfield. Both Ausable Chasm and the Rock of Ages granite quarry charge admission. To omit them would have been a shame, as they are both fascinating places. An abandoned quarry at the Rock of Ages Visitor Center can be viewed without charge.

Vermont State Parks

Vermont state parks open for the season in late May. Kingsland Bay, Knight Point, and North Hero close after Labor Day; Mt. Philo, Little River, and Button Bay close after Columbus Day weekend. Ferry service between Burton Island and Kill Kare State Park runs from Memorial Day weekend through Labor Day weekend. For exact dates call the Vermont Department of Forests, Parks, and Recreation or the park itself (see Organizations: Useful Names and Addresses, p. 253).

Day-use parks are open from 10:00 A.M. until sunset. Restrooms and phones are available. No dogs are allowed in day-use areas. Park amenities include swimming, boating, picnic tables and shelters, camping, play areas for children, and, at Burton Island, a full range of marine services.

Daily admission is $2.00 for adults, age fourteen and over. Children ages four to thirteen are charged $1.50. Vermont resident seniors presenting the Green Mountain Passport are admitted free. A ten-punch, transferable pass represents a 35 percent discount and can be used over several seasons. Frequent park users may buy an $85.00 Vehicle Season Pass for unlimited admissions by all passengers in the vehicle.

Campers registered at any Vermont state park may use day facilities at any other park in the system (except Sand Bar) for the duration of their stay.

Vermont state parks receive no General Fund tax money for operations and maintenance. Costs are covered exclusively by park fees and the leases of seven ski areas located on state land.

The parks are closed and facilities unavailable off-season. Gates are locked, but the land may be accessed on foot. Please do not block the park gates.

Winooski Valley Park District

The district manages eleven properties on 1,722 acres, including more than twelve miles of shoreline, in seven towns of the lower Winooski River valley. The properties are open, free of charge, from dawn until dusk daily. All dogs must be leashed. The district properties offer nature trails for walking and cross-country skiing, picnic facilities, public garden plots, and canoe and fishing access.

The Last Word

Nature is a dynamic force. The ice storm of January, 1998, swept across many of the places described in the book. More than an inch of icy glaze coated Grand Isle and Chittenden Counties, snapping trees, power lines, and utility poles. Tens of thousands of homes were without power for almost a week. Red pines on Mt. Philo became jagged poles. For several days, the diesel generator at the Ed Weed Fish Hatchery in Grand Isle kept the fish alive. The historic Gordon-Center House, adjacent to the fish hatchery and home of the Lake Champlain Basin Program, was gutted by fire, possibly caused by the use of a generator to power the building's furnace.

The legacy of the storm will likely be evident for decades. Final assessments of the storm's impact may take years as tens of thousands of trees struggle to survive and re-establish adequate canopies. As you tour the walks listed in the book, look for evidence of both Mother Nature's fury and her ability to recuperate from such natural disasters.

The final selection of walks was difficult. In a region where northern hardwood forests dominate and Lake Champlain sits boldly astride the map, variety and balance were considerations. Off-season access was another. Don't put this book on the shelf in November—many of these outings are accessible in winter boots or on cross-country skis or snowshoes. Snow is the perfect canvas for animal tracks. Identifying trees without leaves is easier than I'd imagined and, best of all, there are no bugs!

How, my friends asked, could I encourage people to visit some of our favorite places? My hope is that the beauty and bounty of the landscape and an understanding of it will inspire each of us to become more active in efforts to conserve and preserve these precious resources. Individuals can make a difference. The foresight, generosity, and determination of many have given us the privilege of enjoying these special places.

Quick Reference Chart:

REGION	WALK	PAGE	DIFFICULTY
Northern Lake Champlain and the Islands	Missisquoi Natural Wildlife Refuge	1	easy
	Burton Island State Park	8	easy/mod
	Knight Point State Park	14	easy
	North Hero State Park	19	easy
	Ed Weed Fish Culture Station	25	easy
Burlington and Central Lake Champlain	Old Mill Park	31	easy/mod
	Intervale	36	easy
	Ethan Allen Homestead	42	easy
	Winooski Nature Trail et al	49	moderate
	East Woods Natural Area	55	moderate
	Mud Pond Conservation Land	60	easy
	Colchester Bog Natural Area	65	very easy
	Delta Park	71	easy
	Sunny Hollow	76	easy/mod
	Colchester Pond	82	moderate
Southern Chittenden County	Shelburne Farms	88	moderate
	LaPlatte River Marsh Natural Area	94	easy
	Allen Hill	100	moderate
	Williams Woods Natural Area	106	easy
	Pease Mountain Natural Area	111	moderate
	Mt. Philo State Park	117	moderate

Walks and Highlights

Distance	Lake/ Pond	River	Wetlands	Geology	Views	Unusual Plants	Birds/ Animals	History	Wildflowers
1.5			✔			✔	✔		
3.0	✔		✔		✔		✔		✔
0.7	✔				✔		✔		✔
1.3	✔		✔		✔	✔	✔		
0.8	✔				✔		✔		
0.8		✔	✔	✔		✔	✔	✔	✔
1.5		✔	✔			✔		✔	✔
2.8		✔	✔		✔	✔	✔	✔	✔
2.1		✔	✔	✔	✔			✔	✔
0.6		✔		✔		✔		✔	✔
1.0	✔		✔			✔			✔
0.5			✔			✔			✔
1.2	✔	✔	✔		✔	✔	✔		✔
1.0				✔		✔			✔
2.5	✔		✔	✔			✔		
4.25	✔				✔	✔	✔	✔	✔
1.75	✔	✔	✔			✔	✔		✔
1.5	✔			✔	✔	✔	✔		✔
1.3			✔			✔			
1.5-2.0				✔	✔	✔	✔	✔	✔
1.75			✔	✔	✔	✔	✔	✔	✔

REGION	WALK	PAGE	DIFFICULTY
Southern Champlain Valley	Kingsland Bay State Park	123	easy
	Button Bay State Park	129	easy
	Dead Creek Wildlife Management Area	135	easy
	Snake Mountain Wildlife Management Area	141	mod/diff
	Mount Independence Historical Site	147	easy/mod
	Shaw Mountain Natural Area	152	moderate
Central Green Mountains and Valleys	Green Mountain Audubon Nature Center	158	moderate
	Mad River Greenway	165	easy
	Robert Frost Interpretive Trail	170	easy
	Abbey Pond Trail	176	mod/diff
	Leicester Hollow and Chandler Ridge	181	moderate
	Teas Falls	187	moderate
Montpelier Area	Rock of Ages Granite Quarry	193	very easy
	Hubbard Park	198	moderate
	North Branch Nature Center and River Park	204	moderate
Waterbury/ Stowe Area	Tundra Trail, Mount Mansfield	211	easy
	Sterling Falls Gorge Natural Area	217	easy
	History Hike, Little River State Park	223	moderate
	Stevenson Brook Nature Trail, Little River S.P.	231	easy/mod
New York	Point au Roche State Park	236	easy/mod
	Ausable Chasm	242	easy
	Coon Mountain Preserve	248	moderate

Distance	Lake/ Pond	River	Wetlands	Geology	Views	Unusual Plants	Birds/ Animals	History	Wildflowers
0.6	✔				✔	✔	✔		✔
1.6	✔			✔	✔	✔			✔
1.0–2.0		✔	✔		✔		✔		
3.0				✔	✔		✔	✔	✔
3.5	✔		✔		✔			✔	✔
2.0			✔	✔	✔	✔	✔		✔
1.5	✔	✔	✔	✔	✔	✔	✔		✔
5.5		✔			✔		✔		
1.0		✔	✔		✔	✔	✔		✔
3.8	✔	✔	✔		✔	✔	✔		✔
3.0-4.0		✔		✔	✔	✔			✔
1.2		✔		✔		✔	✔		✔
N/A				✔				✔	
1.5			✔		✔	✔			✔
2.1	✔	✔	✔			✔	✔		✔
0.75			✔	✔	✔	✔	✔		✔
0.3		✔		✔		✔		✔	✔
4.0		✔	✔		✔		✔	✔	✔
0.75		✔	✔	✔		✔	✔	✔	✔
3.0	✔		✔		✔	✔	✔		✔
1.0		✔		✔	✔			✔	
2.0				✔	✔	✔	✔		✔

Northern Lake Champlain and the Islands

 ## Missisquoi National Wildlife Refuge

Black Creek and Maquam Creek Trails
Swanton

1.5 miles

1.5 hours

easy

Wildlife and bird-watching along two old channels of the Missisquoi River. Wear waterproof boots in spring and bug repellent in summer. Bring binoculars. Dogs must be leashed.

Established in 1943, Missisquoi is a 6,338-acre refuge on the eastern shore of Lake Champlain and includes most of the Missisquoi River delta. Quiet waters and wetlands attract flocks of migrating waterfowl, while upland areas are home to songbirds and mammals. Peak waterfowl viewing is during the fall migration when thousands of ring-necked ducks feed and rest in the company of hundreds of green-winged teal, black ducks, and mallards.

The wetland trails, which are very wet in spring, follow the banks of Maquam and Black Creeks, long-abandoned channels of the Missisquoi River. The swamp is rich in plant diversity and attracts a wide range of animals. The refuge is actively managed: water level in impoundment areas is

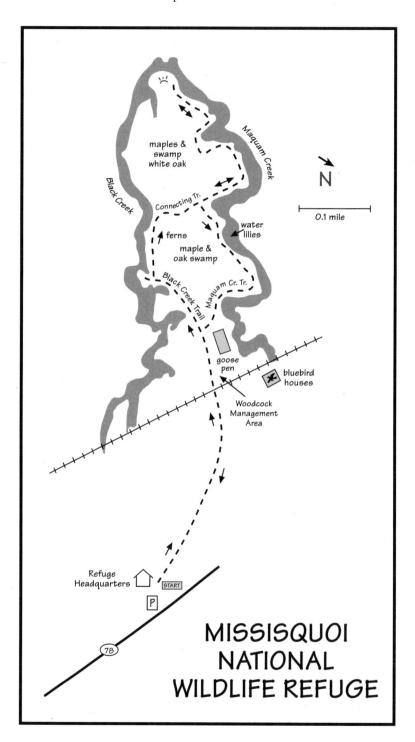

maples &
swamp
white oak

Maquam Creek

Black Creek

Connecting Tr.

N

0.1 mile

ferns

water
lilies

maple &
oak swamp

Black Creek Trail

Maquam Cr. Tr.

goose
pen

bluebird
houses

Woodcock
Management
Area

Refuge
Headquarters

START

P

78

MISSISQUOI
NATIONAL
WILDLIFE REFUGE

manipulated and fileds are hayed, mowed, or burned to keep them from reverting to woodland.

Portions of the refuge are open to hunting and fishing, boats and canoes may be launched from two landings, and cross-country skiing is permitted. Brochures are available at the trailhead. Make sure to take the leaflet for Black Creek and Maquam Creek Trails.

T he trail begins as a mowed path across a hayfield, nesting habitat for field sparrow, bobolink, and red-winged blackbird. Along the edge of the field is a row of bluebird boxes, although they are often used by tree swallows. (See Bluebirds, p. 60.) Look for red-tailed hawks soaring over-head in search of mice and voles.

The trail rises over the railroad track and enters young woods. In some years frogs are so prolific that they bound away at every footfall. Eastern garter snakes slither through the grass.

The woods are a mix of shrubs and young trees: speckled alder, but-tonbush, elm, pin and chokecherry, willow, gray birch, and sumac. Moisture-loving sensitive fern is the dominant ground cover. In spring the fronds have a reddish cast, and they wither at first frost—hence the name. In August or September beaded fertile stalks appear.

In about five minutes we pass a woodcock management area on the right. Woodcock, which thrive in scrubby young growth of alder and aspen, do not find food or camouflage in mature woods. As Vermont becomes increasingly forested, woodcock are threatened. (See North Hero, p. 21.)

The now-abandoned goose pen, also on the right, was used in the 1950s to establish a resident population, similar to efforts at Dead Creek (see p. 135). Unfortunately, the pinioned birds were hunted and the pro-ject was discontinued.

Where the Maquam Creek Trail goes right, walk left on the Black Creek Trail. Swamp white oak, willow, and silver and red maple dominate the swamp, and bright green duckweed coats the open water. Look for east-ern spiny soft-shelled turtles sunning themselves on warm days.

The trail reaches the creek and turns right. Beware of poison ivy. Ferns are prolific and robust. The size of a fern is more dependent on the ecology of its home than is that of a flowering plant. The four ferns in this damp soil—royal, sensitive, cinnamon, and interrupted—are clearly happy here.

Royal fern, with oblong leaflets, looks like a locust tree. It grows to six feet in bogs and swamps and near bodies of water. By contrast the sensitive fern grows to a maximum of two feet. Its wavy-edged, once-cut leaflets often look as if they were not fully cut to the frond.

Interrupted fern gets its name from the absence of greenery in the middle of the fertile fronds. The dark brown spore cases interrupt the bright green leaflets along the frond. Interrupted fern, not particular about habitat, resembles cinnamon fern, which prefers damp locations. Rusty

Royal ferns grow to great size along the perennially moist Black Creek.

wool covers the spring stem of cinnamon fern, and its separate fertile fronds also turn to a cinnamon color.

The trail bends right, away from the creek, and an elevated boardwalk crosses swampy ground. A bridge passes over an inlet and wood-duck boxes dot the creek. Silver maple and swamp white oak, the latter ringed with chicken wire for protection against beaver, tower over sensitive and royal ferns. Across the creek a red maple can be identified in spring by the pendulous red seed keys already dangling before the tree leafs out.

At the end of the boardwalk turn right on a gravel walkway that connects to the Maquam Creek Trail. This connector may not be passable in spring.

At the T-intersection go left on Maquam Creek Trail. Winterberry, dogwood, northern wild raisin, and highbush cranberry are abundant, their fruit and twigs eaten by grouse, pheasants, songbirds, deer, and rabbits.

Along both creeks you may see beaver runs, which look like worn footpaths. These are used by beaver when they leave the safety of the water to seek food and building materials. Beaver also build scent mounds, spraying piles of mud in order to establish their territory.

The creek is on the right and the tree swamp on the left, still dominated by silver maple and swamp white oak. A swamp, or red, maple on the left has a characteristic bird's-eye pattern on its bark. Red maple leaves have three shallow lobes, toothed edges, and red stems. Silver maple leaves are more deeply cut, longer and lighter green, with silver-white undersides. They generally have five lobes. Both trees, when mature, can have shaggy or peeling bark and often have many trunks in a swampy setting.

The trail bends to the left and passes over very wet ground. You may need waterproof boots to continue to Lookout Point, a spectacular wildlife observation spot at the end of the trail. Colorful songbirds flit through the canopy. Wood duck, hooded merganser, osprey, and great blue heron are commonly seen in the marsh or creek. Deer, muskrat, beaver, and rabbit leave their marks.

Return toward the headquarters by retracing your steps. At the trail junction, continue straight or left on the mowed grass of the Maquam Creek Trail. Buttonbush grows along the creek, and by late summer a carpet of white pond lilies floats on the water. The trail leaves the creek behind and returns toward the railroad crossing.

🦅 BLUEBIRDS

Bluebirds are not blue, nor are many other blue birds. They owe their appearance to Tyndall scattering. Their feather structure bends lightwaves so that we see predominantly blue light. Grind up a bluebird's feather and the result is not blue. Bluebirds appear bluer on a sunny day when there is more light.

Bluebirds, like woodcock, are victims of lost habitat and competition. Their traditional homes, farms with open fields, fences for perching, and old tree cavities for nests, are fast disappearing. Bluebirds Across Vermont was established in 1986 to encourage the placement of bluebird boxes as homes to the small population returning each spring to nest. Through good and bad years, these volunteers across the state have nurtured a growing number of fledglings. (See Organizations:Useful Names and Addresses, p. 253.)

🌿 LIFE CYCLE OF FERNS

Ferns are ancient nonflowering plants that lack true leaves, stems, and roots. Ferns have two generations, the gametophyte and the sporophyte, which look very different from each other. The sporophyte is the stage we recognize as a fern.

The cycle begins with a spore, a dustlike speck containing chlorophyll and moisture, which germinates on damp ground. The resulting gametophyte, a tiny plant which most of us would never see or recognize, eventually produces egg and sperm cells. A drop of rain or dew allows the sperm to swim to the egg and fertilize it. (This is a link to primitive plants that required water for reproduction. More-evolved flowering plants do not need water.)

The fertilized egg drops to the ground and takes root, sending up a green shoot which becomes a frond. As the fern develops it produces a case of spores, usually found on the underside of the frond. When the spores are ripe, these one-celled particles of life spill to the earth and begin the cycle anew.

Fern spores scatter by the millions and can remain viable for many years, quite impervious to climatic conditions. Ferns enjoy great mobility, as spores can travel much farther on the wind than seeds of the higher-order plants. Ferns also propagate from their rootstocks, creating an underground branching network. Some cinnamon fern rootstocks are a century old, standing like islands on swampy ground.

Hours, Fees, Facilities

Dogs must be leashed. A waterless toilet is available year-round at the parking area.

Getting There

Take Exit 21 from I-89. Go west into Swanton where Route 78 turns right. The parking and trailhead for the nature trails are on the left 2.3 miles from the turn in Swanton.

For More Information

Missisquoi National Wildlife Refuge
P. O. Box 163
Swanton, VT 05488
802-868-4781

Burton Island
State Park

St. Albans Bay

3.0 miles

2–3 hours

easy

Circumnavigate an island in Lake Champlain with ever changing lake and mountain views. A great walk for kids.

Burton Island is a unique state park. Accessible by boat, the park is a 253-acre island in St. Albans Bay. Its many campsites are clustered along the northern shore, leaving most of the land open to exploration.

As recently as 8,000 years ago, Burton Island was the tip of a peninsula. The land, compressed by mile-thick glaciers during the Ice Age, rebounded after the ice melted and the island was born. Until the 1950s, the land was farmed. Trees are now reclaiming the island. If left alone, Burton Island will be forested within a generation.

Two short nature trails are easily incorporated into a circuit of the island. The views alone justify the journey. The southwestern point of land, its shoreline wild and exposed, has several large shade trees, benches, and a mowed swath for lingering—the perfect destination for an afternoon picnic.

When you disembark from the ferry, stop at the park office for maps and trail guides. Then take the gravel path along the marina to the left. Within a few minutes it reaches an intersection of several gravel roads. Follow a sign, left, to the nature center. When the paths fork, do not go toward the water but right, toward the ranger's house. You will pass the small brown house and then see another just a few hundred yards distant.

The nature center is home to an informal collection of animals, rusty farm implements, and small educational exhibits. I particularly liked a meticulously labeled collection of rock samples from across the state.

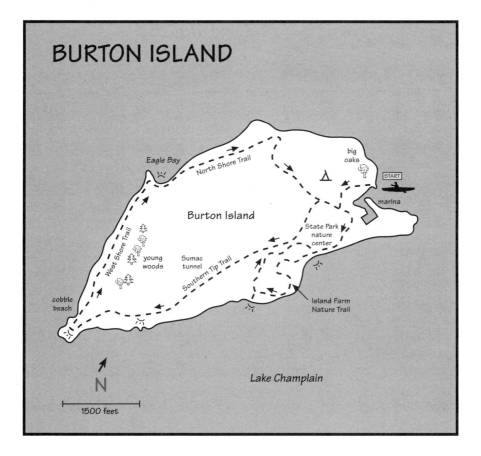

The Island Farm Nature Trail begins at the water's edge overlooking St. Albans Bay. This was an important eighteenth-century port for both lumber and potash, a byproduct of the clearing and burning of forested land. Glacial erratics litter the beach, which is composed of cobbles of shale smoothed by years of water action. Silverweed, a creeping plant named for silvery hairs on the underside of its leaves, thrives on the rocky beach. A single yellow flower blooms in midsummer on this hardy plant, which grows as far north as the edge of the Arctic.

Back on the trail, look for monarch butterflies in the milkweed. They lay their eggs on only the healthiest plants, assuring their offspring an optimal food supply. Goldenrod and hog peanut are abundant in the tangle of grasses and flowering plants. Ash, basswood, silver maple, cottonwood, and black locust trees grow along the shore at the edge of the meadow. The trail crosses a swampy area, a thicket of jewelweed, cattail, red raspberry, cow vetch, and thimbleberry. A rusty plow on the left is a reminder of the not-so-distant farm days. In one generation brush and saplings have overtaken the fields, a process we will witness again and again on Burton Island.

Within ten minutes the trail turns right to go inland, rising slightly through a grove of sumacs. We continue left, past the barn foundations barely visible through the thicket of raspberry canes. The trail continues downhill, bearing right to a splendid view of the lake.

We pass through a young forest of quaking aspen, a fast-growing, sun-loving tree. These will be replaced eventually by more shade-tolerant trees: maple, oak, hickory, and elm.

The trail rises past some large shagbark hickories and into mature woods of northern white cedar, sugar maple, and hickory before turning right toward the middle of the island.

We cross a marsh on a boardwalk. Farm stock watered at this pond, now filling with wetland plants: cattail, red osier dogwood, wild bergamot, and smartweed, its spike of tiny pink flowers encased in a sheath of leaves around the stem. Wild bergamot has a pale lilac flower and looks like domestic bee balm, to which it is related. The August-flowering plant stands about three feet and has opposite, lance-shaped leaves that are serrated. If you have bee balm in the garden you will recognize it immediately. Spotted touch-me-not, or jewelweed, grows next to stinging nettle. Jewelweed's leaves and stems are thought to be a remedy for stinging nettles and poison ivy.

Still on marshy ground, you'll see several spiky hawthorn trees. Their simple, alternate leaves are toothless and vary in shape, even on the same tree. Hawthorns produce a red, applelike fruit and frequently hybridize, making it difficult to identify a species.

This trail will take about a half-hour of leisurely walking. Just before it returns to the nature center, look for a passageway on the left to a dirt road. Turn left on the dirt road and, at the sign for Southern Tip Trail, walk left.

The grassy path, leading generally west, passes through a nearly continuous tunnel of impressively large sumac. Red raspberries—enough to snack on—ragweed, thistle, thimbleberry, and saplings attract choirs of songbirds. Occasional lake views open on the left.

Within twenty minutes the trail reaches the spectacular Southern Tip. Several specimen trees, wide-spreading red oak, sugar maple, and ash, shade benches on the mowed grass. To the south lies Ball Island, and the peaks of the Adirondacks stretch to the southwest. The Green Mountains lie to the east.

Look for osprey and green and great blue heron at Eagle Bay.

A shoreline of black shale wraps around the promontory, exposing the thin and brittle layers that, with erosion, become the beach cobbles. The sedimentary layers were metamorphosed under the pressure of deep layers of earth and ice, subsequently removed by passing glaciers.

When you are ready to leave this view, turn to the right, continuing clockwise around the island. The trail goes along the beach, edged with gnarled white cedars and red maples. In about five minutes, look for a large paper birch with multiple trunks and contorted roots at the edge of the woods. The narrow track begins here and meanders into young woods of red oak, white birch, green ash, elm, basswood, cottonwood, dogwood, quaking aspen, cherry, hickory, and maple.

After about ten minutes the trail comes to another cobble beach littered with glacial erratics. The shale bedrock has wavy stripes of black and orange. Notice the view to the west and how abruptly New York state flattens north of the Adirondacks.

The trail continues along the beach until it reaches a tiny peninsula that forms the western edge of Eagle Bay, a picturesque cove bordered by white cedars. While you probably won't see an eagle here, look for green and great blue heron and osprey. At a large rock outcropping, a path leads inland and joins the North Shore Trail. (We walk the trail in reverse order of the brochure.)

The trail heads east, never far from the shore, through young forest predominantly of paper birch, green ash, cottonwood, and northern white cedar. The canopy then thickens and evergreens become dominant, white pines and hemlocks mixing with the cedars. Hemlock is one of the longest-lived trees in our area, and many of these trees are 200 years old. This is one of the few parts of the island that was not cleared for farming.

A marshy area on the right, once a pond, is now filling with plants and sediment, and the immediate area is drying up. The poor, thin soil is home to red and white cedars as well as poplars and birch. The shrubs and saplings offer food and protection to wildlife. Pencil-point stumps are evidence of beaver. Other mammals that have swum or crossed the ice to Burton Island include deer, red fox, muskrat, and raccoon.

On the final stretch the trail passes through more sun-loving actors in the drama of early succession. Red raspberry, staghorn sumac, goldenrod, and willows dominate these abandoned fields. The North Shore Trail takes less than a half-hour at a leisurely pace.

At the end of the nature trail the campground stretches to the left. Take the mowed path to the right through a swampy area. When the path joins a gravel road, follow the road to the right until it reaches an intersection with other gravel roads. Turn left to return to the marina.

Near the marina at the edge of the woods, look for several large bur oaks, one with a diameter of more than 3.5 feet.

❦ SUCCESSION

When farm fields are abandoned, sun-loving shrubs and saplings move in. These pioneers may include sumac, poplar, white pine, and gray and white birch. They, in turn, are eventually replaced. Much of the sumac on Burton Island is poised to be replaced, as the shady conditions created by the parent trees make it unlikely that a new generation will be as successful. Pioneer trees succumb to shade-tolerant species including maples, shagbark hickory, ash, and oaks.

Grasses and herbs also diminish with decreasing sunlight. As young trees thicken and less sunlight reaches the forest floor, mosses and ferns return. Only in a mature climax forest, where the leafy canopy is at great height, do prolific spring wildflowers find enough sunlight to flourish.

❧ SUMAC

The fuzzy branches of staghorn sumac resemble the antlers of a deer in velvet, hence the name. Its leaves are long, with up to thirty-one toothed leaflets. The shrub grows to thirty feet, often in thickets. Native Americans made a lemonade-like drink from the red fruits, and its tannin-rich bark and foliage were used to tan leather.

The rare poison sumac causes a severe rash. With care, it can easily be distinguished from staghorn sumac. Poison sumac is generally found in swamps and bogs and its twigs are hairless. It has fewer leaflets, a maximum of thirteen, and they are not toothed.

Hours, Fees, Facilities

The ferry runs from Friday before Memorial Day through Labor Day, subject to weather conditions and lake levels. Six departures from Kill Kare State Park run from 9:00 A.M. to 6:30 P.M., with service from Burton Island six times daily, 8:30 A.M. to 6:00 P.M. The trip takes ten minutes. The fare is $4 per person, round-trip, for passengers over age four.

Getting There

Take I-89 Exit 19. At the stop sign turn right, following signs to Vermont 36. At a stop sign at 0.6 mile, turn left onto Vermont 36 west. Continue to the Green in St. Albans at 0.8 mile. Turn right at the light and jog *immediately* left, staying on Vermont 36 west. In 3.0 miles go right when the road comes to the lake, still on Vermont 36. After 0.9 mile, turn left onto Hathaway Point. This access road meanders 2.7 miles to the entrance of Kill Kare State Park. The ferry for Burton Island is on the left.

For More Information

Department of Forests, Parks, and Recreation
Burton Island State Park
P.O. Box 123
St. Albans Bay, VT 05481
802-524-6353

Knight Point State Park

North Hero

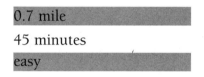

0.7 mile

45 minutes

easy

A quiet stretch of Lake Champlain shoreline. Some grand old sugar maples and shagbark hickories shade the grassy trail.

At first blush Knight Point looks an unlikely place for a nature walk. Yet beyond the stately brick Knight Point House, rolling lawns, and picnic tables, a narrow stretch of lakeside forest sits on a bluff above the lake. Cries of gulls mix with songs of woodland birds, and the trail has several benches at scenic spots.

The islands of North and South Hero commemorate Vermonters who fought in the Revolutionary War. Knight Point is named for its first resident, John Knight, who began ferry service between the islands in 1785. His family ran this service until the first bridge was built in 1892.

The wooden wing of the Knight Point House is a replica of Knight Tavern, an inn for ferry passengers built in 1790. Its two-story porch was an unusual architectural feature in its time. The historic building now accommodates park staff.

The nature trail meanders above the shore to the northern border of the fifty-four-acre park. The trail makes a loop, and several spurs lead back to the meadow and picnic shelter.

Start your walk on the south shore, west of the swimming beach. The mowed trail goes immediately into a thicket. The trees along the water's edge are those that don't mind wet feet: ash, cottonwood, and red maple. The shrubs, on slightly drier ground, include red cedar, red osier dogwood, and young shade-tolerant saplings like sugar maple and the hickories.

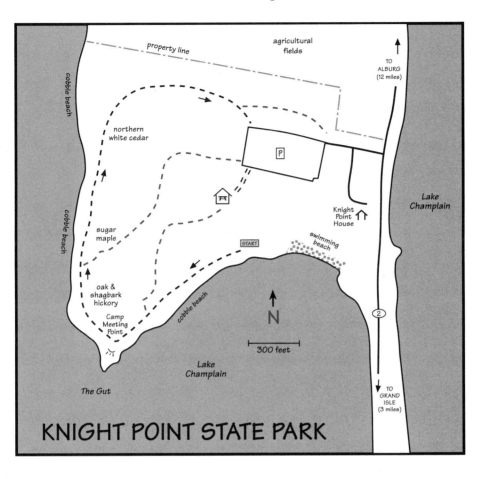

KNIGHT POINT STATE PARK

Choking these trees, or trying to, are Virginia creeper and wild grapevines. Both opportunists twine their way upward to reach the sunlight, and in so doing block the sun's rays to the trees that support them. While these vines provide food for birds and small mammals, they exact their price. Scouring rush, or horsetail, looking like its namesake, grows on damp soil. (See Horsetails, p. 17.)

Mature sugar maple, shagbark hickory, and red and white oaks are scattered along the shore, some thought to be more than 200 years old. One spreading sugar maple has a diameter of more than four feet. Shagbarks, found only in warm microclimates near the lake, are at the northern extreme of their range here. Red oak, recognizable by the pointed lobes of their leaves, sometimes grow to 70 or 80 feet. The red is the northernmost of our oaks, growing in well-drained soil, rich or poor. Its acorns do not ripen until the second autumn and in northern Vermont it is found at elevations of less than 1,400 feet.

About ten minutes into the walk, a side trail branches to the right. The main trail stays left and soon arrives at Camp Meeting Point. With mowed grass, benches, and a picnic table, this is a lovely spot to savor views of the lake and Adirondacks. Great blue heron frequent the shallows off the point. To the south is the "gut," a nautical term for a narrow passage like this one between the two islands.

For nearly a half-mile along the shore, a cobble beach stretches below the bluff. This beach is the most extensive of its type in Vermont. The cobbles, the result of lake action on black shale, are small and smooth and harbor little vegetation. The beach is maintained by wave action, ice scouring, and seasonal flooding.

Spotted sandpipers, with long, spindly legs, are thought to nest on this beach in grass- or moss-lined depressions. While most of our familiar shorebirds breed farther north in Canada, this one nests in the area.

As the trail heads north the understory thickens. Some big, old field trees—oaks, shagbarks, and maples—dot the woods thick with saplings: hickory, maple, poplar, ash, elm, oak, and red osier dogwood. Staghorn sumac, a pioneer that prefers full sun, is on the decline, being replaced by more shade-tolerant trees.

Several small trails fork right while the main path continues left. Northern white cedar, a tree that thrives on lakeside bluffs, become thick, and hop hornbeam appear for the first time. I was enchanted on a May day as a scarlet tanager flitted from maple to maple with bright flashes of red. The footing can be damp as the trail turns away from the lake, a perfect place to look for animal tracks in the mud. Deer, red fox, and raccoon frequent these woods. Basswood, an indicator of fertile soil, grows among abundant spring wildflowers: yellow and purple violets, Canada violets, wood nettles, white trillium, jack-in-the-pulpit, and hepatica.

The trees thin out and a cedar-rail fence borders agricultural fields on the left. The trail passes through a grove of saplings—poplar, ash, quaking aspen, and sumac—before returning to the meadow.

🕷 *NATURE'S WEAVERS*

On a late-summer morning the woods and meadows are a sticky tangle of spider webs. Spiders create these architectural and structural marvels to trap prey, provide transportation, and encase their eggs.

Webs come in several designs: the familiar orb or circular web (of *Charlotte's Web* fame), sheet, and funnel. Spiders produce seven or eight specialized types of silk. It has great strength and elasticity; a one-inch-thick rope of spider silk would be stronger than a steel cable.

Late in the season huge insects, entangled in sticky silk, destroy the webs, forcing the hungry spider to spin anew as often as once a day. A female spider's final act may be the weaving of an intricate egg sac, an effort that expends her silk-producing energy. Without silk a spider starves. The egg sac, tough on the outside and lined with the softest of silks, protects the eggs through winter. Baby spiders hatch out in spring when food is readily available.

Humans have used spider silk for centuries, packing wounds and making fishing nets and thin hairline sights on telescopes. Ruby-throated hummingbirds also use spiders' webs, to glue together their nests.

✳ HORSETAILS

Horsetails, or scouring rushes, are primitive fern allies. Their prehistoric relatives, the *Calamitales*, were large and abundant treelike plants that lived nearly 300 million years ago. The bounty of their spores produced great beds of coal which are still mined today!

Horsetails are found in wet places, often on sandy or gravelly soil. When the stems branch, they do so in regular whorls—picture a bottle brush. Both stems and branches perform photosynthesis, a function usually reserved for leaves.

The most common horsetail is the field horsetail, which has as many as seventeen different forms and grows like a weed. The fertile stem grows to only about six inches in height and generally has no branches or very stunted ones. The infertile stems, resembling a brush, grow to eighteen inches, with regular whorls of branches along its length.

Like other fern relatives, horsetails have a two-stage life cycle. Spores are produced at the end of fertile stems and are carried by the wind. Horsetail spores, containing chlorophyll and moisture, live only a few days and must germinate quickly. When they do, they produce either male or female gametophytes, which are dependent on moisture for fertilization. Once the sperm fertilizes the egg, a sporophyte is produced and the cycle begins again.

✖ *KILLDEER DRAMA*

In the meadows and parking area you may hear the plaintive cries of a killdeer circling overhead.

A brown-and-white shorebird the size of a robin with very long legs, the killdeer frequents open fields, golf courses, gravel lots, and rooftops (including schools and shopping centers!). In May, the male cries out as he stakes his territory. After a pair has made a nest, a depression scraped in the ground, the female feigns injury to distract from it, crying piteously and dragging her wings.

The fully feathered hatchlings are precocial, meaning they can walk and find food at birth, a necessary adaptation for ground nesters who cannot remain in the safety of a treetop nest.

Getting There

Coming from the north on Route 2, the park is 3.4 miles south of the town hall in North Hero. From the south on Route 2 the park is immediately on your left after you cross the drawbridge from Grand Isle. It is approximately 17.0 miles from I-89 at Exit 17.

For More Information

Knight Point State Park
RD 1, Box 21
North Hero, VT 05474
802-372-8389

North Hero State Park

North Hero

1.3 miles

1–1.5 hours

easy

An unusual flood-plain forest on the shore of Lake Champlain. Beautiful lake and mountain views. Bring bug repellent, a bird book, and, in spring, waterproof boots.

In anticipation of a bounty of campers attracted by the Montreal Olympics, the state acquired North Hero State Park in 1963. To the chagrin of environmentalists, portions of a rare flood-plain forest were filled to create roads, tent sites, and services. Nearly one-third of the park's 400 acres sit below the 100-foot elevation mark (the unregulated water level of Lake Champlain fluctuates seasonally between 95 and 101 feet), and each spring the lake rises to cover the campsites, leaving low-lying areas waterlogged and buggy.

Apart from the camping areas, the forest remains quite undisturbed. This type of lakeside flood-plain forest is found in Vermont only around Lake Champlain, and this is one of the largest. The annual spring flooding ordains the vegetation and animal life.

While the flood-plain forest lacks plant diversity, it is an interesting habitat. It is a spawning area for northern pike and pickerel, and signs of beaver and muskrat are found. Deer are frequently spotted in the adjacent fields, and the shore is a good place to observe waterfowl.

The nature trail is a loop. Take the mowed path to the right beyond the Nature Trail sign. The meadows are mowed periodically to keep them from succeeding to woodland. Occasional cutting allows grasses, flowering herbs, berries, and saplings to flourish. Insects, snakes, small mammals,

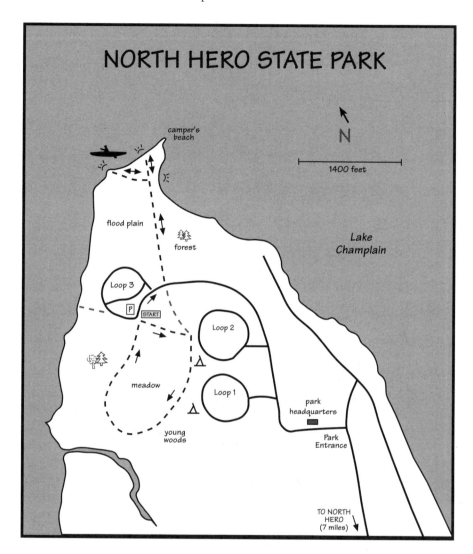

and birds are attracted by the rich mix of food, shelter, and camouflage. Breeding birds include the veery, blue-gray gnatcatcher, warbling vireo, yellow-throated vireo, and Baltimore oriole. The vulnerable woodcock (see Woodcock, p. 21) can be spotted here with its comical round body, spindly legs, and long beak.

Continuing straight on the mowed path, you reach a shady bench under several large shagbark hickories. The trail soon bears left, passing through young woods that include willow, basswood, quaking aspen, gray birch, bitternut and shagbark hickory, red and silver maple, and a hybrid of the two maple. The trail can be soggy early in the season.

As the trail continues curving to the left, several large swamp white oaks, ash, and shagbark hickories tower over the meadow, perhaps shade trees left when this land was farmed.

When the trail reaches an intersection take a left, passing through meadows of milkweed, grasses, goldenrod, Queen Anne's lace and wet meadow sedges. You will complete the loop in thirty minutes or less.

Back at the starting point, follow the road right along the edge of the campsites. When you reach the main road, turn left toward the beach and boat launch. If the ground is dry walk beneath the trees, but beware of poison ivy.

Unlike a swamp, where hummocks and pools provide a variety of growing surfaces, the flood-plain forest lies on flat ground. This forest, at or below lake level, has less diversity than most plant communities in Vermont. The trees, green ash, swamp white oak, and maple hybrid, are tall with few side limbs. Many maples have multiple trunks, the result of extensive firewood cutting several decades ago. There is almost no shrub layer, and the ground vegetation is primarily sensitive fern and wood nettles. Along the road a few winterberry shrubs grow. Natural debris from spring high water covers the ground: stumps, leaf litter, broken branches, mud, and sand.

A ten-minute walk leads to the lake. To the right is a marshy area. In the summer it's possible to venture amidst cattail, arrowroot, purple loosestrife, and rushes. At the end of the road is a cobble beach facing due north. In the distance cars cross between Swanton and Alburg on the Route 78 bridge.

In June, map, snapping, and painted turtles lay their eggs on this beach. The area is roped off during nesting season.

A detour to the left leads to the boat launch area. A few footpaths meander away, one to the woods and another to a tiny picturesque bay, its shore littered with mollusk shells. Shorebirds skittle along the water's edge and great blue heron fish in the shallows. This is a good place to observe waterfowl unnoticed.

🦅 WOODCOCK

The woodcock is a long-legged shorebird with an unusually long, three-inch bill. It has moved to upland scrub from shoreline mud flats. Its feathers, resembling dead leaves, are camouflage against the overhead menace of hawks and owls as well as weasels and other ground predators. It lives on

The aquatic arrowhead blooms in the shoreline wetlands. Known as duck potatoes, its tubers are eaten by ducks and muskrats.

worms and insects in moist, fertile soil. Being a ground nester adds to the woodcock's vulnerabilities.

As shrubs grow into trees, the habitat no longer protects and provides for the woodcock. Historically fires and the abandonment of farmland provided a continual supply of scrubby habitat. The woodcock is now dependent on human intervention for land management or logging.

🐜 PONDER THE INSECT

Between swats at black flies or mosquitoes, consider the insects. Without them we would have few flowers or fruits and no silk or honey. What would frogs eat and how would swallows, swifts, and bats fuel their flights? There are more than a million known species of insects.

Unlike mammals, reptiles, birds, and fish, with internal bony skeletons, insects have an exoskeleton. This tough, protective layer covers the entire body, including legs, feet, eyes, and antennae. This layer allows for little growth, so insects must molt in order to grow. Many times in their lives insects shed a replica of themselves, right down to the claws of their feet.

Insects have six jointed legs and wings which allow them to escape danger and search for food. Unlike warm-blooded mammals, insects are cold-blooded. When the temperature drops, their metabolism slows. Very dependent on the sun's warmth, they spring to life on the first spring day.

An insect begins life as an egg. It hatches into a larva, usually a grub or caterpillar, which undergoes a metamorphosis, or change. The larva feeds and molts repeatedly, eventually becoming an adult quite different from the larval stage. The winged adult, like familiar bees, butterflies, dragonflies, and grasshoppers, has the mobility to lay eggs in spots favorable to the next generation. The monarch butterfly, for example, lays her eggs on the larva's favorite food, a milkweed plant.

Hours, Fees, Facilities

Day users may rent boats and canoes at the park office. Oars or paddles and life jackets are available at the office, and the boats are kept at the boat launch area.

Getting There

From the north on Route 2, cross the bridge onto North Hero and take an immediate left on Bridge Road. After 0.5 mile the road turns right and continues to a T-intersection at 1.8 miles. Turn left onto Lakeview Drive. The park gate is 1.6 miles on the left.

From the south on Route 2, pass through the town of North Hero. From the town hall drive north 3.5 miles to a fork. Bear right on Lakeview Drive. Continue 3.7 miles to the park entrance on your left.

Inside the park, drive 0.7 mile on the main road to Loop No. 3. Follow the loop counterclockwise 0.3 mile to the water spigot, where there is parking.

For More Information

Vermont Department of Forests, Parks, and Recreation
North Hero State Park
RD 1, Box 259
North Hero, VT 05474
802-372-8727

In the Area

Alburg Dunes State Park

A new acquisition on the southern coast of the Alburg peninsula, this park has a half-mile white-sand beach strewn with sea grass and mollusk shells. Sand dunes have been destroyed by foot traffic and are fenced in the hope that they will rebuild over time. At the end of a long stretch of open lake with prevailing south winds, the beach is the recipient of wind- and water-carried sand.

Hidden in the acreage is an inaccessible black spruce swamp and bog, a very northerly feature in one of the most moderate of Vermont's climates, a demonstration of the extraordinary insulating ability of peat.

The park is south of Route 129 on the western side of the peninsula. From the junction at Route 2, take Route 129 west to a left turn at 1.2 miles. Follow this road 1.6 miles until it ends at the park.

Ed Weed Fish Culture Station

Grand Isle

0.8 mile

1–1.5 hours (including time at the visitor center)

easy

Vermont's largest fish hatchery produces 260,000 pounds and more than a half-million fish each year for the state's lakes and rivers. A lakeside exploration through the process of fish rearing. Children's activities in the visitor center.

Vermont's five hatcheries rear more than a million fish each year. They stock 400 locations for recreation and to support populations threatened by overfishing, pollution, erosion, dams, and loss of habitat.

The Ed Weed Fish Culture Station raises landlocked Atlantic salmon and brook, brown, rainbow, steelhead rainbow, and lake trout. About a quarter-million of these fish go directly into Lake Champlain each year.

In addition to the hatchery, an "upstream path" has been constructed for adult salmon and trout returning to spawn. Each year thousands of fish jump and swim upstream in an environment designed to mimic their native habitat. The best viewing is in April and May and again in October through December.

Be sure to pick up a brochure for the self-guided tour just inside the door.

Take some time in the visitor center, where the hatchery is fully explained. A fish census lists the number and types of fish delivered across the state each spring from all of the state hatcheries. (In 1997 more than

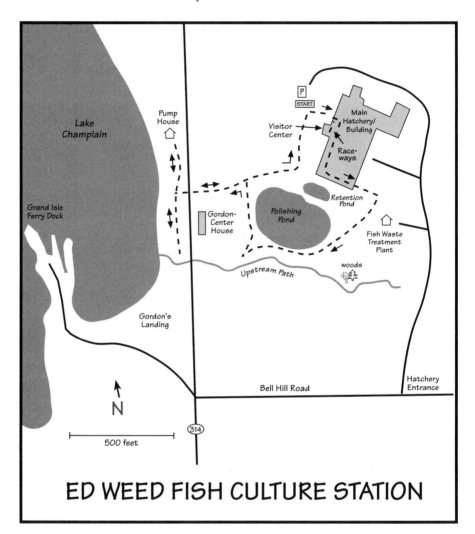

ED WEED FISH CULTURE STATION

286,000 fish were stocked to Lake Champlain and more than 540,000 to inland waters across the state.) Historic exhibits begin with the paleo-Indians and end with the colonial history of Vermont. A film demonstrates the entire process of fish culture. There are also several activities for young children.

You will exit to the raceways where fish spend most of a year before being stocked. They are moved here when they are about two inches long. The fish in the ten pairs of raceways are labeled by species. Often you will see the fish being hand-fed. The raceways are enclosed to protect this tempting dining site from otters, minks, great blue herons, and kingfishers.

Follow the fish stenciled on the sidewalk. A gravel path leads to the fish-waste treatment plant and a facility where all trucks used to transport fish are thoroughly cleaned. The trail skirts the polishing pond. On the left are trees typical of the warm Lake Champlain lowlands, including white oak, basswood, hickory, maple, and ash.

A short spur on the left leads to the outfall where treated water returns to the lake. The channel is designed with strategically placed cobbles and boulders to prevent scour and erosion.

The trail continues to a driveway and turns left, passing beneath several impressive ash and shagbark hickory trees. The Federal-style Gordon-Center House on the left was built in 1824 of Isle La Motte limestone and is listed in the National Register of Historic Places. It houses the Lake Champlain Basin Program, which focuses on the environmental, historic, economic, and cultural life of the lake.

Cross the road and turn left onto the gravel path leading to the man-made stream. The culvert that carries the hatchery outflow has been adapted for returning trout and salmon. Concrete baffles create resting pools en route. The pool on the right of the culvert, at the top of an eighteen-inch jump, allows fish to rest before continuing the uphill journey. The metal rakelike projection prevents lampreys from spawning in the stream. (See Pests of the Lake, p. 29.)

Retrace your steps and continue north on the gravel path toward the pump house. Ferries have operated here since 1796. During cold spells, water under pressure is circulated around the hulls to prevent overnight ice formation. Once the boats are moving they can break through a thin accumulation of ice, but if they freeze in the slip they cannot move.

About 4,400 years ago, eight to ten Indian families summered nearby. The site, to the north of the pump house, is protected from further development.

Three-quarters of the pump house is built into the bedrock below. Two intake pipes, at different levels, control the temperature of the 11 million gallons of water that pass through the hatchery each day. This enormous volume is required to maintain water quality where fish are raised in such crowded conditions.

In addition to pumps, the building houses an emergency diesel generator to produce electricity for the entire hatchery in the event of a power outage. This generator was used for several days after the ice storm of January 1998.

The trail returns to the gravel driveway and back to the visitor center. A small depression on the right is the retention pond, where any medication or disinfectants can biodegrade before the water is returned to the lake.

🐟 LIFE IN THE FISH LANE

Each fall more than two million freshly spawned eggs are delivered to this hatchery. Hunters and fishers hand-strip the brood fish to collect eggs. At the hatchery additional fish are anesthetized and stripped and their eggs and milk collected. The male milk remains viable for only thirty seconds.

The fertilized eggs are bathed in chilly water for four to eight weeks as embryos develop. Once the eggs hatch, the fry are transferred to start tanks. In late spring, as two-inch fingerlings, they are transferred to the outdoor raceways, where they will spend eight to ten months. The fish will be eight to ten inches long when they are stocked.

Many species of ducks stop at the polishing pond during migration.

✳ PESTS OF THE LAKE

Many nonnative plants and animals have been introduced to Vermont over the centuries. An absence of natural controls—predators, weather, or disease—allows uncontrolled reproduction of these pests.

The sea lamprey, *Petromyzon marinus,* has adjusted to life in fresh water by developing a taste for salmon, trout, and northern pike. Decades ago this eel-like vertebrate devastated commercial fishing in the Great Lakes, and now it consumes a significant portion of the species in Lake Champlain.

The adult spawns in streams, where up to 100,000 eggs hatch into ammocoetes. These burrow into the stream bed, where they thrive on plankton and decayed material for three to fourteen years. When the six-inch lampreys emerge, they swim to the lake where, with a disklike mouth, they feed on the blood and flesh of host fish.

It takes only two days for a seven-ounce lamprey to kill a lake trout more than twice its size. Larger fish have a higher survival rate, but their size, health, and reproduction are ultimately at stake.

Eurasian water milfoil (*Myriophyllum spicatum* L.) is a nonnative aquatic plant that infests many Vermont lakes, including large areas of Lake Champlain. Growing up to twenty feet a year from a fibrous root, it outcompetes and eliminates beneficial native plants. Its dense growth discourages fish spawning and recreation, while the plant is rarely used as a food source.

Eurasian water milfoil spreads whenever a broken fragment travels to a new location. Boat owners have unwittingly transported fragments from lake to lake across the state.

Currently the plant can be only controlled, not eliminated. Divers use suction hoses and hydrorakes or remove roots and shoots by hand. The grass carp, a natural predator native to China and partial to Eurasian water milfoil, is currently illegal in Vermont. Other biological controls, such as insects, bacteria, and fungi, are being tested.

Zebra mussels, with striped clamlike shells usually smaller than one inch, are making a similar assault on the lake. Discovered in Lake St. Clair in 1988, the zebra mussel entered Lake Champlain from the south in 1993. A female can produce a million eggs each season, and, in the absence of predators, the tiny mollusks disrupt the ecosystem and clog water intakes, boat hulls, and cooling systems. Great care is taken to filter hatchery water in order not to infest other lakes.

Hours, Fees, Facilities

The visitor center is open every day of the year from 7:30 A.M. to 4:00 P.M. Admission is free and restrooms are available.

Getting There

From I-89, Exit 17, take Route 2 west for 10.2 miles. Turn left on Route 314 north and continue for 2.3 miles. Turn right on Bell Hill Road. The hatchery entrance is on your left at 0.2 mile. The gravel drive loops left around the building and brings you to the parking area in 0.3 mile.

For More Information

Ed Weed Fish Culture Station
802-372-3171
Vermont Department of Fish and Wildlife
(See Organizations: Useful Names and Addresses.)

In the Area

Hyde Log Cabin, Route 2, Grand Isle
Built in 1783 of logs hand-hewn by Jedediah Hyde Jr., an engineer and Revolutionary War veteran, the cabin was one of the first buildings on the islands. It was home to the Hyde family for more than 150 years.

Burlington and Central Lake Champlain

 ## Old Mill Park

Jericho

0.8 mile

1 hour

easy, with a few hills

A river with potholes and striking bedrock erosion on a woodland walk. An exhibit of Snowflake Bentley's photographs.

Six mills were once located along this stretch of the Browns River, the earliest built in the 1820s. In the 1880s the adjacent Chittenden Mill was one of the first in the country to convert from traditional grinding stones to the roller process for making flour. The mill was named for Thomas Chittenden, first governor of Vermont and ancestor of owners Lucius and Frank Howe. Early in this century, as competition from the midwestern states grew, the mill converted to making animal feed. In 1946 it was closed.

Both the river, with its beautiful potholes, and the woods are cool and welcoming. There are several benches along the river at particularly scenic spots.

The Winooski Valley Park District (WVPD) manages this park. A coalition of seven towns in the lower Winooski valley, it preserves and maintains historic and natural areas. Several other walks in this book are on WVPD properties.

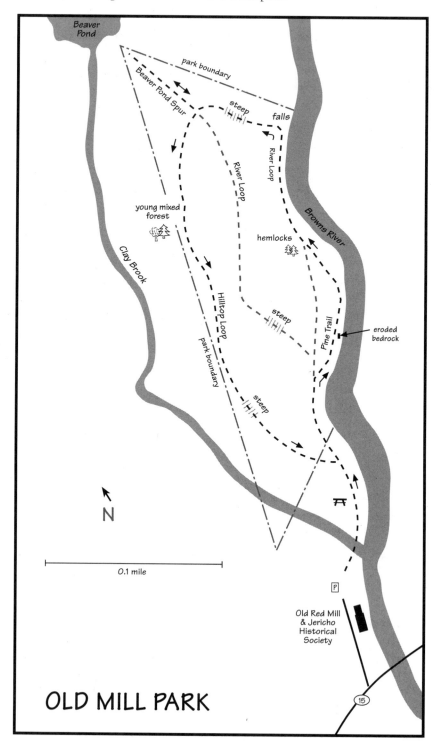

Beaver Pond

park boundary

Beaver Pond Spur

steep

falls

River Loop

River Loop

young mixed forest

hemlocks

Browns River

Clay Brook

Hilltop Loop

steep

park boundary

Pine Trail

eroded bedrock

steep

N

0.1 mile

P

Old Red Mill & Jericho Historical Society

15

OLD MILL PARK

The walk begins behind the map. The wetland on the left once lay beneath the millpond behind the dam. Through the 1960s the pond was used for ice-skating. With the dam gone, cattails and other marsh vegetation took root. These plants create a mat of vegetation, which in turn allows other plants to establish themselves on drier ground. The process continues as water-loving shrubs and trees invade. Willow, box elder, and speckled alder thrive here now. This land will become drier and eventually return to woods.

Across Clay Brook the trail enters the woods. Go straight rather than left at the sign for the Hilltop Loop. Tall meadow rue, alternate-leaved dogwood, and sensitive and interrupted ferns are lush here. Indian pokeweed, or false hellebore, dies back in early July, its huge, conspicuously veined leaves yellowing until the entire plant withers away. Native Americans once used the leaves to make cigars.

On the drier left side of trail, the twice-cut New York fern grows. Its fronds taper to both ends. It is unusual among ferns in not preferring wet sites.

Take the Pine Trail right toward the river. We pass through thick banks of jewelweed and cinnamon, sensitive, and bracken ferns before the trail rises under a thick canopy of hemlocks. The river, with beautifully sculpted bedrock, is on the right. One stretch looks like the inside of an abalone shell. Don't miss the water skaters or striders on the quiet pools, trolling for dinner.

Water skaters (and water boatmen) are true bugs, a group of insects with feeding tubes adapted to piercing and sucking. They inject their prey with digestive juices and then suck out the resulting potion. Like all insects, water skaters have six legs: the front pair grasp prey, the middle set propel the skater, and the rear ones steer. They skate across the surface of quiet water, patrolling for potential victims, dead or alive.

Skaters can walk on water because of surface tension, a phenomenon that allows some objects with a greater density than water to float. The bond between water molecules at the surface is greater than between those beneath it. Only if the insects do not break the water's surface can they stay on top of it. Legs covered with thick pads of water-repellent hair facilitate this feat.

Returning to the Pine Trail, we continue beneath thick hemlocks. Unlike white pines, which need sun, hemlocks grow in shady ravines or beneath a leafy canopy. Once they are established, little can grow beneath them. The few ferns here are beneath small sunny openings.

The Pine Trail bends left and rejoins the other trails. We follow the River Loop to the right.

As the deciduous trees thicken, wildflowers bloom, especially those tolerant of acidic conditions. Pink lady-slippers, with a pair of heavily ribbed, lance-shaped leaves, are one of the great beauties of the forest. Wood sorrel, partridgeberry, starflower, Indian cucumber, goldthread, bunchberry, trillium, Clintonia, and wild lily of the valley are thick here. Goldthread has bright, gold-colored roots and astringent properties. Once chewed for mouth sores, it is also called canker-root. Its shiny evergreen leaves resemble flat-leaf parsley, the three leaflets both toothed and scalloped.

Trailing arbutus, becoming less and less common, hugs the trail. It prefers open edges to deep leaf litter, making it vulnerable to traffic. Also called Mayflower, trailing arbutus is the earliest bloom of spring, with tiny, sweet-scented pink or white flowers.

The trail rises and falls over eroded sections of hillside as it continues along the river. Tree roots are exposed and the footing can be slippery. Several pools of clay have slumped out from beneath the mossy hillside, creating light gray puddles.

Just below the falls, the trail turns left and climbs away from the river. Follow signs for both loop trails. The understory flourishes in inverse proportion to the hemlocks in the canopy as we rise through the woods.

A spur to a beaver pond goes right. At the end of the short trail a beaver dam and lodge are visible upstream to the right. It's not possible to be sure from year to year where beaver will live, but their operations are fascinating whenever we get the chance to observe them. (See Beavers, p. 179.)

Return from the detour and go right onto the Hilltop Loop. The trail continues on higher ground, where maples and white pines dominate old pastures. This is a common pattern of succession, as sun-loving white pines quickly colonize open land. A photo in the Jericho Historical Society shows Jericho Village from this hill when fields rolled down to the village.

A large white pine on the right side of the trail is a wolf, or field, tree. Its strong side branches grew in an open field, something not possible in the confines of crowded woods. Like a wolf, such trees once stood alone in the field. Both names are commonly used.

At a fork in the trail, stay right on the Hilltop Loop. Red and sugar maples, beech, white oak, and yellow and paper birch dominate the woods. Several gray birches are dead or dying, perhaps for lack of sunlight. Beech saplings sprout from the roots of parent trees. Striped maple, or moosewood, is plentiful and conspicuous with its pale green striped bark. Its leaves are huge to catch enough sunshine in the understory.

Several water bars cross the trail to keep it from eroding as we descend to the valley. At the base of the slope the trails merge near a picnic table and the spur returns to the parking area.

▦ SNOW AND SNOWFLAKE BENTLEY

Jericho is the home of Snowflake Bentley. For nearly half a century, W. A. "Snowflake" Bentley (1865–1931), a farmer and self-taught photographer, shivered through the winters in an unheated shed, capturing snow crystals on film for science and posterity.

After catching a snowflake on a black board, Bentley hurried to shelter. With a magnifying glass he identified a promising specimen and then nudged it into position on a microscope slide using a small wing feather. His camera fitted with a microscope, Bentley pointed it to the sky to capture the snowflake with light coming through it. The average exposure time was twenty seconds!

Snow is crystallized water that forms on a particle of dust, its underlying structure too small for the naked eye to see. When we see snowflakes, in various six-sided forms, we are seeing a mass of individual crystals.

Many plants and animals depend on an insulating blanket of snow for winter survival. As snowflakes fall, landing every which way, air is trapped between them. Not only does the snowy layer retain warmth, it hides animals and their food caches from predators.

Snow can lift shorter animals up to branch tips, and a snow crust may support white-tailed deer as they search for food. A deep dump of powder is a problem for deer, with their thin legs and tiny, cloven hooves. Small animals, like mice and voles, are light enough to stay on the surface while larger predators—foxes, coyotes, and the cats—may be hampered by deep accumulation.

A thick coating of snow on an ice-covered pond keeps the ice from thickening and gives beaver and muskrat more room to maneuver to their stored food. Snow protects plant roots from deep cold spells as well as from damaging freeze-and-thaw cycles.

A history of Snowflake Bentley and a selection of his photographs are on display in the Jericho Historical Society located in the Old Mill.

Getting There

From the Five Corners in Essex, at the intersection of Route 15 and Route 2A, take Route 15 east. Follow Route 15 5.3 miles to the Old Mill on the left. Parking and the trailhead are to the rear.

For More Information

Winooski Valley Park District
(See Organizations: Useful Names and Addresses.)

Intervale

Rena Calkins and Bike Trails
Burlington

0.6 mile on Rena Calkins Trail, plus about 1.0 mile, round-trip, on Bike Trail

1–1.5 hours

easy (Bike Trail to Ethan Allen Homestead, 2.1 miles, one way)

One-sixth of all open land in Burlington is in the Intervale. Fertile farmland in the Winooski River flood plain is an incubator for sustainable-agriculture projects.

The dictionary defines *intervale* as low, flat land between hills or along a river. Near the Winooski River, in the towns of Burlington, Colchester, and Winooski, the Intervale is 3,900 acres of fertile agricultural and wetland. This flood plain was first inhabited at the end of the Ice Age, about 10,000 years ago.

Archaeologists have dated a settlement near the Ethan Allen Homestead to 4,500 years ago. Six hundred years ago in the Intervale, Abenakis experimented with cold-resistant corn hybrids while growing the traditional three sisters: corn, beans, and squash.

In colonial days, the Intervale became a breadbasket, producing grains, flax, meat, dairy products, and lumber for export. Later, with competition from western states, dairy farms became dominant, a situation that prevailed into this century.

In the last hundred years, commerce and industry took advantage of the underappreciated land. Paupers camped and dumps and a slaughterhouse dotted the landscape. Since 1950, a landfill, the Northern Connector (Route 127), an electrical generating plant, and several radio towers have been constructed.

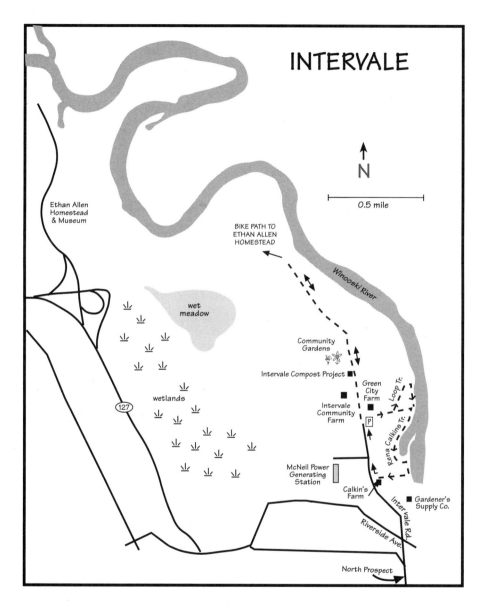

Today, the Intervale is being renewed. In the 1970s the Winooski Valley Park District began acquiring land for public access and the city of Burlington established community gardens. In the early 1980s, Gardener's Supply, a catalog company committed to organic gardening, located in the Intervale, spearheading cleanup efforts and the restoration of the soil to organic certification. In 1988, the nonprofit Intervale Foundation was established to continue these efforts and to revitalize the area as a social, economic, and natural resource. The foundation serves as a laboratory for sustainable, community-based agriculture and has a goal of supplying 10 percent of Burlington's food needs.

To fully appreciate the Intervale, I recommend a walk along the river, past the businesses, and through the farmlands. The bike path is a series of pedestrian-friendly dirt trails and farm roads that follow the river two miles to the Ethan Allen Homestead (see p. 42).

Begin on the Rena Calkins Trail. Walk through the split-rail fence and look for white blazes with the interlinked letters RC. A strong musty smell is a reminder that the compost project is not far away. On the left is the Green City Farm, a market garden growing organic produce for Fletcher Allen Health Care and the New England Culinary Institute.

Water-loving trees dominate the fertile river-bottom soil. Cottonwood, ash, black willow, elm, silver and red maple, and box elder are the dominant trees, the cottonwood growing to greatest height. Box elder usually does not grow beyond forty feet and often has multiple trunks at odd angles. Jewelweed and wood nettles join sensitive and ostrich ferns to create a tall, lush understory. Remember, wood nettles have alternate leaves and stinging nettles opposite leaves.

River flooding is a regular spring occurrence, coating everything in mud and littering the flood plain with leaves and branches. For thousands of years the Winooski has carried topsoil downstream, dropping it in the delta.

The Loop Trail, blazed LT, makes a detour to the left. The trail turns right and then bears right again, continuing along the riverbank through the flood-plain forest. A tangle of vines adds to the feeling of a forest primeval. Hog peanut, with three leaflets, usually creeps near the ground, while wild cucumber and Virginia creeper climb high in the trees. Virginia creeper leaves, with five toothed leaflets, turn a deep red in fall, and the plant produces blue berries eaten by birds, mice, chipmunks, and skunks. Its foliage and twigs are browsed by deer. Wild cucumber, also called balsam apple, has maplelike leaves and produces a spiny fruit containing four flat seeds.

In the shallows along the river, you may see shorebirds: great blue heron, green heron, black-crown night heron, Virginia rail, and sandpiper.

Migratory waterfowl may include Canada and snow geese and mallard, American green-winged teal, ring neck, and wood ducks.

Beaver have gnawed a number of trees as the trail continues on the sandy riverbank. Shaggy-barked silver maple and black willow have roots seasonally in the water. This is an opportunity to compare the distinctive barks of three hydrophilic trees. Cottonwood bark is deeply and regularly ridged. Silver maple bark shreds vertically, while black willow bark often curls back from the tree in thick, gnarled chunks.

The river appears to be barely flowing. Water striders skim over the flat pools and falling insects dapple the surface like raindrops. Steps climb the hillside on the right toward Gardener's Supply. Walk to the right of the building.

A patchwork of garden plots flourish on the right—employee, test, demonstration, display, and market gardens. The Cook's Garden is a test and display facility for an organic seed grower. Two commercial organic-flower growers, Stray Cat and Berry & Maxwell, contribute splashes of color.

Turn right on the paved Intervale Road. The McNeil Electric plant is on the left, an innovative facility utilizing wood chips, a forest byproduct. The wood depot, also on the left, diverts scrap wood, brush, and Christmas trees from the landfill into the hoppers at McNeil.

The Calkins Farm, the last dairy farm in the Intervale, is on the right. The 1860 farmhouse is registered with the Vermont Division for Historic Preservation. Continue on the dirt road past the Rena Calkins Trailhead and Green City Farm. The Intervale Compost Project (ICP) is on the right.

ICP is a cooperative partnership between the Intervale Foundation and Chittenden Solid Waste District. It received Vermont's first permit for commercial-scale food composting. Fletcher Allen Health Care composts the hospital's (pre-patient) kitchen waste. Ben & Jerry's adds its sweet input to a soup of leaves, yard waste, food, and horse manure. The compost is used by Intervale farmers and sold to the public.

The Farm Incubator Program provides low-cost land, farm equipment, greenhouse space, irrigation, and compost for small-scale organic farmers. Two of these, Digger's Mirth Collective Farm and Endless Summer Farm, are on the left.

The Intervale Community Farm (ICF) is also on the left, a venture in community-supported agriculture. ICF is a share-based organic garden providing members with weekly allotments of produce throughout the growing season. Members' shares pay for labor, equipment, and seed.

Beyond ICF on the left are community gardens. One of many such locations in Burlington, these community gardens provide an important bit

Cook's Garden is a test and display facility for the organic-seed catalog merchant.

of earth and continuity to Burlington's growing population of immigrants, many of whom arrive bearing seeds from the old country.

Although the road is blocked to vehicles by a metal gate, the walking and bike paths continue. Corn, hay, and alfalfa fields stretch toward the river on the right. An algae-covered, tire-filled pond is a reminder of the Intervale's past. The farm road turns to gravel and winds through agricultural land, some of which is fallow, to arrive eventually at the Ethan Allen Homestead.

Turn around where you wish and retrace your steps.

✳ LOOK BEFORE YOU TOUCH

Stinging and wood nettles look similar and it's best to recognize them without doing a touch test, because stinging nettles leave raised welts that sting and itch.

Both plants have coarsely toothed oval leaves. Leaves of the stinging nettle are opposite each other along the stem, while wood nettle leaves come off the stem alternately. Stinging nettle leaves have heart-shaped bases. Very young shoots and leaves of stinging nettle can be made into soup!

Getting There

From Main and South Prospect Streets at the University of Vermont, take Prospect Street north. It jogs slightly to the left at 0.3 mile as it crosses Colchester Avenue (becoming North Prospect Street). Continue 0.6 mile to a traffic light at Riverside Avenue. Go straight, although you are now on Intervale Road, which crosses the railroad at 0.1 mile. The road turns to dirt in 0.3 mile. The parking area is another 0.1 mile on the right.

For More Information

Intervale Foundation
128 Intervale Road
Burlington, VT 05401
802-660-3508

Ethan Allen Homestead

Homestead and Peninsula Loops to Wetlands Walks North and South

Burlington

2.8 miles

1.5–2 hours

easy

Wetlands and fertile farmland share the flood plain of the Winooski River, land which attracted Native Americans more than 4,000 years ago. The homestead of Ethan Allen and exhibits of early Vermont history are open to visitors.

The Winooski Valley Park District (WVPD) manages one of the largest urban natural areas in Vermont. Seven towns in the lower Winooski watershed—Burlington, Colchester, Essex, Jericho, Williston, Winooski, and South Burlington—share the cost of conservation of these properties.

The final few miles of the Winooski River, as it meanders to Lake Champlain, are a broad fertile plain. The wetlands and fertile soils attracted Native Americans as early as 3000 B.C. Later, the Abenakis relied on the Winooski as a transportation route for canoes in summer and as an icy pathway in winter.

Early European settlers lost no time in exploring the valley for its fish, wildlife, timber, farmland, and water power. Samuel de Champlain first paddled the lake in 1609, and by 1790 a settlement was growing at the falls a few miles upstream.

In 1787 Ethan and Fanny Allen built their home in the Intervale. The homestead was preserved by the WVPD in 1981. Exhibits at the Hill-Brownell Education Center elaborate on early Vermont history and the life of Ethan Allen.

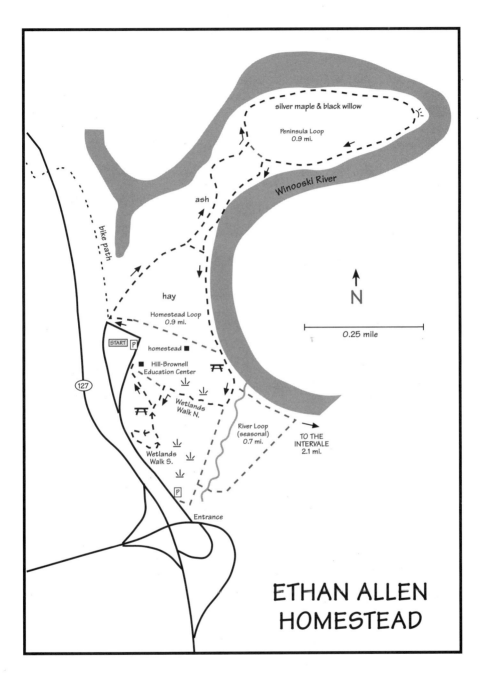

silver maple & black willow

Peninsula Loop
0.9 mi.

Winooski River

ash

bike path

hay

Homestead Loop
0.9 mi.

N

0.25 mile

START P

homestead ■

■ Hill-Brownell
Education Center

127

Wetlands
Walk N.

River Loop
(seasonal)
0.7 mi.

TO THE
INTERVALE
2.1 mi.

Wetlands
Walk S.

P

Entrance

ETHAN ALLEN
HOMESTEAD

The Homestead and Peninsula Loops, each less than a mile, give the flavor of the lazy meanders of the Winooski. Two wetlands walks occupy long-abandoned river channels now evolving into drier land. The seasonal River Loop lies at the edge of meadow, young woods, and river. A pedestrian-friendly bike trail links the homestead with the Intervale (see p. 43) two miles distant. We will walk around the peninsula and through the wetlands.

Make sure to pick up a map and wetlands walk brochure at the outdoor information board near the parking area.

Begin by taking the Homestead Loop, which crosses a grassy hayfield. Go left and then right across the fields toward the end of the peninsula. After about ten minutes, the Homestead Loop circles right and the connector to the Peninsula Loop goes straight ahead. Go straight, passing through low, oft-flooded woodlands. These willow, green ash, cottonwood, and silver maple trees spend part of each spring with their roots submerged. After about five minutes the trail reemerges into another field. This is the Peninsula Loop, which follows a meander of the Winooski. Walk this loop clockwise, looking for blue heron in the shallows.

Along the perimeter of the peninsula are black ash trees. Their blossoms attract mourning cloaks, dark brown butterflies with a band of yellow-and-white trim along the edge of their wings. Mourning cloaks overwinter as adults and warm up with the spring sunshine. They can be found looking for sparse nourishment in early flowers or tree sap.

Cottonwood and black willow grow to great size in this moist environment, their huge trunks rooted near the water's edge. Several red or swamp maples, with shaggy bark, have multiple trunks. The river is slow and tranquil, and the scene of cows, grassy fields, and picturesque silos across the river could be an English landscape painting.

Look for animal and bird tracks in the mud at river's edge. The trail bends right at the end of the peninsula after about ten minutes. The riverbanks are steeply cut, and sediment has been dropped on the inside of the turn. Sun-loving sumac grows on the left as the trail returns toward the Homestead.

After another five to ten minutes the Pond Trail goes left, passing through the low wooded stretch again. Beaver are active here. Poplar trees are among their favorite foods. Sandy soil is evidence of river flooding. In another five minutes the trail rejoins the Homestead Loop. Bear left and beware of crumbling banks along the river; the soft soil is eroded every year

Skunk cabbage poking through the leaf litter in early April.

by high water. After another five minutes the trail arrives at a canoe launch and a picnic table in a shady grove.

Turn your back to the river and follow signs to the River Loop Trail. Do not cross the stream on the wooden bridge to your left. Look for signs to the Wetlands Walk North. Ignore a right turn that leads to the education center and parking lot.

Shortly the Wetlands Walk North trail branches to the right. It passes briefly through young woods before arriving at the boardwalk. This is an old channel of the Winooski River, which is returning to dry ground. Slow your pace to a crawl, as the wetland is teeming with life.

A marsh and field on the left are a tangle of smartweed, milkweed, joe-pye weed, ragweed, box elder, elm, wild cucumber, sensitive fern, and orange-spotted jewelweed.

As the ground becomes more waterlogged, wetland plants dominate: silver maple, box elder, willow, speckled alder, turtlehead, and cattails. Duckweed coats the open water. Arrowhead (*Sagittaria latifolia*) is a wetland beauty. Its leaves are shaped like arrowheads and in late summer a leafless stalk bears small, three-petaled white flowers. Underwater tubers, or rhizomes, are eaten by ducks and muskrats. Another stunning denizen of the wetland is water arum, or wild calla (*Calla palustris*). Related to jack-in-the-pulpit and philodendron, which it resembles, water arum produces a broad white bloom similar to the calla lily. It looks surprisingly tropical for Vermont.

A boardwalk crosses very wet ground and frogs scatter at our approach. Patrons of the marsh range from grasshoppers and green frogs to raccoon and muskrat. Marsh and red-tailed hawks may soar overhead. Red-winged blackbirds nest in cattails. Aggressive males fight for territory in the spring and are very protective through the nesting season.

At the end of the boardwalk take the steps up the bank. Follow signs left toward Wetlands Walk South. Walk past the Children's Discovery Garden and picnic shelter, across a grassy meadow to the trail. If you plan to follow the self-guided tour with numbered stops, follow the gravel road left 0.1 mile to a second sign on the left for Wetlands Walk South. The trail begins down the steps.

On the bank several musclewood trees present quite a sight. As many as twenty young trunks spring from the roots of each tree.

Skunk cabbage (*Symplocarpus foetidus*) is abundant in the drier reaches of this wetland, emerging in early spring. When the plant is bruised an odor resembling decaying flesh attracts insects to pollinate it. Skunk cabbage sprouts so early in the spring that respiration resulting from its rapid growth can melt surrounding snow.

Its flower is a remarkable sight. A deep-red-colored cup, the spathe of which resembles a leaf, opens to reveal a golf-ball-sized knob, called the spadix, covered with tiny yellow flowers. The leaves are bright green and resemble a loose head of cabbage. Skunk cabbage, near the northern limit of its range, is found only in the Champlain Valley of northern Vermont.

To the right is a remnant of open pond, filling rapidly with nonwoody or herbaceous plants like cattails, jewelweed, and arrowhead. This first stage of wetland succession is a marsh. Insects and amphibians breed in the open water.

Water-loving ferns flourish. Cinnamon, sensitive, and royal fern are robust. By late summer, sensitive fern sends up its beady fertile frond and royal fern sports feathery tips on its fertile fronds.

The second stage of wetland succession is a swamp, which includes woody trees and shrubs: speckled alder, witch hazel, red osier dogwood, red or swamp maple (with many trunks), and willow. Black, or swamp, willow (*Salix nigra*) can tolerate several feet of standing water, as its roots resist rot. It often resembles a giant shrub with multiple trunks. Black willow branchlets are very brittle at their base and, when they are broken off by the wind, readily take root. Willow provides drier islands where less water tolerant plants can grow.

The middle section of the wetland is very wet indeed. Cattails tower overhead and water-loving plants create a luxuriant tangle. Among the ferns, arrowhead, jewelweed, skunk cabbage, and cattails, turtlehead (*Chelone glabra*) bloom extravagantly in late summer. A wetland plant, its white, pink, or lavender flowers resemble turtle heads. They bloom at the end of a stalk, which can range from one to four feet.

A set of steps lead out of the wetland. At the top, next to a picnic table, notice a red maple with a diagonal design around its trunk, which grew with a vine entwining it.

⚘ WETLANDS

Wetlands may be marshes, swamps, swamp forests, fens, or bogs, all of which occur in Vermont. They occur where upland and aquatic environments meet, either beside bodies of water or in isolation. Wetlands exist where soil is waterlogged for any part of the growing season, from one week to year-round. Once the soil becomes waterlogged, its oxygen is quickly depleted. Even after the water has receded, oxygen is slow to return to the soil.

A marsh develops when nonwoody plants take root in the shallows of open water. A swamp follows as woody shrubs and trees invade, eventually becoming a swamp forest when the trees thicken to form a canopy of leaves. A bog (see Colchester Bog, p. 65) is an acidic wetland with little or no flow of fresh water. Sphagnum peatlands and heaths dominate bogs. Fens host similar plants, but a flow of ground water supports a wider range of vegetation.

Upland plants die in wetlands, while plants adapted to a waterlogged environment thrive. Adaptations of wetland plants include shallow root systems with significant above-ground sections to maximize contact with the air, multiple trunks for the same purpose, and a biochemical ability to thrive in anaerobic (without oxygen) conditions. Carnivorous plants also live in bogs and fens.

Surface water is filtered and absorbed in wetlands, making them important to flood control. Wetlands provide food, camouflage, and shelter to birds and animals not available in other habitats.

Hours, Facilities

Open from dawn to dusk. A waterless outhouse near the picnic shelter is open year-round. Restrooms in the foyer are open seven months of the year. The Ethan Allen Homestead has separate hours and an admission charge.

Getting There

From Burlington take the Northern Connector, Route 127, north for 0.9 mile to the first exit, North Avenue and Beaches. While still on the exit ramp you will see a sign to the Ethan Allen Homestead at 0.4 mile. Turn right and follow the entrance road past the first small parking area to the welcome center and main parking areas at 0.5 mile.

For More Information

Winooski Valley Park District
(See Organizations: Useful Names and Addresses.)

Ethan Allen Homestead Trust
1 Ethan Allen Homestead, Suite 2
Burlington, VT 05401-1141
802-865-4556

Winooski Nature Trail, Winooski One, and Salmon Hole

Winooski and Burlington

Winooski Nature Trail

1.4 miles

1 hour

moderate

Walk to Winooski One, 0.5 mile, easy

Walk to Salmon Hole, 0.2 mile, easy

The Winooski Nature Trail is a scenic walk along the Winooski River including some dramatic cliffs. A half-mile away, Winooski One is a modern, 7.4-megawatt hydroelectric dam that incorporates a fish lift. Across the river, in Burlington, the Salmon Hole is a traditional fishing spot that was once at the base of the natural falls. The river has carved potholes and other formations in the limestone. Salmon Hole is connected by a 0.7-mile walking path, the River Walk Foot Path, to Intervale Road, just a short distance from the Intervale (see p. 36).

As early as 3000 B.C., the Great Falls on the Winooski River were a focus for human settlement. *Winooski* means "wild onion" in the Abenaki language. Until about 1000 A.D., hunter-gatherers spent time in the area

Winooski Falls was attractive to early European settlers because of its close proximity to farmland in the Intervale, pine woodlands, and water to power mills. In 1772, Ira Allen, youngest brother of Ethan Allen, built a log cabin here with Remember Baker. By 1790 a community, including an iron foundry, had grown up around the falls. At the Salmon Hole, deeper than it is today, small ships were built and barges loaded with logs for Quebec. The only way to cross the river was on the ice or Ira Allen's ferry.

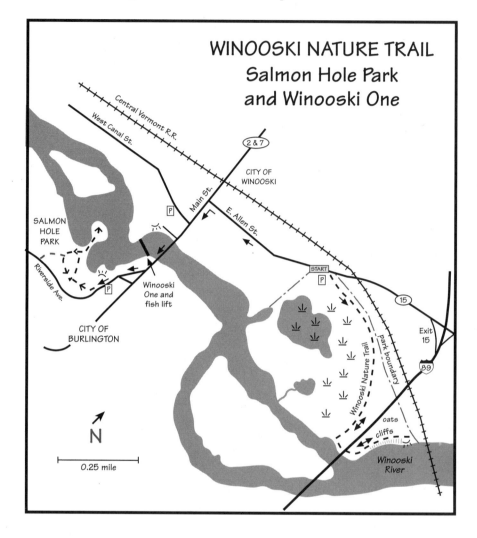

WINOOSKI NATURE TRAIL
Salmon Hole Park
and Winooski One

Over the years mills clustered around the upper and lower falls: flour, grist, paper, saw, textile, and mills that turned flaxseed into linseed oil. In 1870, a gristmill produced 500 barrels of flour each twenty-four hours.

Villages grew up on both sides of the river, but fire and successive floods on the Burlington side eventually spelled an end to industry there.

Woolen mills prospered intermittently. During the Merino sheep boom in the 1830s, Vermont's woolen mills exploded from 33 to 334. In 1837, the Burlington Woolen Mill had nine buildings, among them the largest in Vermont. It was powered by a water mill thirty-six feet in diameter.

Unskilled immigrants living in mill-owned tenements worked long hours in poor conditions. Business ebbed and flowed over a century, booming as wool was used for Civil War uniforms, railroad and police uniforms, and again during both world wars. In 1954 the last mills closed.

In the late 1970s, civic and business groups joined forces to renew the area. The Champlain Mill now is home to a mix of offices and retail space, the Colchester Merino Mill was transformed into the Woolen Mill Apartments, and Winooski One produces renewable energy.

The Winooski Nature Trail starts behind the wooden barrier, plunging from a busy street into the woods. A distant urban cacophony lingers in the air: airplanes; helicopters; car and truck traffic; a railroad symphony of horns, whistles, diesel engines, screeching wheels, and crossing bells; and the peel of midday church bells. Young, sun-loving trees grow in the damp soil: box elder, big-toothed aspen, elm, dogwood, and sumac. An open cattail marsh and tree swamp are visible to the right as the trail descends and traffic noise disappears.

Boardwalks cross a few wet sections and false Solomon's seal grows to large dimensions, producing cascades of rosy berries. A stream bursts from a culvert at the top of a hillside and rushes toward the swamp. Cattails, orange-spotted jewelweed, hog peanut, and ragweed form a wetland thicket.

The trail crosses a bridge, rises slightly, and passes a huge red oak with a double trunk. Swamp maple, shagbark and bitternut hickory, red oak, hop hornbeam, paper birch, ash, cherry, and blue beech (or ironwood) fill the woods. The marsh towers with enormous phragmites, tall reeds topped with showy tufts of seeds. Duckweed flourishes on open water and speckled alder thrives in the wet soil.

The path arrives at the edge of the Winooski River and turns left. The river is wide and lazy with sandy patches of shoreline. The trail, on large chunks of rock, passes beneath a gargantuan interstate-highway bridge. It then regains the bank, with lovely views upriver to the falls and railroad trestle. Sheer limestone cliffs dotted with northern white cedar form the opposite bank.

The trail rises through young woods dominated by multitrunked red oak, hop hornbeam, and alternate-leaved dogwood. A detour to the right ends at the sandy riverbank. The main trail continues uphill to the top of the cliffs through woods of northern white cedar, white pine, and red and white oak. Bracken fern dominates the understory, and beware of poison ivy.

Limestone cliffs along the Winooski River near the Salmon Hole.

Hang on to young children here! The trail, which ends just before the railroad track, affords magnificent views of the falls and limestone cliffs of the Winooski Gorge. Linger for a moment on this sunny perch, listening to the water crashing over the falls.

Retrace your steps to the trailhead and walk or drive to Winooski One.

At Winooski One a fish trap combined with a truck program enables migratory salmon to return to their upriver spawning grounds. The fish lift is a cooperative program involving federal and state fish and wildlife agencies along with Green Mountain Power and the Winooski One Partnership. Installation and operation of the fish-passage facility is a requirement of Winooski One's license. If you are lucky, you may see fish being measured and tagged before trucking. (Call ahead for information.)

Until the early 1800s, salmon was abundant in Lake Champlain. Each fall, adult salmon swim up the tributaries of their birth to spawn. Heavy logging in the colonial era caused erosion and silt buildups. Silt suffocated incubating eggs, and the loss of forest cover allowed the sun to heat streams to temperatures threatening to young salmon. Dams prevented salmon from returning to spawn, and the huge population of salmon blocked below the dams made for easy harvests.

Restoration programs began in 1973. These many-faceted programs include stocking, sea-lamprey control, monitoring of land-use practices, pollution reduction, and fish transport. The stocked fish are raised at the Ed Weed Fish Hatchery in Grand Isle (see p. 25). Trucked fish are placed upstream of Winooski One and two other dams, where they have access to twenty miles of the Winooski and more than eight miles of tributaries.

Playing with nature is tricky business. Over the years the Department of Fish and Wildlife has introduced young fish to multiple locations at various ages to find the most successful combination of age, location, and flow patterns. If the fish are not introduced to the tributaries at a time of high flow, they will not smolt, or leave the mouth of the river to live in the open lake. Experimentation continues in the hope of maintaining a stable population of migratory fish in Lake Champlain.

Salmon Hole, a favorite fishing spot, is just across the Winooski River in Burlington. Many of the game fish of Lake Champlain spawn here. Among the species caught are walleye, pike, steelhead trout, and land-locked salmon. Potholes and other interesting formations have been carved by the river in the 500-million-year-old limestone.

Getting There

From I-89, take northbound Exit 15. Turn left on Route 15 and continue west for 0.3 mile. Parking area is on left.

From the Winooski Nature Trail to Winooski One, continue 0.4 mile on Route 15 (East Allen). Turn left at Route 7. Take your second right on West Canal Street at 0.1 mile. The pedestrian entrance is immediately on the left. Parking is at meters on the street.

From Winooski One to the Salmon Hole, cross the Winooski River on Route 7 and go immediately right at the light. Parking is on the right, 0.2 mile from West Canal Street. A path leads down to the Salmon Hole.

For More Information

Steelhead, an introduced sport fish native to the Pacific, spawn in the spring and migrate upstream from April through June. Salmon return to spawn in October or November. You may call for information on the migrating fish at the Winooski One lift.

Department of Fish and Wildlife
111 West Street
Essex Junction, VT 05452
802-878-1564 or 800-640-3714

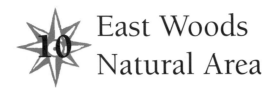

East Woods
Natural Area

Interpretive Trail
South Burlington

0.6 mile

45 minutes

moderate

Old woods and a brook saved from suburban sprawl. A nice winter destination and good for children.

East Woods Natural Area is testimony to a committed community. In 1930, neighbors raised $4,000 to protect the woods from being cut for saw timber. At the urging of Dr. H. E. Perkins, botany professor at the University of Vermont (UVM), the school contributed the additional $7,500 needed to buy the land. The original preserve was more than twice its current size. In the 1960s the interstate connector bisected the land and the parcel north of the highway was sold.

This isle of natural beauty, surrounded by highways and sprawl, is one of UVM's Natural Areas and is used as an outdoor laboratory by students. East Woods has been said to support as many as fifty six species of woody plants on its current forty acres. The area contains some of the largest hemlocks and red and white pines in the Burlington area and has the richest flora of any known area of comparable size in northern Vermont. A mixture of forest types nestle in its contours, and Potash Brook flows between sandy banks.

The interpretive trail was developed in 1986 by Jennifer Murphy, a student in the Environmental Program at the university.

Follow the path to the sign-in ledger and map. Take a copy of the informative brochure.

The trail begins to the left, bordered in late summer by sprays of red elderberries. It's a short distance to Stop 1. On the left is a huge and

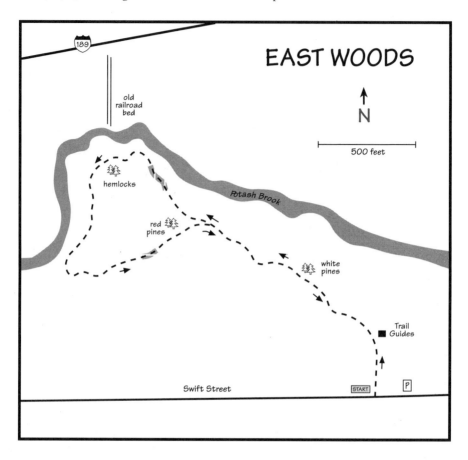

uncharacteristic white pine. White pines are easy to identify, with their single trunk and bundles of five (remember w-h-i-t-e) long needles. When this pine was young, the white-pine weevil, an insect, attacked its terminal shoot. The side branches, usually small and horizontal, compensated to produce this unusual tree. White pine, like northern white cedar, contains vitamin C in its bark. Before the availability of year-round fruit, those who suffered from scurvy, a deficit of vitamin C, consumed these barks.

Spring wildflowers that tolerate acidic conditions thrive beneath the thick canopy of pines: starflower, partridgeberry, and wild lily of the valley.

After a small clearing, the trail descends a sandy gully. Eastern hemlocks are thick on these banks of sand. (See Eastern Hemlocks, p. 59.) At Stop 4, Potash Brook gurgles below to the right. Potash was one of the first exports of the United States. As farmers cleared the forests and burned the trees, tons of wood ash resulted. This ash was boiled and the resulting potash was sold to Europeans to make fertilizer and soap.

Here and across the brook we see a prepared railroad bed. In 1898, a small commuter railway was being constructed until funding was cut. A century later, a new and controversial commuter service is planned on tracks less than a mile from here.

Make a left turn and follow the railroad's path beneath the hemlocks. There is very little understory, and the ground is thick with needles and rotting trunks of paper birches.

After Stop 6, turn left up a short rise. A few oaks grow with the conifers and as a result there is more of an herb layer. We find goldthread, starflower, partridgeberry, and wild lily of the valley here.

Shortly after Stop 7 you will have to clamber over a fallen giant with deeply furrowed cinnamon bark. Look at the shallow root system of this mammoth hemlock. Somehow it clung to the sandy hillside for many years before a windstorm or the weight of a falling neighbor ended its life.

Growing next to the trunk is wintergreen (*Gaultheria procumbens*), a treat of the woods. The small evergreen heath hugs the ground with alternate glossy, dark green leaves. It bears a white, bell-like flower and eventually a red berry. Wintergreen prefers cool, damp woods and is often found beneath oaks and pines. Its leaves are, of course, aromatic with wintergreen oil!

The trail continues downhill to the sandy banks of Potash Brook. The hemlocks now share the sunlight with beech, red oak, and ash. The sandy path follows the stream for a few minutes.

At the end of the Ice Age about 10,000 years ago, with the land still compressed from the weight of glacial ice, salt water flowed south from the St. Lawrence River to create the Champlain Sea (see Button Bay, p. 129). This sea covered an area greater than that of Lake Champlain. East Woods would have been on its shore, and the sand here is the remnant of an old beach.

The trail leaves the brook and turns left at an arrow. Many trillium and jack-in-the-pulpit grow here as the path climbs. At Stop 10 there are several fallen trees, or blowdowns, due at least in part to the sandy soil. This is another chance to see the shallow root system of the giant hemlocks. At Stop 11, on a steep section, a paper birch grows on an eroded mound of sand. Soon the trail arrives at a plateau with several mature hemlocks and red and white pines. It's interesting to compare the barks of the three in close proximity. You can distinguish the hemlock by its short needles and the red pine by the reddish patches of bark on its trunk.

White trillium is one of many spring wildflowers in East Woods.

Striped maple, with its green and white candy stripes, shades a large patch of partridgeberry on the right. This evergreen ground cover has tiny dark green, heart-shaped leaves with a white central vein. Its red berries are a favorite of the partridge.

The trail makes a left turn past another upended tree. The path dips down before climbing a sandy hillside, then turns left and, at an arrow, turns right again. The worn trail is easy to follow.

At Stop 13, a white pine on the left has been excavated by a pileated woodpecker. This begs the question of whether these woodpeckers are beneficial or destructive to living trees. While they remove harmful insects from beneath the bark they also expose the pulp of the tree to destructive fungi and bacteria. Both theories have supporters.

As the trail approaches the clearing at Stop 3, turn right to rejoin the original trail and return to the trailhead.

🌰 EASTERN HEMLOCKS

Hemlocks often grow in pure stands as they shade out competitors. Their needles are flat, about a half-inch long, and soft to the touch. One of our longest-lived trees, hemlocks can live six centuries and grow to 80 feet (in the Appalachians they have reached 160 feet). They favor cool, shady ravines and will grow in a wide range of soils. Hemlocks can germinate in any moist locale and are often found growing on boulders or rotting stumps.

There is concern for the health of hemlocks, as a devastating insect defoliator, the woolly adelgid, moves north through New England. No hemlock has been known to survive its attack.

Getting There

From Interstate 89, take Exit 13 to I-189. Follow the connector to the end. Turn left onto Route 7 south. At 0.1 mile, turn left at the light onto Swift Street. Park at a turnout on the left side of the road in 0.6 mile. There is space for several cars. Walk about 100 yards west along Swift Street to the sign and trail entrance.

For More Information

University of Vermont
Environmental Program
(See Organizations: Useful Names and Addresses.)

In the Area

Redstone Quarry

Another UVM Natural Area, Redstone Quarry, is nearby. Reddish-brown Monkton quartzite was quarried here for more than 100 years. A rock cliff exposes colorful striations, showing the layering of the sandstone, which, under conditions of heat and pressure, metamorphosed into quartzite. The small wetland at its base attracts birds, frogs, and other wildlife. It's a nice place for a picnic.

From the light at I-189 and Route 7, take Route 7 north for 0.9 mile to Hoover Street. Turn right and continue 0.2 mile to a small parking area.

Mud Pond
Conservation Land
Williston

1.0 mile

45 minutes

easy

*Hemlock woods give way to alder swamp and marsh at the
edge of the pond. Wear waterproof boots to go to the pond's
edge. Skiers welcome.*

Not far from Williston's Tafts Corners, Vermont's often-maligned sym-
bol of sprawl, lies an island of tranquillity. Deep hemlock woods muf-
fle the hum of the interstate and the roar of departing jets. Mud Pond,
headwater of Allen Brook, is surrounded by wetlands and a 223-acre oasis
in one of Vermont's fastest-growing towns.

Mud Pond fills a kettle hole left by receding glaciers of the Ice Age.
The six acres of open water are only ten feet deep, the shallow bottom composed of organic debris. Pollen from core samples of this peat is more than
6,000 years old. In more recent times the land has been used for logging,
agriculture, gravel mining, peat extraction, and ice harvesting. Stands of
white pine have grown up on the old pastureland.

Horses, carts, cars, and kids all have gotten stuck in the legendary
mire that gives Mud Pond its name. The peat mat and bog plants are accessible only to the hardy in waterproof boots.

Take the trail to the right in front of the parking area. White pines are
dense and the cushion of needles thick underfoot. The trail is marked
frequently with orange surveyor's tape. Solid white pines give way to woods
of hemlocks, black cherry, hop hornbeam, yellow and paper birch, oak, and
maple, although fast-growing white pines are the tallest. Canada
Mayflower, partridgeberry, starflower, Indian cucumber-root, goldthread,

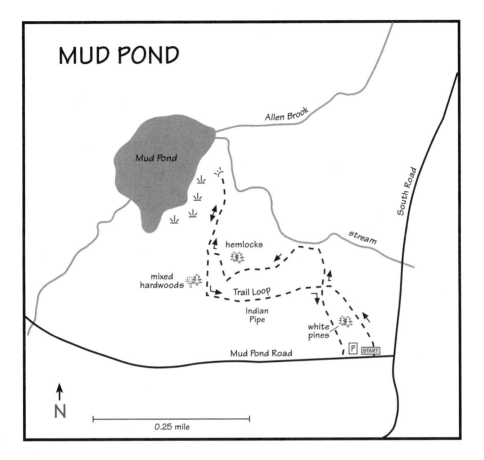

MUD POND

Mud Pond

Allen Brook

South Road

stream

hemlocks

mixed
hardwoods

Trail Loop

Indian
Pipe

white
pines

Mud Pond Road

P START

N

0.25 mile

wood sorrel, and trillium are among the wildflowers tolerant of acidic conditions. The vegetation reflects the underlying soil and bedrock, derived from schist, which is not high in natural fertility. There is no bloodroot or basswood in these woods.

Clumps of club moss, or lycopodium, dot the forest floor. Common names include princess pine, fir club moss, ground cedar, ground pine, and running cedar, sometimes the same name given to two or more species. (See Lycopodium, p. 64.)

Within five minutes the trail goes downhill briefly before coming to an intersection. Turn right toward the pond.

Indian pipe (*Monotropa uniflora*) is prolific in mid- to late summer, its nearly translucent pink or white stems rising from beneath the leaf litter. The plants have no chlorophyll and derive their nourishment from decayed organic matter. The clustered stems turn black as they die.

The trail passes through several wet sections where hummocks of moisture-loving sensitive and cinnamon fern abound. Cinnamon fern can be distinguished from interrupted fern by a woolly tuft at the base of its leaflets. Look carefully at the underside of the frond.

The trail jogs left and right, avoiding a very wet section. The turns are well marked. It then comes to an intersection with a dirt road. Follow the sign right, toward the pond. The track descends through woods of birch, beech, red maple, and hemlock. Striped maple, saplings, and herbs are lush in the understory.

The trail levels out at a mucky section, which explodes in late summer with jewelweed, or touch-me-not. Jog right, then left, over a slippery log bridge. A series of logs cross several sodden stretches.

On drier ground woodland plants return: wild lily of the valley, partridgeberry, wood sorrel, bunchberry, Indian cucumber-root, and goldthread, its glossy parsleylike leaves shimmering in the sunshine.

The trail leads left to the territory of waterproof boots. The University of Vermont uses these peatlands to study bog vegetation. Hummocks of sphagnum moss support black spruce, tamarack, and northern white cedar. Other bog plants include Labrador tea, bog rosemary, leather leaf, and pitcher plant.

Some wetland vegetation is visible from dry land. Cattails fill the marsh, and speckled alder, meadowsweet, and red maple dominate the swamp. One swamp maple has sixteen boles, or trunks. Swamp or red maples show red in every season: buds in winter, flowers in spring, leaf stems in summer, and leaves in fall. Some swamp maples begin to color in August.

Return along the same route through the lowlands. As the road climbs, a sign points left toward the parking area. We came from this path. Do not turn left but continue straight. The woods are mostly deciduous and the trail soon levels off. You may see blue-bead lily, or Clintonia, a cluster of yellow, lilylike flowers on a single stem in spring and deep blue berries in late summer. The plant has a pair of shiny, oblong leaves and prefers moist, acid soils.

At a sign that says Park Ends Here, turn left, following the surveyor's tape. White pines increase and mushrooms flourish in the company of Indian pipes. On the left is a nurse log (a stump, actually), home to moss, ferns, wood sorrel, goldthread, hemlock seedlings, and even a young white pine. The hemlocks likely will survive, as their roots are inclined to reach far and wide for nourishment and support. The white pine is unlikely to fare as well.

A colony of club moss, or lycopodium, can take up to a century to grow. Don't pick them, please!

The path crosses another damp section of ferns. It then rises to drier land, and herbs of the forest return, including vast clumps of Indian pipe. Partridgeberry is also particularly lush, its orange-red berries poking from the tangle of tiny green-and-white leaves.

Two more intersections follow in close succession. Turn right both times. The last short section is through dense white pines. Within minutes the trail meets the road; the parking area is about 100 feet to the east.

❋ *FRIENDS DON'T LET FRIENDS PICK LYCOPODIUM*

Creeping underfoot, usually in the shade of their namesakes, are tiny evergreen plants with names like running pine, ground cedar, and running moss. These members of the fern family are club mosses, or lycopodia.

Fossils of club mosses date to the Paleozoic era, more than 300 million years ago. Their ancestors were a part of vast fern jungles which ultimately produced, largely by their spores, coal still mined today.

Club mosses prefer cool, damp, shady sites with acidic soil. Several species inhabit the sphagnum bog, the ultimate wet, acidic environment.

Club mosses grow very slowly: a sustainable colony may take seventy-five years to develop. They propagate most efficiently by runners, since the reproductive cycle of two generations takes nearly twenty years. The unknowing who pick these diminutive greens for holiday decorations can destroy a century's growth in m inutes.

The spores of club mosses are so minute and uniform in size that they were once used for microscopic measurements. Water-repellent and dust-like, spores coated pills. They were also used for fireworks and photographic flashes, as they give off an explosive flash when lit. The leaves and stems have been used in dying woolens and as emetics and poisons!

Getting There

From Tafts Corner in Williston, the intersection of Routes 2 and 2A, take Route 2 east. In the village of Williston, 2.3 miles, turn right on West Hill Road. Turn left, just past the interstate, onto South Road at 0.3 mile. After 1.9 miles turn right on Mud Pond Road. Parking is on the right.

For More Information

Public Works Department
Town of Williston
722 Williston Road
Williston, VT 05495
802-878-1239

Colchester Bog Natural Area

Colchester

0.5 mile

1 hour

very easy

A boardwalk to the suspended world of the bog and its extra-ordinary vegetation.

Colchester Bog is one of two large peat bogs adjacent to Lake Champlain. The larger, 800-acre Maquam Bog is part of the Missisquoi National Wildlife Refuge (see p. 1). Colchester Bog, at 184 acres, is a University of Vermont (UVM) Natural Area. Several years ago UVM built a 400-foot floating boardwalk, which allows visitors to see the unusual and very fragile vegetation without harming it. A nearby recreational path also passes through a section of the bog (see In the Area, p. 70).

Colchester Bog began forming about 9,000 years ago in an old channel of the Winooski River. When the river shifted, a sandbar developed along the shoreline, cutting off the flow of lake water.

There are no streams entering the bog. A bog evolves when there is no fresh supply of water (see About Bogs, p. 69). Over the millennia a thick carpet of sphagnum moss, or peat, has grown, twenty feet deep in places. Almost none of Colchester Bog is open peatland, as trees and shrubs have grown up over the years.

As the sand barriers are porous, the water table fluctuates with the lake level. The annual spring flooding pours water over the sandbars, providing a yearly surge of oxygen and nutrients.

Walk to the right of the children's playground toward a wooden barricade of posts at the edge of the trees. This stockade protects an endangered plant, downy hudsonia (*Hudsonia tomentosa*). Colchester Point

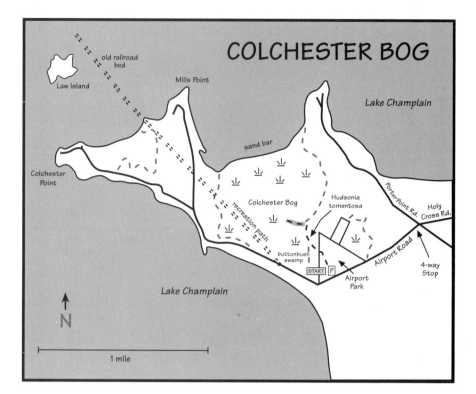

was once mostly dunes and is one of only four sites in Vermont where this low shrub survives. Its long, delicate root fibers enable it to thrive despite shifting sands.

To the left of the barrier locate a small path that passes between an oak on the left and a small cherry tree on the right, then into a tunnel of white pines. Emerging from the trees, you intersect a worn path. Turn left. After about fifty feet, turn right around a medium-sized red oak into an allée of gray birch. The narrow path is sandy and worn. Notice the reindeer moss, tufts of gray-green lichen, along the trail. Lichen thrive in inhospitable environments like this nutrient-poor, sandy soil.

The path slopes downhill through young deciduous woods to the edge of the bog that looks like a wet depression. Turn right, still on a sandy path, and walk a few hundred feet to the wooden boardwalk on the left.

Slow your pace to a crawl on the boardwalk. The bog is exploding with life, much of it quite unfamiliar.

At the edge of the bog, runoff from higher ground neutralizes the acidic water somewhat. Royal ferns, meadowsweet, and jewelweed live in these first few yards along the edge.

Trees on the bog are scrubby: swamp maple; tamarack, or larch, with its soft, bright green needles; gray birch; black spruce; and pitch pine—this last an anomaly, as it usually prefers well-drained, sandy soils.

The shrub layer is at eye level since the boardwalk is elevated. Highbush blueberries, eight or ten feet tall, are laden with an astonishing crop of berries. In midsummer speckled alder still cling to some of last year's tiny wooden cones. Black alder (*Ilex verticillata*), or winterberry, is also here. A member of the holly family, it is not related to speckled alder. Clusters of two or three tiny starlike white blossoms ripen to scarlet berries in the axils of the shrub's oval, serrated leaves.

Near the boardwalk, two to three feet high, are several characteristic, acid-loving bog plants. Rhodora is a member of the heath family and the *Rhododendron* genus, which may help you recognize it. Early purple-pink flowers precede the leaves. The inch-long, gray-green leaves are oblong and roll under at the edges.

Also easy to recognize because of their domestic cousins are the laurels, sheep and bog laurel, both of which have pink flowers and thrive in northern bogs. Sheep laurel, sometimes called lambkill, is poisonous to livestock. Its flowers are in the middle of the stem. Bog laurel leaves are thinner, more like rosemary leaves, and its flowers are at the end of the branch.

One of the dominant shrubs is leather leaf, an evergreen plant two to four feet high. Its leathery, toothless leaves are oblong and between one and two inches long. White, bell-shaped flowers may appear as early as March on this bog pioneer. Leather leaf can advance bog development by forming floating mats around the edges of open water.

Many bog plants are northern species adapted to stressful conditions. Despite the abundance of water, acidic conditions make it difficult for plants to absorb it. Thick, leathery leaves preserve moisture and protect the plants from transpiration.

At the bottom of all this is the deep, underlying mat of sphagnum moss. Over the thousands of years since the shift of the Winooski River channel, the moss has been thriving in this acidic, oxygen-poor environment. Tufts of sphagnum form the floor of this bog and support its specialized vegetation.

In the herb layer you may recognize huckleberry and bog cranberry. The cranberry is similar to cultivated fruit but the leaves are tiny, about a half-inch long. Arrowhead, with leaves shaped like arrows, is also called

Pitcher plants inhabit the suspended world of the peat bog. These carnivorous plants get nitrogen from their insect victims.

duck potato, as its rhizomes are eaten by ducks and muskrats. A rhizome is an underground stem, not a root, which often has enlarged nodes for food storage.

Wild calla, or water arum, is a vine with a showy, tropical-looking flower. Its leaves are heart shaped and the flower a bold white spathe (not a petal, although it looks like one) around a spadix, a spiky growth covered with tiny yellow flowers.

Last but not least, the most spectacular of the bog plants is the carnivorous pitcher plant, whose leaves resemble red-and-green organ pipes. There are quite a number at the far end of the boardwalk, lying low against the sphagnum mat. A single, spectacular purple-red flower on a leafless stem rises a foot or more above the equally extravagant curved leaves. The leaves form tubes, which fill with rainwater for trapping insects. Stiff, downward-pointing hairs prevent the prey from escaping. The captives are eventually broken down by the plant's digestive juices and the nutrients absorbed by the plant. The insects provide nitrogen not otherwise available in this suspended, soilless world.

⬂⬃ BOGS AND SPHAGNUM MOSS

While most bogs in Vermont are kettle bogs, formed when retreating glacial ice left depressions in the bedrock, the state's two largest bogs are the result of shifting river courses.

A relative of jack-in-the-pulpit and philodendron, the exotic water arum, or wild calla, looks remarkably tropical for Vermont.

Bogs occur in an environment of stagnant water. As plants grow, die, and decay, the dissolved oxygen in the water is depleted and bacteria can no longer live. Decay ceases and the water becomes sterile. Most plants cannot live in this highly acidic, nutrient- and oxygen-poor environment.

Over thousands of years, special bog vegetation has evolved. Sphagnum moss is one of the most successful of these plants and generally provides the surface on which other plants grow. It can absorb up to a hundred times its weight in water and floats on the surface of the bog. As the moss dies it does not decay but accumulates as peat. Nearly 10,000 years of sphagnum have filled Colchester Bog to a depth of twenty feet.

The surface of the bog is spongelike and jiggles underfoot. Mats of sphagnum are sometimes called quaking mats. The peat can be dried and used in gardens and as fuel for fires. Because of the absence of decay, peat bogs preserve historic records. Bodies, tools, artifacts, and pollen found in bogs can reveal remarkable information.

Getting There

Coming from Burlington, take the Northern Connector, Route 127 north. The road crosses the Winooski River into Colchester and is no longer a limited-access highway. Turn left at the first traffic light onto Porter's Point Road. When the road forks, stay left and continue 1.4 miles to Airport Road. Turn left and drive 0.6 mile to Airport Park on the right.

For More Information

University of Vermont
Environmental Program
(See Organizations: Useful Names and Addresses.)

In the Area

The Recreation Path begins 0.3 mile farther along Airport Road. This path cuts across a corner of the bog on an old railroad bed. A tree-dominated swamp stretches into the distance. Runoff feeds many nonbog plants at its edge: ash, pussy willows, red osier, and buttonbush. Blooming in late July, buttonbush dominates the shrub layer with thousands of suspended white pompoms.

Delta Park

Colchester

1.2 miles, no elevation gain

1 hour

easy

A glimpse of the sandy shore and dunes once common along Lake Champlain. Expansive lake views and sunsets. A good walk for even the youngest children.

From its vast drainage basin to the east, the Winooski River carries a huge volume of water and sediment to Lake Champlain. As the riverbed widens and the water slows down, the smallest of these suspended particles settle out and a river delta is created. At the mouth of the Winooski, deposited silt has created extensive marshes and swamps on both sides of the river.

Delta Park preserves a large marsh, silver maple swamps, and sandy shoreline. Over thousands of years wind-whipped waves have deposited sand here at the widest section of open lake. The southern shore of Colchester Point was once covered by sand dunes. At Delta Park, vestigial sand dunes and several rare plants give us a chance to imagine that landscape.

Walk through the wooden barricades past a pair of black locust trees. Their lower bark is furrowed, and leguminous seed pods dangle from the branches. The trail passes a sandy berm, a tangle of prickles and vines, among them rosa rugosa, raspberries, blackberries, grapevines, and Virginia creeper.

The Winooski River is to the left across a swamp. Cottonwoods, willows, silver maples, and red osier dogwood grow near the water's edge, all at home with wet feet. Box elder thrives here, too. A member of the maple family with opposite, compound leaves, this sturdy tree grows to thirty or

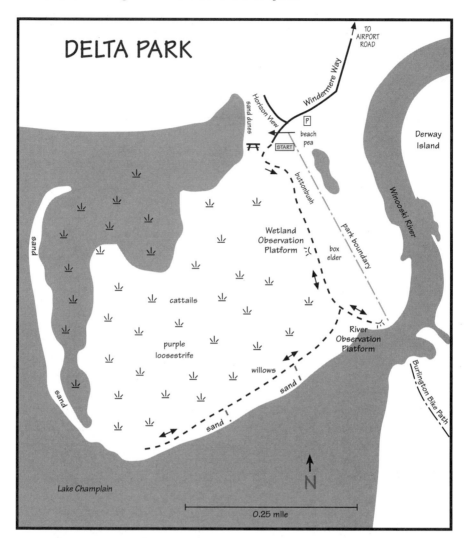

DELTA PARK

TO
AIRPORT
ROAD

Windermere Way

Horizon View
sand dunes

P

beach
pea

START

Derway
Island

Winooski River

buttonbush

park boundary

Wetland
Observation
Platform

box
elder

sand

cattails

River
Observation
Platform

purple
loosestrife

willows

sand

Burlington Bike Path

sand

sand

N

Lake Champlain

0.25 mile

forty feet. Its seeds and leaves recall the ash family, but its leaflets can be irregular and multilobed, unlike the ash.

Throughout Delta Park there are many pencil-pointed stumps, indicating beaver activity. Many of the poplars have resprouted.

Make sure to detour to the left on one of the worn trails to see buttonbush in the swamp. Its white flowers resemble tiny pincushions and its fruit is a pale brown spherical ball. This water-loving shrub, often found near rivers and lakes, can grow to about twenty feet. Irregular branches may lean every which way, giving the plant an odd shape. Shiny, poisonous foliage remains untouched, while its seeds are a delicacy for ducks, water birds, and shorebirds.

Vines entangle every vertical and horizontal surface in midsummer. The hog peanut, with its three (remember h-o-g) yellow-green leaflets, twines along the ground. Honeysuckle, groundnut, Virginia creeper, wild grape, Queen Anne's lace, red raspberries, and milkweed all contribute to the chaotic thicket.

An observation deck on the right looks across a cattail marsh ablaze with purple loosestrife in mid-summer (see p. 74).

A leisurely fifteen-minute walk leads to the river-observation point, a bridge abutment on the old railroad line. We look across the Winooski River toward the northern end of the Burlington Bike Path. Snapping turtles are said to lay their eggs in the sand along the river channel.

Retrace your steps, and after a minute or two take the path to the left. The lake is now on your left and the marsh to the right. Willows at the edge of the marsh spend at least part of the year submerged. You can recognize their long, brittle twigs even in winter. Jewelweed, a lover of wet places, grows to over four feet here and looks limp in the midday heat.

Turn left when you see a path to the beach (there are several). Imagine that miles of sand once stretched along the shores of Lake

When buttonbush blooms in mid- to late summer, it dots the swamps with its showy white pompoms.

Champlain. High water has washed stumps and dead tree trunks onto the beach, and a few remarkably tenacious trees cling to life. Several red maples and willows, more dead than alive, have clumps of leaves. Red maple saplings have sprouted just above the high-water mark. At a safer distance from the water some silver maples thrive, with multiple trunks and deeply lobed, silvery leaves. Red osier dogwood is robust as well.

When the beach becomes impassable, return to the trail and retrace your steps back to the parking area.

When you reach the gate, take a detour toward the water. Several passageways lead through the fencing, which protects the vestigial sand dunes from traffic. The endangered beach pea grows here. Its vines look similar to those of a garden pea; likewise its purple flowers and leguminous pods. It will look familiar to visitors to Cape Cod, where the beach pea thrives on the dunes.

Another walkway leads to a stretch of driftwood-covered shore.

✳ PURPLE LOOSESTRIFE

Its purple-pink stalks waving over a cattail marsh on an August day, purple loosestrife is colorful, even pretty. But this introduced plant is conspiring to starve waterfowl across Vermont.

Introduced from Europe to the United States nearly two centuries ago, purple loosestrife (*Lythrum salicaria*) has no enemies on this continent and is spreading through wetlands at an alarming rate. An aggressive species, it crowds reeds, grasses, and other wetland plants that are food for ducks, geese, and other denizens of the marsh. Waterfowl cannot eat purple loosestrife, and if the invader crowds out their native foods, they will starve.

The problem is more severe in other states than in Vermont, and the U.S. Department of Agriculture has developed a strategy now being tried here. A beetle that feeds exclusively on purple loosestrife, the *Galerucella*, has been introduced in several locations. If the strategy is successful, the beetle will reproduce and eventually keep the loosestrife invasion in check.

Getting There

From Burlington, take the Northern Connector, Route 127 north. The road crosses the Winooski River into Colchester and is no longer a limited-access highway. Turn left at the first light, Porter's Point Road, 4.4 miles from the beginning of Route 127. When the road forks, stay left and continue 1.4 miles to a stop sign at Airport Road. Turn left and drive 0.5 mile to Windermere Way on the left. The park is 0.7 mile at the end of Windermere.

The sandy beach of Delta Park is littered with tree trunks, some dead and others still clinging to life.

For More Information

Winooski Valley Park District
(See Organizations: Useful Names and Addresses.)

In the Area

Half Moon Cove

One of the few lakeshore wetlands on the northern shores of Lake Champlain, Half Moon Cove is an important fish-spawning and waterfowl-breeding habitat. As a result, it's also a great place to watch hungry muskrats, turtles, and great blue heron. Once a meander of the Winooski River, the cove is now isolated except in spring floods. Several short paths lead to the edge of the cove.

On Route 127, after crossing the Winooski River bridge into Colchester, take the second left, 0.6 mile, into Holbrook Court. Walk down the path at the end of the residential cul-de-sac.

Sunny Hollow

Colchester

1.0 mile

1 hour

easy to moderate

A Cape Cod walk in Vermont: pitch pines, oaks, and heaths on glacially deposited sand. Can be buggy.

Don't be put off by the neighborhood —light industry and megastores— or the ten-minute walk through a natural-gas-pipeline right of way. This walk is one of the best-kept secrets of Chittenden County.

The unusual feature, for Vermont in any case, is a remnant of a pitch pine–black oak–heath woodland like that which once covered the sand plains of Colchester. Deposited by the receding glacier, this sand has the same Ice Age pedigree as many of the sand and gravel pits in Colchester and neighboring towns. The sand-plain forest contrasts sharply with the adjacent ravines leading to Sunderland Brook, where moisture and nutrient runoff support a greater diversity of trees, shrubs, and herbs.

The trails are not well marked, but all of them eventually return to the gravel access road. The area is small and bounded by industry, highways, Camp Johnson, and Sunderland Brook. If you go astray you will not get lost.

Take the gravel road behind the gate. An industrial building sprawls on the left and a scruffy thicket of poplar, gray birch, and willow is on the right. The land is maintained for access to a buried natural-gas pipeline. Common wildflowers bloom along this stretch, including black-eyed Susan, Queen Anne's lace, cow vetch, and bird's-foot trefoil. The latter has a cheerful yellow pealike flower on stems with three leaves—hence its

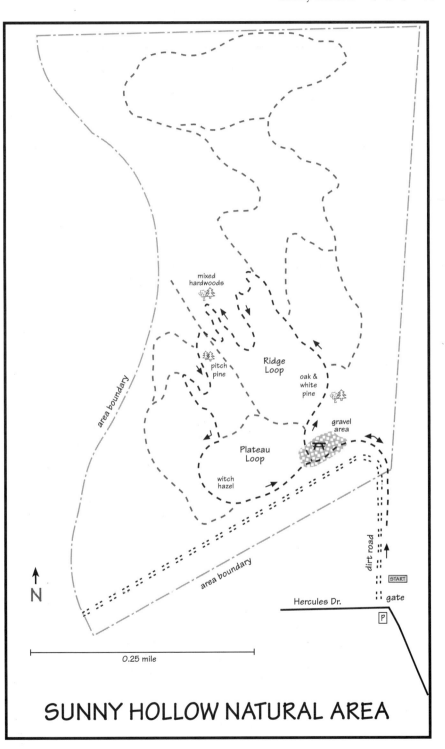

mixed
hardwoods

pitch
pine

Ridge
Loop

oak &
white
pine

gravel
area

Plateau
Loop

witch
hazel

area boundary

area boundary

dirt road

N

0.25 mile

Hercules Dr.

START

gate

P

SUNNY HOLLOW NATURAL AREA

name. The plant is low, usually less than one foot tall, and is found in sunny fields and roadsides.

The road ends at a gravel circle. Look to the right for an unmarked trail, the Ridge Loop, that enters the woods. Within the first few feet a wider dirt track goes left. Stay right on the smaller trail.

Red and white oak share the canopy with white pine and the occasional gray birch or maple. None of the trees is very large because of the dry, sandy soil. Oak leaves, slow to decompose, litter the ground. Acid-tolerant plants grow well in this soil, among them several heaths; the rare trailing arbutus; sheep laurel, a small shrub with pink flowers similar to its cultivated cousin; wintergreen, with glossy, dark-green leaves; and lowbush blueberry. Bracken fern, its three-part fronds lying nearly horizontal, shuns

Pitch pine trees can sprout from the trunk, enabling them to quickly recover after a fire.

the limy soils usually favored by ferns and is abundant here, as are wild sarsaparilla, sweet fern, and partridgeberry.

The trail soon slopes downhill and the vegetation changes before our eyes. The soil in the ravine collects moisture and nutrient runoff from the sandy plain. Sand particles are too big to retain water well. Maple and paper birch join the oak and gray birch, and all of them are suddenly taller. Hemlocks grow in the shade. Red, mountain, and striped maple saplings grow in the understory along with starflower, wild lily of the valley, goldthread, and Clintonia. Clintonia is acid tolerant but prefers damp soil.

A few small trails branch to the right. Stay left on the main trail, which descends into a stream bed. Hobblebush and cinnamon fern both proliferate in the damp soil.

The trail goes over a stump bridge before rising again. Water bars cross a steep section. Along the steep banks, look for tree roots and moss holding the soil against continued erosion.

The trail passes through another wet section where jewelweed flourishes. An array of mushrooms grow on a steep climb with numerous switchbacks. Large oak, beech, and maple dominate.

At the top of the rise two paths intersect. Jog briefly to the right then turn immediately left. This is the Pitch Pine Loop, the heart of the dry sand plain. Trees are scrubbier and the canopy more open. Pitch pines mix with oak, gray birch, red maple, and white pine.

Pitch pines are small trees that grow to sixty feet and have bunches of three needles, two to five inches long. The hard, nearly round cones have prickles and may remain on the trees for up to a dozen years. Pitch pines grow more slowly than many of their competitors, especially white pine, and depend on fire to survive. After a fire, pitch pines sprout from the stump and from tufts of needles along the trunk. No other pine can do this. Fire also releases nutrients as it burns fallen needles, providing clear ground for seed germination. Blueberries benefit from periodic burning as well. Old wood is destroyed and the plant puts forth new, prolific branches.

Black oak, at the northern extreme of its range in the Champlain Valley, also grows here. With pointed rather than round lobes, its leaves resemble those of red oak. Unlike the red oak, it produces acorns in two years, not one. Black oak, sometimes confusingly called yellow oak because of its yellow or orange inner bark, thrives on dry, upland, sandy soils. It was once used as a source of tannin, medicine, and yellow dye.

The heaths, early and late lowbush blueberries, sheep laurel, and black huckleberry are abundant, as are bracken fern and sweet fern

Sweet fern is an indicator plant found on poor, often acidic soils.

(*Comptonia peregrina*). Despite fernlike foliage, sweet fern is a flowering plant. Grouse and white-tailed deer feed on its aromatic twigs and leaves.

Turn right onto the Plateau Loop. The dry, sandy soil continues to support vegetation that doesn't require rich soils. Such faster-growing trees as gray birch, oak, maple, and white pine have surpassed the pitch pines without benefit of fire. Witch hazel joins the understory as the trail returns to the gravel lot.

Retrace your steps on the dirt road to the entry gate.

⚡ FIRE IN NATURE

Lightning has always caused fires in nature. Only in recent years have humans intervened, usually to protect human habitation. Without fire, nature's balance is jeopardized in communities like Sunny Hollow.

Some types of forests are more vulnerable to fire than others. Where pine needles and oak leaf litter accumulate, few herbaceous plants can grow. The combination of flammable debris and the absence of a damp, green ground cover makes oak-pine communities especially fire prone.

Fire has long been an effective forest-management tool. In *Reading the Forested Landscape,* author Tom Wessels maintains that Native Americans in the Northeast used fire to help control insects, maintain berry production, make the forest floor quiet for stalking and hunting, and encourage the growth of nut-bearing trees. Several of the region's most prolific nut producers have the most fire resistant bark: white oak, shagbark hickory, and the nearly extinct American chestnut.

Getting There

Take I-89 Exit 16, Routes 2 and 7. Turn right and follow the combined routes north for 0.4 mile. Turn right onto Hercules Drive. At the bend in the road, 0.3 mile, park on the left at the turnout near the gate. Walk down the gated road about ten minutes to the trailhead.

For More Information

Town of Colchester
Recreation Department
Blakeley Road
Colchester, VT 05446
802-655-0811

Colchester Pond

Colchester

2.5 miles

2 hours

moderate with steep, rocky sections

A lakeside walk in the near-wilderness of inner Chittenden
County. All dogs must be leashed.

Colchester Pond is the newest acquisition of the Winooski Valley Park District. Surrounding a mile-long pond with 2.4 miles of shoreline, this park provides a greenway link to Indian Brook Reservoir, a scenic overlook of the Champlain Valley, and a wilderness home to deer, bobcat, fisher, and fox. The 693 acres were dedicated in 1997 after a nine-year effort to combine eight separate acquisitions.

The trail leads down the grassy slope to the water's edge and turns left along the shoreline. Hayfields rise to the left and a hedgerow grows along the pond. Jewelweed abounds near the shore and milkweed spreads through the hayfield, attracting monarch butterflies. The trail tunnels through hedgerows where several spreading basswood and shagbark hickory trees tower over sumac, a few intimidating hawthorns with two-inch thorns, opposite-leaf dogwood, honeysuckle, and spirea.

In the shallow water bur reed, cattails, wild celery, stonewort, spike rush, and bulrush flourish. In the adjacent wetland, jewelweed and spotted joe-pye weed are lush.

As the trail leaves the open fields sweet fern grows on left, an indicator of dry, acidic sites. A flowering plant with fernlike foliage, it has a woody stem. Sun-loving white pines give way to deciduous woods as the trail rises and falls following yellow-green blazes. The blazes are clear until the trail reaches the ridge on the far side of the pond. Plans call for more trail blazing in the spring of 1998.

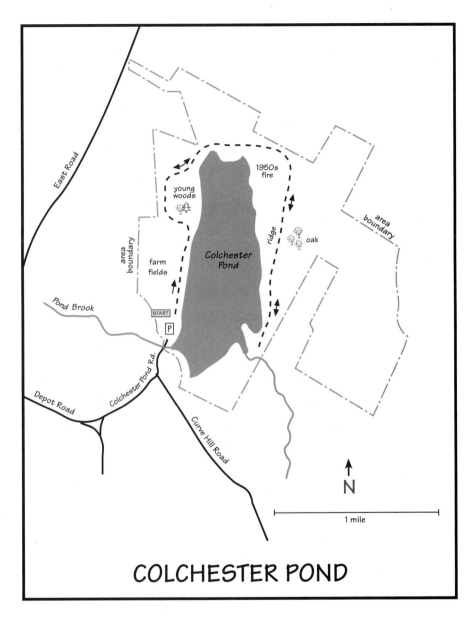

COLCHESTER POND

False Solomon's seal is abundant in the understory, along with partridgeberry, meadow rue, and jack-in-the-pulpit. The woods are a mix of young red and white oak, paper birch, hop hornbeam, serviceberry, elm, big-toothed aspen, red and sugar maple, and ash. The footing is rocky as the trail climbs gently.

Pussy willow is among the hydrophilic plants at Colchester Pond.

The trail makes a right turn and follows a damp course downhill. Bloodroot, an indicator plant, grows in what must be fertile soil. A left turn at the pond edge is marked by an arrow about twenty-five minutes along the trail.

Shortly a boardwalk crosses a wet section where sensitive fern and jewelweed flourish. The trail turns left and rises, climbing stone steps. Herb Robert flowers beneath a grove of white pine.

Another fifteen minutes brings us to a bridge over a rivulet before a steep and rocky hillside. The vegetation changes as we climb. American beech, maple, paper birch, basswood, and hemlock grow among the rocky outcroppings. Many trees with multiple trunks and a few charred stumps are remnants of a fire that raged here about fifty years ago. While multiple trunks are often a sign of logging, it is unlikely that every species would have been logged at the same time.

As the trail rises over rocky ledges, hemlock perch precariously on ledges. Three evergreen ferns grow: Christmas, polypody, and spinulose wood fern.

Yellow blazes mark the path as striped maple, a favorite of deer, becomes abundant in the shrub layer. After a final steep section the trail goes right at an arrow and picks up an old logging road along the quartzite ridge. The drier, less fertile soil supports fewer plants than the more moist and fertile lower slopes. Red and white oak and hop hornbeam dominate with the occasional hickory. There are no large-diameter trees. We pass a red maple on the left with a bird's-eye pattern on the bark. Understory plants that tolerate either dry or acidic conditions predominate, including wintergreen, lowbush blueberry, starflower, bracken fern, Indian pipe, Indian cucumber-root, and partridgeberry. Masses of club moss grow and many asters flower in September.

Bobcat den among the rocky ridges, where the undulating topography provides isolation and protection. These secretive predators are not tolerant of human interference. Please stay on the trail.

The trail continues, unblazed, along the ridge until it reaches open fields near the south end of the pond. Signs indicate the end of the trail. Retrace your steps to the trailhead. On the return, look for the left arrow off of the logging road and back onto the blazed trail.

AMPHIBIANS

Spring is announced by the mating call of frogs—the male's distinctive aria to females of the same species. Even while ice lingers on the ponds, the couple produces a jellied mass of beadlike fertilized eggs. The dark yolk within the clear orb will divide and divide until, several weeks later, a tadpole swims free.

Amphibians live on land and in water and, like fish, reptiles, birds, and mammals, are vertebrates. Unlike birds and mammals, however, they do not need to maintain their body temperature in winter. Coldblooded animals merely decrease their activities as the temperature plunges.

In the Devonian period, 360 million years ago, close relatives of fish may have been attracted to land by ample food and fewer enemies. Lungs evolved for breathing and fins evolved into limbs. Most of these animals became extinct, but a few evolved into modern amphibians.

*Found in a wide range of soils, false Solomon's seal
is a common flowering plant of the woodlands.*

Three groups of amphibians are frogs and toads; newts, salamanders, and sirens; and the little-known tropical wormlike caecilians. Tailed amphibians—newts, salamanders, and sirens—include 360 species, most found in temperate, forested regions of the Northern Hemisphere. There are 3,500 species of frogs, a term often used to include both frogs and toads.

Frogs tend to be more active than toads; live in or near water; and have smooth skin, long hind legs, and fully webbed feet. In contrast, less active toads prefer land and have dry, warty skin, short legs, and little or no webbing.

Amphibians have naked skin—no hair, feathers, or surface scales—and can breathe through their skin as well as their lungs. This distinguishes them from reptiles, which have dry, scaly skin.

Water is essential to amphibians because porous skin allows for great loss of moisture. Most require water for reproduction, as their eggs are laid in water and the larval stage is waterbound.

Among their adaptations, most amphibians are dark colored above and light below, making them less visible to both overhead and underwater predators as they blend into their respective backgrounds. Their dark-colored backs also absorb heat better from the sun.

While their diet includes insects, spiders, snails, slugs, and earthworms, amphibians represent dinner to turtles, otters, and snakes, among others.

Getting There

Take I-89 Exit 16. Go right on Route 7 for 1.7 miles. Turn right on Severance Road. After 1.0 mile, turn left on Mill Pond Road. At a stop sign in 1.6 miles, go straight onto East Road. Turn right on Depot Road, 0.2 mile. You will cross the railroad and the road turns to dirt. Fork left on Colchester Pond Road at 1.1 miles. The parking area is on the right in 0.2 mile.

For More Information

Winooski Valley Park District
(See Organizations: Useful Names and Addresses.)

Southern Chittenden County

Shelburne Farms

Farm Trail

Shelburne

4.25 miles

3 hours

moderate

(Lone Tree Hill, 2.0 miles and 1.5 hours, round-trip, moderate)

On the shores of Lake Champlain, a Vanderbilt Webb agricultural estate is now a nonprofit educational foundation and working farm. A wonderful walk for children to Lone Tree Hill. No dogs allowed in season.

Shelburne Farms was created by Dr. William Seward Webb and his wife, Lila Vanderbilt Webb, during the Gilded Age. With the Champlain Valley on hard times after the collapse of the wool market, the Webbs began buying failed sheep farms on Shelburne Point. By the turn of the century they had acquired thirty-two farms totaling 3,800 acres.

Shelburne Farms was more than a luxurious retreat for the wealthy; it was a model farm and an expression of the new conservation movement. Landscape architect Frederick Law Olmsted, designer of Central Park, created the visual landscape with ponds, lawns, fields, and forests. No view

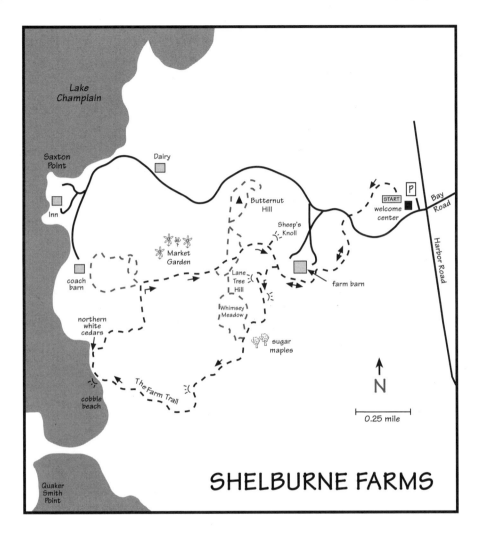

SHELBURNE FARMS

was left to chance as 10,000 trees and shrubs were planted every year for ten years.

The first head of the U.S. Forest Service, Gifford Pinchot, began his career at Shelburne Farms. Pinchot developed a plan to maximize yield and sustain productivity of the wood lots.

The years between 1895 and 1910 were the heyday of Shelburne Farms. The five-story farm barn, with its two-acre courtyard, was equipped with gas lights and steam conveyors and elevators. Two hundred and fifty workers and forty teams of horses and mules tended to herds and crops. A breeding barn was built, then the largest barn in the country. Steam green-

The Farm Barn, once the focus of agricultural activity, is now home to an educational center, children's farmyard, raptor care facility, and cheese-making operation. Photo by Margaret Campbell, courtesy of Shelburne Farms Collection.

houses were filled with flowers and more than 100,000 trees and shrubs grew in the nursery.

A who's who of social luminaries visited Shelburne Farms. The 110-room Queen Anne Revival "cottage," designed by Robert H. Robertson, had velvet lawns and gardens spilling down to the lake. During extreme weather the house consumed a railroad car of coal each day. Plans called for a grander, Newport-style mansion to be built on Lone Tree Hill.

Alas, times changed, and when federal income taxes were introduced in 1913 it became more difficult to maintain such wealth. In 1914, Dr. Webb gave half of the farm to his son James Watson Webb as a wedding present. (The latter's wife, Electra Havemeyer Webb, founded the Shelburne Museum in 1947 on some of this land. See In the Area, p. 93.)

The decline of Shelburne Farms accelerated with the death of Dr. Webb in 1926. Only in 1938 did his grandson Derrick reenergize the farm. Derrick Webb experimented with herds and crops and built a pole barn for cattle, then a novel idea with its open design.

By the late 1960s the Webbs could no longer remain on the farm.

Despite the financial realities, they refused to sell the farm for development. Over a period of fifteen years, Derrick Webb and his children created the nonprofit Shelburne Farms, a foundation that teaches stewardship and sustainable agriculture through continued farming of the property.

Today, Shelburne Farms is a 1,400-acre working farm maintained by gifts, grants, and revenues from cheddar cheese making, a mail-order business, and the Inn at Shelburne Farms. Each year, thousands of teachers and students of all ages participate in a wide range of educational programs.

As you enjoy the woods, fields, and lakeside bluffs, take a moment to appreciate that this spectacular property is performing a vital mission and is not a subdivision of lake-front mansions. The entire property, both land and buildings, is on the National Register of Historic Places.

The loop from the Welcome Center to Lake Champlain via Lone Tree Hill is more than four miles long. While it is too long for young children, they might happily stay behind (with an adult) at the Farm Barn, where they can milk cows and goats, collect chicken eggs, comb an angora bunny, and watch piglets romp in their pen. Lone Tree Hill is a perfect destination for a family walk and picnic.

The walking trail begins at the Welcome Center and crosses a hayfield to the right before turning left beneath an arch of trees. The trail crosses the main road and then hugs the woods along the edge of a field. The massive Farm Barn towers ahead. The cheese-making operation, classrooms, offices, and children's farmyard are here.

The trail goes left around the Farm Barn and continues uphill on a dirt road. As you climb take a backward glance at the stretch of the Green Mountains beyond the clock tower.

Take a left when the dirt road forks. Look for the blue blazes and arrows of the Farm Trail. Just past a picnic shelter on the left, blue arrows point left and the trail leaves the road.

These woods host maple, birch, ash, white pine, basswood, and hickory. Red elderberry is a frequent shrub. Its compound leaves, with five to seven oblong leaflets, resemble those of the ashes. The leaves are opposite and the clustered flowers recall the viburnums, to which red elderberry is related. Its scarlet berries color the woods as early as July.

The trail emerges from woods at Lone Tree Hill. Linger awhile over the view: farm fields, the Inn at Shelburne Farms, Lake Champlain, and the Adirondacks.

The trail continues uphill, across a grassy field. Keep your nose alert for the warm fragrance of wild strawberries and red raspberries!

Just before the trail enters the woods, look left. This is the sort of signature tableau, in this case a portrait of Camel's Hump, with which Frederick Law Olmsted punctuated Shelburne Farms. Your eyes are drawn across the meadow to the mountain framed between banks of trees.

The woods are primarily sugar maples, with little understory other than maple saplings. Deer graze these woods heavily. The trail is a farm road and easy to follow as it rises and falls through the woods. Stay on this road as the yellow-blazed Whimsey Meadow Trails go right.

Within fifteen minutes of Lone Tree Hill, the Farm Trail, still a dirt road, leaves the woods and passes along the edge of a meadow. On the left is another of Olmsted's framed vistas of Camel's Hump. The trail passes between woods on the right and a clump of trees on the left. When it emerges yet another view is framed, this time of the lake and the Adirondacks.

The cluster of trees atop the knoll is another Olmsted hallmark. The path crosses a farm road and enters this clump of trees. Another orchestrated view, to the south-southwest, features Pease Mountain with Mt. Philo beyond. The sheep-back shape of Mt. Philo is particularly visible from here.

Huge bitternut hickories grow in this stand of trees; the bigger ones have vertical fissures on their gray bark. Bitternuts are an indicator of fertile soil. At the edge of the woods a bench on the left has a lovely view toward the lake and farm on Quaker Smith Point.

After passing through more farm fields, the trail leads toward the woods and turns right, continuing on a mowed swath along the edge. The rich woods include beech, maple, oak, elm, hop hornbeam, ash, and cherry.

The trail jogs to the right along a fence line before blue arrows indicate a left turn across the hayfields toward the lake. A mowed spur leads to a lovely cobble beach. On a May day, I watched blue heron, ducks, loons, swallows, and geese from this spot. You might want to bring a bird book and lunch.

The trail continues along the shore through young woods. It jogs right, then reemerges into fields, rising slightly as it leaves the lake. After about ten minutes blue arrows point left onto a gravel farm road. This is a working farm with fragrant mounds of hay and manure; old, rusting equipment; beehives; and compost piles. We pass beneath several large cottonwood trees, the largest of which has a diameter of more than four and a half feet!

The Farm Trail turns right while the Market Garden Trail, blazed purple, goes left. The latter visits the organic gardens of David Miskell and the Coach Barn.

Continuing on the Farm Trail, we go straight at an intersection where a private dirt road goes right and the main road goes left. Look for the blue markers.

Basswood and bitternut hickory, indicators of rich soil, are scattered through the woods beside less particular trees: maple, beech, hop hornbeam, black and paper birch, black cherry, and oak. The beech here are falling victim to the beech blister. Among the flowering herbs are trillium, jack-in-the-pulpit, and false Solomon's seal. Stinging nettles are also abundant.

As the road rises through the woods the red-blazed trail to Butternut Hill leads left and the yellow-blazed trails to Whimsey Meadow go right. Eventually we emerge from the woods and look over open fields. On the left is a final vista at Sheep's Knoll before the road descends to the Farm Barn.

Hours, Fees, Facilities

In season, mid-May to mid-October, trails are open from 10:00 A.M. to 4:00 P.M. Admission of $5 for adults; $4 for seniors; $3 for children; and under three free includes the walking path, children's farmyard, and the cheddar cheese operations.

Off-season, trails are open without charge, weather permitting. Visitors must check in at the Welcome Center.

Water and restrooms are at the Welcome Center and Farm Barn.

Getting There

From Shelburne drive north on Route 7. At the second light, 1.9 miles, turn left onto Bay Road. The road ends in 1.5 miles at the Welcome Center.

From the north, travel south on Route 7 from South Burlington. Bay Road is on the right, 3.0 miles from the I-189 interchange.

For More Information

Shelburne Farms
Harbor Road
Shelburne, VT 05482
802-985-8686

In the Area

Shelburne Museum

America's premier collection of its arts, architecture, and artifacts. The historic collection, spread over forty-five acres, ranges from quilts to children's toys and a merry-go-round to Monet's haystacks. A country store, a side-wheel steamboat, and a Shaker barn are among the thirty-seven structures at this unique museum. On Route 7 in Shelburne.

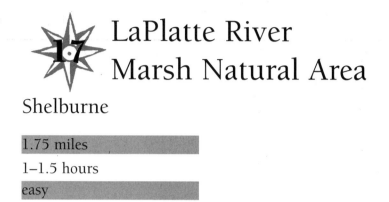

LaPlatte River
Marsh Natural Area

Shelburne

1.75 miles

1–1.5 hours

easy

The channels and wetlands of two rivers as they enter Lake Champlain. A great place to observe wildlife and to ski or snowshoe. Please leave pets at home.

One of many protected parcels on Shelburne Point, the 211-acre preserve is at the confluence of McCabes Brook and the LaPlatte River. Shelburne Farms sold the LaPlatte River Marsh in 1975 to the Nature Conservancy, which in turn transferred it to the town of Shelburne. The Vermont Chapter of the Nature Conservancy currently manages the property.

In 1985 Christopher Fastie, a student in the University of Vermont Field Naturalist Program, wrote a master's thesis on the LaPlatte River Marsh, an area larger than but including this preserve. Fastie estimated that sixty species of birds; twenty species of mammals; and fifty species of reptiles, amphibians, and fish breed in or near these wetlands. This meeting of swamp, marsh, forest, river, delta, and lake is rich territory indeed!

The town of Shelburne owns adjacent Shelburne Bay Park (see Allen Hill, p.100), and Shelburne Farms has preserved more than 1,400 acres to the west. A few sizable private holdings adjoin these properties, creating a large area of wildlife habitat stretching from lake to bay across the peninsula.

Begin your walk under the electrical wires that follow the Ticonderoga Road. In 1955, over frozen ground, workers laid temporary railroad tracks from Shelburne Bay to the Shelburne Museum. They then towed the

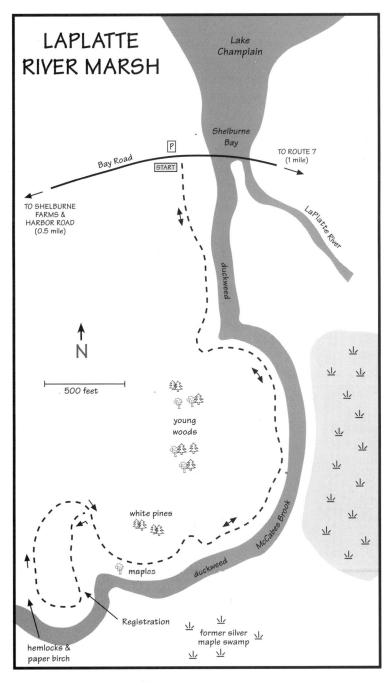

Base map information courtesy of The Nature Conservancy—
Vermont Chapter.

huge, nineteenth-century side-wheel steamboat, the *Ticonderoga,* to its home at the museum.

The white-blazed trail turns left, toward the water, through a thicket of red osier dogwood, honeysuckle, staghorn sumac, and ash saplings. The only trees are fast-growing white pines.

The trail follows the west bank of McCabes Brook. The channel is wide as the brook joins the LaPlatte River. Yellow-green duckweed flourishes from the earliest warm days of spring and soon covers the water. Air pockets keep duckweed leaves afloat, and new plants are produced by shoots that break off and float away. The tiny fronds of this flowering plant provide food for snails and insect larvae.

Keep an eye out for cormorants drying their wings on dead branches.

A young forest of sun-loving pioneers is growing on abandoned farmland: poplar, gray birch, white pine, maple, and ash. Young sassafras trees grow knee-high on the left. The untoothed leaves come in three patterns: one lobed, or egg-shaped; two lobes like a thumb and mitten; and three-lobed, more like fingers. The leaves and bark are very fragrant when crushed and tea can be made from the roots. Bark extract can be used as an orange dye. Its fruits are eaten by songbirds, bobwhite, wild turkey, and black bear and its twigs browsed by marsh and cottontail rabbits and white-tailed deer.

After ten minutes we overlook the channel and an assortment of water-loving plants: cattails, purple loosestrife (see p. 74), arrowhead, white waterlilies, and pink flowering rush. There's a lot going on here. Frogs jump, turtles sun themselves on rocks and logs, and, in spring, bullfrogs sound like the rhythmic sawing of logs. Ducks nest along the banks, great blue heron wade in shallow water, and a pileated woodpecker frequents the woods.

Along the banks a hybrid maple grows, with characteristics of both silver and red maple. Both trees are swamp and river-edge dwellers. The leaves of the hybrid are deeply cut and five-lobed like the silver maple, but without the characteristic silver underside. The stems are rosy like those of the red maple.

Increasingly white pines are in the woods, while honeysuckle and buckthorn are the dominant shrubs. White pines grow quickly, especially when there is abundant water. This was pastureland until the 1950s. The trail turns right to bypass an inlet and continues through piney woods.

Several turns in the trail are marked by arrows, although the path is obvious. A left arrow points to the first of two wooden bridges, and the trail leads to a peninsula and the sign-in box. There are some hemlocks and

A former silver maple swamp, drowned by a colony of beaver before they moved on.

paper birch mixed with the pines. Several herbs characteristic of an acidic, evergreen forest grow here: partridgeberry, wild lily of the valley, goldthread, and starflower. Fringed polygala provide a bright burst of pink in May.

The trail makes a counterclockwise loop around the small peninsula. There is a long view up McCabes Brook, a nice place to watch birds or wait for turtles to appear.

Across the channel, in the midst of the cattail marsh, is a forest of dead stumps. While silver maples (*Acer saccharinum*) are adapted to a damp environment, they cannot live underwater. Why did these trees, once so large and healthy, drown? The clues are scattered about in the sharpened stumps of trees. In the 1980s a population of beavers, (See Beaver, p. 179), attracted by abundant poplars and gray birch, drowned the silver maple swamp with their dams. The beavers have since moved elsewhere.

As the trail bends away from the brook, look for the brilliant, August-flowering cardinal flower. The bright scarlet flowers are fertilized primarily by hummingbirds, since most insects cannot navigate the long, tubular blooms. These beauties are threatened by overpicking.

The path crosses a wooden bridge next to a large-diameter white pine. It turns right at an arrow and rejoins the outbound trail.

As you return, look for animal tracks in this rich edge habitat. *Edge* is where two or more plant communities meet. Each habitat attracts animals to its unique mix of food, cover, and denning or nesting sites and materials. These assets multiply where communities meet, attracting a variety of wildlife. The wetlands in this preserve also provide access to water necessary for the courtship and reproduction of many species.

🐻 TRACKING

Tracks can be found in dust, mud, snow, and grass, but for the inexperienced, snow and mud are best. Tracking is a detective game as you look for prints, scat, nibbled or broken twigs, claw marks, fur, quills, feathers, blood, and bones.

Tracking books use a distinct vocabulary: *print* is the mark made by one foot, *track* is a series of prints, *straddle* is the width of the track, *stride* is the distance between prints of a walking animal, and *leap* is the distance between sets of four prints made by hopping or bounding animals.

The pattern of tracks reflects the animals' gaits. Deer; moose; canines—foxes, dogs, wolves, and coyotes; and felines—cats and bobcats—all have regular walks. Canines often leave toenail marks, while cats usually keep their claws retracted.

Bounders include weasels, mink, marten, fisher, otter, and squirrels. Their tracks are clumped, leaving two or four prints as they hop from place to place.

The prints of leapers and hoppers have hind feet positioned ahead of the front feet, the hind being the larger of the two. This happens as the animals propel themselves with strong rear quarters and land on their front feet. You will become familiar with this pattern because rabbits are prolific and their tracks so abundant on a snowy morning. Hares, raccoons, chipmunks, and mice hop similarly.

By contrast, waddlers are heavy and lumbering and include a range of animals. Generally awkward, they use means other than speed and agility to escape danger. We know the weapons of skunks and porcupines!

Woodchucks escape to their burrows; beaver and muskrat into water; and raccoons, porcupines, and bears climb trees. These animals often leave drag marks, from dragging feet or tails.

Look for location clues. Are the tracks near water, in the protection of woods, or leading to a hole in the snow? Look for nibble or claw marks. Bears claw beech trees while porcupines will strip bark in neatly gnawed, irregular patches, some very high off the ground. Just inches off the ground, a cottontail will gnaw twigs or the bark of fruit trees.

Positive identification from tracks and signs is both an art and a science. But there's no law against guessing. Put a tracking chart in your pocket and enjoy!

Getting There

From Shelburne drive north on Route 7. At the second light, 1.9 miles, turn left onto Bay Road. Just after crossing the LaPlatte River, turn right into the state fishing access at 1.1 miles. The trailhead is directly across Bay Road.

From the north, travel south on Route 7 from South Burlington. Bay Road is on the right, 3.0 miles from the I-189 interchange.

For More Information

The Nature Conservancy
Vermont Chapter
(See Organizations: Useful Names and Addresses.)

Keeping Track
P. O. Box 848
Richmond, VT 05477
802-434-7000

Keeping Track trains high school groups and community organizations involved in habitat monitoring. Some local conservation commissions offer tracking classes in cooperation with Keeping Track.

Allen Hill

Shelburne Bay Park
Shelburne

1.5 miles, 180-foot elevation gain

1–1.5 hours

moderate with a few steep sections

*A lakeside hill with a rare stand of chestnut oaks, nice views
of Lake Champlain, and early spring wildflowers. Wear sturdy walking shoes or hiking boots. Dogs must be leashed.*

On a small peninsula in Shelburne Bay, rising abruptly 180 feet over
Lake Champlain, sits Allen Hill. Its south-facing, lakeside slopes are
unusually warm, even for the Champlain Valley. As a result, Allen Hill is
one of the few places in northern Vermont where the chestnut oak grows.
Spring wildflowers bloom early on the hill's dry summit, a good vantage
point for watching the comings and goings of waterfowl at the mouth of
the LaPlatte River.

The 93-acre Shelburne Bay Park adjoins other large holdings of preserved land on Shelburne Point: LaPlatte River Marsh, 1,400 acres at
Shelburne Farms (of which this property was once a part), and several large
private parcels.

Two trails lead to Allen Hill, the Clarke Trail and the Recreation Path.
The Clarke Trail follows the shore and has many nice views. It can also be
very muddy in spring and early summer. The Recreation Path, to the west,
is a smooth gravel trail that is less interesting to walk but is always passable.

I recommend the Clarke Trail except for muddy times. Allen Hill
itself is very dry except during active rains.

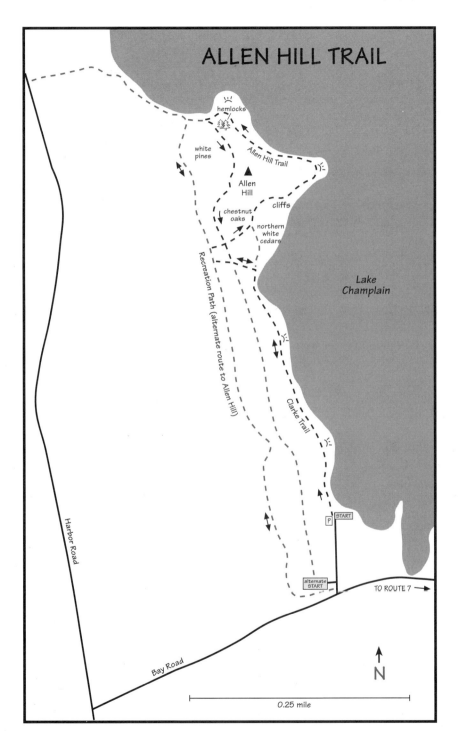

ALLEN HILL TRAIL

hemlocks

white
pines

Allen Hill Trail

Allen
Hill

cliffs

chestnut
oaks

northern
white
cedars

Recreation Path (alternate route to Allen Hill)

Lake
Champlain

Clarke Trail

Harbor Road

P START

alternate
START

TO ROUTE 7 →

Bay Road

N

0.25 mile

The Clarke Trail begins at the north end of the northernmost parking area, next to the lake. It enters mixed woods of white pine, hemlock, and deciduous trees. Two large cottonwoods grow next to the lake. To the left of the trail polypody ferns grow on a white quartzite outcropping. This small evergreen fern with leathery leaves prefers damp, shallow soil, usually on rocks or cliffs.

The understory, all the vegetation beneath the canopy of tree leaves, is varied. Young maples, honeysuckle, and buckthorn are the dominant shrubs, while marginal wood ferns, hepatica, wild lily of the valley, and ground pine are in the herb layer.

Several lichen-covered rock outcroppings border the lake. Lichens are pioneer plants needing nothing but occasional moisture to survive. They perform photosynthesis while clinging to nearly any surface, including bare rock. Lichens are a composite plant, a combination of algae and fungi. Chlorophyll provided by the algae allows them to manufacture their own food. Lichens lack true leaves, stems, or roots and absorb moisture across their entire surface. Plants can be dry for many years and will spring back to life when moistened.

Lichens, in turn, provide a surface where moss spores can germinate. Several patches of moss grow on these rocks, the next actors in the drama of plant succession. As moss dies and decomposes, it adds organic matter to the mat. Seeds that germinate in the damp moss now have a chance at survival. Someday, wildflowers and grasses will bloom on these rocks.

The trail crosses a small stream after about twenty minutes. Follow the path left and slightly uphill to the confluence of several trails.

Look for a huge red oak with barbed wire embedded in its west side. In May the oak is surrounded by a sea of trout lilies. Take the trail that goes right, uphill of the tree, in the direction of the lake. It climbs gently before making a left turn and then climbing steeply.

The woods are now a mixture of beech, sugar maple, shagbark hickory, hemlock, hop hornbeam, and cherry as we continue a steep scramble over rocky shards. Red and white pines are still occasional.

We begin to see chestnut oaks, on both sides of the trail, many with multiple trunks. They seem to relish growing at odd angles to the hillside, often in defiance of gravity. These remarkable trees have deeply furrowed bark, and their leaves are toothed, like the elm, rather than lobed, like most oaks. Chestnut oaks are an indicator species, plants found almost exclusively in their preferred habitat, limy soil. (See Limy Soils, p. 104.) They rarely are seen in this part of Vermont, the northeastern extreme of their range. Only in the warmest lakeside location with a southern exposure do we find chestnut oaks in the Burlington area.

Allen Hill's limy dolomite cliffs are home to a population of mature northern white cedars.

The trail jogs right, then left, and continues its climb past many chestnut oak, hop hornbeam, shagbark hickory, red and white oak, and basswood trees. None of these is extremely tall because of the shallow, dry soil on the rocky summit. This hill was one of the many sheep farms bought by the Webbs for Shelburne Farms, and it's likely that sheep had overgrazed this pastureland, thus exposing the bedrock.

The limy soil supports a variety of wildflowers. Because this hilltop is dry, spring wildflowers bloom early, especially those sheltered from the cool spring winds off the lake. White trillium, hepatica, bloodroot, false Solomon's seal, and early meadow rue bloom in April or early May.

At the crest of the hill look west, before the trees leaf out, for a view to the open lake. The trail continues along the ridge as white cedars and the occasional hemlock begin to mix in. Below the trail on the bay side, the rocky hillside is densely forested with mature northern white cedar, another tree partial to limy soils.

The trail begins to descend, bearing slightly to the right, toward a rocky promontory. There are nice views to the south and east, often with good bird-watching. I've seen and heard geese, cormorants, heron, and one day, at very close range, a turkey vulture. As I approached this spot it perched on the edge of the promontory, its back to me as it scanned the lake below. I was not prepared for its shrunken red head.

The trail turns to the left and the footing is rocky, although not slippery. On a cool day, the north wind tells us we've changed exposure. Waves from the more open water to the north splash against the shore below. There is less sunlight on the north side of the hill and more hemlocks, moss, and ferns as a result. There are occasional large white oaks, perhaps left as shade trees when the land was farmed. There are lovely vistas, especially in summer, with sailboats crisscrossing the bay.

The trail follows the shoreline and soon reaches an intersection. The Recreation Path is about 100 yards to the right and the Allen Hill Trail turns left, going inland.

Under a dense canopy of white pines, the Allen Hill Trail rises. This section of trail can be wet. (If it's muddy, you might want to reconsider the Recreation Path.) A few scraggly cherries struggle to reach the light, but there is very little understory.

As the trail approaches the drier hillside on the left, deciduous woods of maple, ash, shagbark hickory, and oak replace the dense white pines. The understory returns, and within a few minutes we are back at the barbed-wire-fence oak and the junction of the trails.

To return on the Recreation Path, turn right and then left when you reach the gravel trail. To return on the Clarke Trail, bear left toward the lake. You will be back at the parking lot in twenty minutes.

✳ LIMY SOILS AND THEIR FLORA

Allen Hill is one of several in the area with a summit of calcareous, or limy, bedrock. It joins nearby Pease Mountain in Charlotte in supporting plants that thrive in these limy, alkaline conditions.

The underlying bedrock of much of the Champlain Valley is limestone and dolomite. These rocks were once sea-bottom sediments and are composed of calcium-rich layers contributed by the shells of marine creatures. Calcium is an important nutrient for plant growth. Magnesium, another critical nutrient, is also available to plants in limy soil.

Calcareous soil usually produces a higher diversity of plants, which in turn attract a greater number of animal species.

This, in a nutshell, is why the Champlain Valley supports a diversity of flora not seen in granite mountains. The sandy soil eroded from granite cannot support this wide range of plants. It is not by accident that the Champlain Valley is the historic breadbasket of Vermont.

Hours

The park is open from dawn to dusk.

Getting There

From Shelburne travel north on Route 7. At the second light, 1.9 miles, turn left onto Bay Road. Just past the fishing access, turn right at 1.2 miles, Shelburne Bay Park. The parking area straight ahead is closest to the Clarke Trail. On the left is the beginning of the Recreation Path.

For More Information

Town of Shelburne
Parks & Recreation Department
Shelburne, VT 05482
802-985-9551

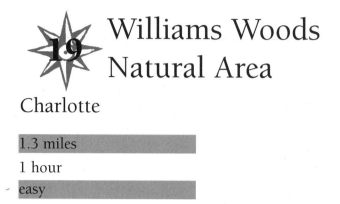

Williams Woods
Natural Area

Charlotte

1.3 miles

1 hour

easy

One of the best remaining examples of the lowland forests once common in the Champlain Valley. Wear boots in wet seasons. Ideal for snowshoes.

Bounded by working dairy farms, Thorp Brook, and the Vermont Railroad, Williams Woods is an island of old forest in the flat and fertile Champlain Valley, land which has been extensively farmed since precolonial times. It is the rare wood lot that has grown unmolested for more than a century.

A stone's throw from Lake Champlain, forests like these would have been among the first to be cleared for timber in the late eighteenth and early nineteenth centuries, when sawmills dotted the lake's tributaries. Lewis Creek, just to the south, was home to a number of mills.

In deeds dating back to the 1850s, Williams Woods was referred to as a "greenbush," a piece of land used for selective firewood cutting. Perhaps the wet soil and undulations of the terrain made the land undesirable for corn or hay. The wood lot was isolated from grazing cattle when the railroad was built in 1850. Arthur Williams, who owned the property until 1983, deliberately protected the trees for at least the previous forty years.

The fertile, moisture-retentive clay soil and relatively long growing season combine to provide favorable growing conditions for these trees.

The trail begins in the filtered light beneath a canopy of large hemlocks. Frequent white blazes indicate the route, which is not always obvious where the understory is sparse.

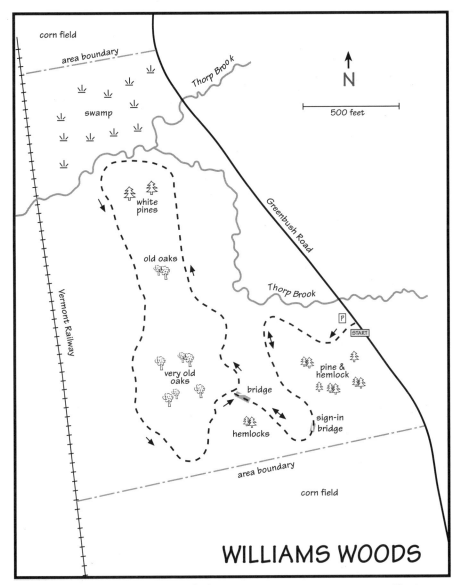

corn field

area boundary

Thorp Brook

N

500 feet

swamp

Greenbush Road

Thorp Brook

white
pines

old oaks

P

START

Vermont Railway

very old
oaks

pine &
hemlock

bridge

sign-in
bridge

hemlocks

area boundary

corn field

WILLIAMS WOODS

Base map information courtesy of The Nature Conservancy—Vermont Chapter.

You will notice immediately, perhaps by tripping, that the tree roots grow along the surface. Yellow birch and hemlock roots often spread across a rocky hillside, but in Williams Woods waterlogged soil is the cause. A high water table and clay soil make for very damp ground. The shallow root systems account for the numerous blowdowns throughout the woods.

When soil is waterlogged, even briefly, its oxygen is quickly depleted and it becomes anaerobic (without oxygen). Even after the water recedes, oxygen is slow to return to the soil. Such wetland trees as willow, silver and swamp maple, and cottonwood have evolved shallow root systems with significant above-ground sections to maximize contact with the air. Multiple trunks can perform the same function.

Towering hundred-year-old hemlocks dominate the beginning of the trail. Only spinulose wood fern grows in the understory. The many blow-downs have created sunny openings and pocket wetlands in the water-logged soil. Young, fast-growing white pines have seized these opportunities and are overtaking the hemlocks.

Trout lilies prefer rich, moist soils like those in Williams Woods.

The trail turns left. Hardwoods are more common and several ash trees with deeply furrowed bark grow near Thorp Brook on the right of the trail.

The trail bends left and beech trees increase. The trail turns right and reaches the sign-in box within ten minutes of the trailhead. Cross the wooden bridge and turn right at a double blaze.

An increase in deciduous trees provides more sunlight to herbs. Bloodroot, jack-in-the-pulpit, and common elderberry, all indicators of fertile soil, make appearances. The trail crosses another wooden bridge, goes up a slight rise, and turns right. Red and white oak, ash, shagbark hickory, hop hornbeam, bur oak, sugar maple, beech, and birch grow in the rich clay. Some very large, old oaks are scattered in the woods, some still standing, others victims of blowdown.

The trail jogs back and forth over a tangle of roots. A yellow birch with spectacular roots is on the left. The understory waxes and wanes inversely with the hemlocks in the canopy.

The trail passes through a white pine plantation near the edge of the Thorp Brook swamp. Next to the swamp a huge old bur oak (*Quercus macrocarpa*) stands with a diameter of nearly three and a half feet. A stately tree indeed!

The trail bends to the left, keeping the swamp on the right. The canopy is mostly hemlocks and white pine. A wolf tree, a white pine that was free to grow wide branches in a field, is on the left.

The trail emerges from the dark coniferous woods to mixed woods again. Basswood, another indicator of fertile soil, and shagbark hickory join the other hardwoods.

The trail makes a number of turns, always indicated by double blazes. After several left turns the trail crosses a plank bridge. Cross one more bridge and rejoin the outbound trail for the last ten minutes.

Coyote, white-tailed deer, and wild turkey are plentiful in these woods. Look for scat, prints, feathers, browsed twigs, or the animals themselves.

🌿 OLD TREES

New England's rigorous climate makes it difficult for trees to grow to old age, as wind, snow, ice, lightning, and pathogens conspire against longevity. Many native species have life spans of 300 to 400 years, eastern hemlock, northern white cedar, eastern white pine, and white oak among them.

What, then, are *old* trees, and what constitutes old growth?

The term *old growth* implies a lack of human disturbance—no logging, pasturing, tilling for crops, or roads at their feet, although such trees may be victims of natural calamities. Experts disagree about where *old-growth* trees exist in Vermont, but that there are some *old trees* is certain. Williams Woods has some oaks that may approach 200 years of age.

🌳 EUROPEAN BUCKTHORN

An introduced species that escaped cultivation, buckthorn (*Rhamnus cathartica*) is spreading like a weed through New England woods. Its seeds spread by birds, buckthorn squeezes out plants that provide benefit to a wider range of wildlife. One competitive advantage of the buckthorn is its ability to photosynthesize for a longer season than many of its competitors. It is one of the few plants in the woods holding its leaves through November.

🏭 ABOUT CLAY

Clay soil, the waterlogged underpinning of Williams Woods, owes its fertility to its small particle size and the many negatively charged ions on its surface. Important minerals for healthy plant growth, like calcium and magnesium, are positively charged and attach to the clay molecules while remaining accessible to the plants.

Getting There

From the north take Route 7 south and turn right at the stop light in Charlotte, Ferry Road or F-5. There are signs for the ferry to New York state. Drive 0.3 mile to the stop sign. Turn left on Greenbush Road. After 2.0 miles you will swing to the left—be careful! Greenbush Road continues, paved, to the south. (If you cross the railroad, turn back. You missed the turn.) After 1.0 mile you will find a wooden sign, tucked under the trees, for Williams Woods. Pull to the side of the road to park.

From the south on Route 7, turn left at Stage Road in North Ferrisburg. The Ferrisburg post office is on the southwest corner. Drive 1.0 mile to Greenbush Road. Turn right. The entrance to Williams Woods will be 1.0 mile on the left.

For More Information

The Nature Conservancy
Vermont Chapter
(See Organizations: Useful Names and Addresses.)

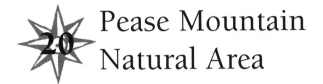

Pease Mountain
Natural Area

Nature Trail
Charlotte

1.5 miles, 200-foot elevation gain

1 hour

2.0 miles, 400-foot gain to summit ridge

1.5 hours

moderate with rocky footing

A prominent hill in the Champlain Valley with a rich diversity of plants and a large flock of wild turkeys. A great place to cross-country ski or snowshoe.

A series of newspaper articles written in the 1890s by William Wallace Higbee provide historical texture to many local haunts. His collected writings were compiled by the Charlotte Historical Society in *Around the Mountains*, and from it we glean some details about Pease Mountain.

Higbee writes that Pease Mountain was twice "denuded of its forestry" in the nineteenth century. Its trees fed the boilers of the Rutland and Burlington Railroad, yet by 1897 the land was once again forested. So it is with forests in Vermont.

The 800-foot-high mountain was home to the town's first settled minister, who built his house on the sunny, southeast side of the mountain. In 1841, Charlotte town selectmen leased a large section of the mountain to George Pease for 999 years. The family returned that generosity in 1949, when trustees of the Pease estate donated 180 acres to the University of Vermont (UVM).

Pease Mountain is a UVM Natural Area. Forestry students use it for plant identification and mapping exercises. A group from Charlotte Central School, working with the university, designed a nature trail in the 1980s. Some of the markers are still in place.

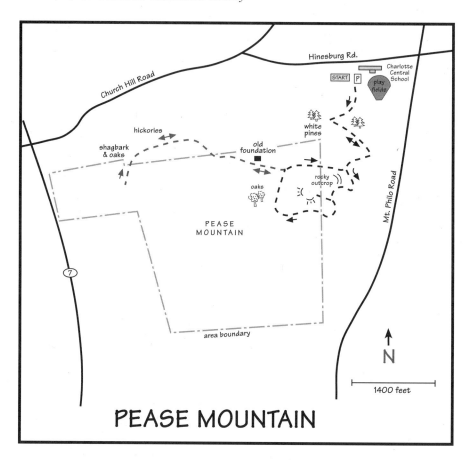

PEASE MOUNTAIN

W alk south across the playing fields to the right of the backstop. Follow the gravel path up the slope to the trailhead and sign-in box.

The trail begins in a dense stand of white pines. Because of abundant runoff at the base of the mountain, these well-watered trees have grown quickly, erasing grazing and agricultural fields. Notice that many of the pines have multiple trunks. The white pine weevil probably infested the young trees.

The trail turns left at an arrow and continues a gradual climb. Partridgeberry and purple-flowering herb Robert peek from beneath lush ferns. As the trail turns right, sensitive ferns are abundant on the left. Constant moisture keeps the ferns happy.

Several young black birch, moderately shade tolerant trees, grow beneath the white pines. Their leaves and twigs taste of wintergreen and the sap can be used to make birch beer.

We begin to see bitternut hickory saplings with vertically striped bark and relatively few stubby, alternate branches. Bitternut buds are unmistakable: large, saffron-colored swellings already conspicuous in August for the next spring. Its compound leaves fairly explode from the bud with as many as eleven leaflets. Bitternuts are found only in fertile soil.

These woods are home to a wide variety of deciduous trees, among them paper, yellow, and black birch; red and white oak; American beech; hop hornbeam, with its shreddy bark and lacy twigs; elm; poplar; maple; white ash; basswood; and bitternut and shagbark hickories. Among the shrubby trees we find serviceberry, striped maple, and the occasional blue beech. Many of these trees are generalists and will grow in a variety of conditions, but basswood and bitternut hickory are indicators of fertile soil.

In early May a bounty of wildflowers bloom in the rich soil, including white trillium, hepatica, trout lily, spring beauty, and bloodroot.

Where the trail forks, go left. Although the trail isn't blazed, it is well worn. After a minute or two of gentle rise an arrow marks a sharp right turn.

We pass a number of serviceberry trees (*Amelanchier canadensis*) with wavy vertical lines on their smooth gray bark. These early-flowering trees never grow beyond thirty feet. As early as April their five long, white petals

The saffron-colored bud of a bitternut hickory unfurling.

burst forth. The name refers to the time when burial services could be held in the spring for those who had died in winter (when the ground was frozen). Its other names, shadbush and Juneberry, also refer to the season: the spawning of shad and the tree's June berries.

The trail rises over rosy quartzite outcroppings. The bedrock of Pease Mountain is very old metamorphic rock. This Monkton quartzite, called redstone, was used in many local buildings in the nineteenth century. The quartzite formed when sandstone was subjected to enormous heat and pressure. The mineral content is not altered by this process, and the quartzite has the same calcareous or limy characteristics as the original sedimentary rock.

When glaciers melted at the end of the Ice Age, much of the Champlain Valley was inundated, first by freshwater Lake Vermont and later by the salty Champlain Sea (see Button Bay, p. 129). Thick deposits of sediment left by these bodies of water became the rich, clay soils of the valley. Only the islands that stood above water, including Pease Mountain, Mt. Philo, and Snake Mountain, are not mantled in clay.

After about twenty minutes on the trail, we arrive at a clearing. This fragile rock outcropping has thin soil, so please stay on the bedrock.

This is a lovely place to tarry, a place of color, texture, and bird song. The soft, gray-green tufts of reindeer moss, really a lichen, grow in pretty patterns on the maroon quartzite. Sun-loving plants tolerant of the dry conditions on this shallow soil are low and compact: lowbush blueberry, huckleberry, and juniper. Pease Mountain is a great place to see and hear spring warblers.

Two medium-sized oaks grow side by side, a red and a white. The red oak has leaves with pointed lobes, while white oak leaves have rounded lobes. The bark of the white oak has a light, almost whitish cast, while the red has a rich brown bark. White oak acorns ripen the first autumn, while the reds take two years to mature.

Follow white blazes on the rock to the left toward a worn path into woods dominated by shagbark hickory and hop hornbeam trees. Many paper birch have died here, perhaps due to lack of sunlight. There's also a patch of the yellow-flowered barren strawberry. The trail bends right as it descends over more scrabbly rock. On the left is a five-trunked red oak, which sprouted from a stump after logging. The central trunk, measured from the center of each sprout, would have produced a huge piece of timber.

After a steep descent, the trail turns right at an arrow. The trees are taller because more moisture is available, but none is very mature. The trail curves gradually to the right.

Stop 11 is a patch of red and white trillium, both of which prefer rich,

The tidy, evergreen polypody ferns.

moist soils. White trillium are more common in the Champlain Valley and red in the higher elevations.

In less than ten minutes an arrow points left and a sign welcomes us to the Pease Mountain Natural Area. Take the trail on the left. (We will return later to the right fork.) Walk straight ahead for just a few minutes. Look for Stop 13 on the right, an old redstone foundation. (The signs have been vandalized and may be missing.) This may have been the home of Charlotte's early minister. This once sunny location would have been protected from the prevailing south winds, and several springs for water are nearby.

The nature trail turns around here but a walking path continues. It's a leisurely fifteen minutes to the summit ridge. When the leaves are off the trees there is a view to the lake, and the dry conditions produce early spring wildflowers. Hepatica blooms early in April, one of the first joys of spring. Its flowers, on hairy stems, range from deep purple to white, and the evergreen leaves have three lobes. The ability of evergreen leaves to use every ray of spring sunshine may contribute to the plant's early flowering.

The summit forest, a mix of hickories, oak, ash, sugar maple, and hop hornbeam, has a ground cover of sedge. With few side branches on the trees, minimal understory, and the vertical markings or strips on the trunks of bitternut, shagbark, hop hornbeam, and ash trees, these woods are a vertical vision.

When you turn around, follow the trail back past the UVM Natural Area signposts and bear left. (We came from the right.) A stand of honeysuckle grows on rocky ground as the trail descends gently. Honeysuckle's bright, prolific berries are attractive to birds. A stream spills over the ground on the left. The bedrock is so close to the surface that the runoff from nearby springs cannot be absorbed.

The trail turns sharply to the right at an arrow and continues on the level. One more right turn, marked with an arrow, takes us back to the outbound trail. Turn left and continue downhill to the trailhead.

🦃 *TURKEY TROT*

A maze of wild turkey tracks covers the winter snows on Pease Mountain. These three-pronged prints appear gigantic, six inches from front to back and three inches from side to side, as melting snow exaggerates their dimensions. The stride, distance from one print to another, is about a foot.

The wild turkey (*Meleagris gallopava*) was hunted nearly to extinction before habitat management, controlled hunting seasons, and calculated reintroduction helped reestablish the giant bird. The male averages forty-eight inches from beak to tail, the female thirty-six inches. The turkey is predominantly brown and white, with many beautiful, striped feathers.

Ground nesting makes turkeys vulnerable to predators. They lay ten to fifteen eggs in a shallow, leaf-lined depression in the vegetation.

Getting There

Take Route 7 to Charlotte. At the stoplight, the intersection of Ferry Road to the west and Church Hill Road to the east, turn onto Church Hill Road. At the stop sign in 0.7 mile, turn right on Hinesburg Road. Turn right in 0.3 mile to park in the lots west of Charlotte Central School.

For More Information

University of Vermont
Environmental Program
(See Organizations: Useful Names and Addresses.)

Mt. Philo
State Park

Charlotte

1.75 miles, 600-foot elevation gain

1.5 hours

moderate with some steep sections

The view from Mt. Philo is special any month of the year. Its geology is intriguing and visible, and its spring wildflowers are spectacular.

M t. Philo is Vermont's oldest state park. The 968-foot summit has love-ly, gentle views of the Champlain Valley, and its spring wildflowers are early and prolific. Hawk viewing is excellent and there's even a great sledding hill!

The original carriageway was built in 1903 by owners of the Mt. Philo Inn. In the 1930s, the Civilian Conservation Corps (CCC) constructed the current road, which makes Mt. Philo's summit so accessible. Young, old, and the physically challenged can enjoy the same view. When April turns the countryside to a sea of mud, the pavement leads to a bounty of wildflowers and the songs of migrating warblers.

Hiking trails recently have been developed, but they are not for everyone and certainly not for every season. The trails are steep and often muddy, and they can be icy in winter. They are maintained for summer use only. The road is passable much of the year, open to cars in season and foot traffic year-round. The asphalt access is an off-season gift.

The road wastes little time in beginning its climb, which continues steadily to the top. On the lower slopes, plantations of conifers were planted by the CCC in the 1930s to reforest the mountain's bare slopes. Look for tamarack (or larch), Scotch and red pine, and Norway spruce. The short needles of Scotch pine, usually less than two inches long, are

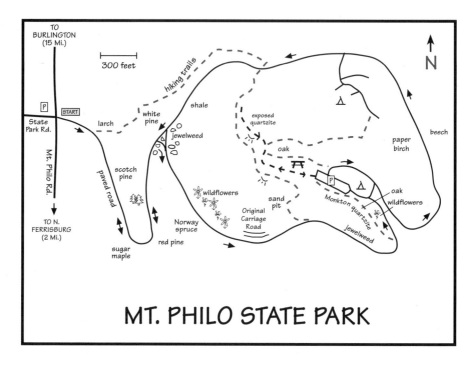

MT. PHILO STATE PARK

in bunches of two. The upper bark on the trunk glows a salmon color, like a perpetual sunset. Red pine also has bunches of two needles, but they are long, dark green, and brittle. The mature trunk has rosy patches peeking from beneath brown scales of outer bark. Tamarack, or larch, is our only deciduous conifer. Other evergreens keep their needles from three to ten years and shed them gradually. Tufts of short, bright green needles give tamarack a soft look. In late autumn they glow a butterscotch yellow. Norway spruce, with drooping boughs, looks altogether different. Its short, spiky needles are not bunched but arranged spirally around the twig.

The road makes one switchback before coming to a fork within ten to fifteen minutes. In late April or early May, bloodroot blooms along the roadside. A member of the poppy family, the plant gets its name from the red-orange juice in its roots and stems. It was used by Native Americans as an insect repellent and dye. You can recognize it by its eight to ten white petals surrounding a golden orange center. Its single leaf curls around the stalk. The blossoms open in full sun and close at night.

The road forks around a boulder field on the right. These chunks of maroon Monkton quartzite have fallen from the top of the mountain (more about this shortly). Go uphill to the right.

Any time from late fall until midspring, Mt. Philo is a great place to learn the basics of fern identification. Four evergreen ferns grow on Mt. Philo. With no other leaves, flowers, or summer ferns as a distraction, the task is quite manageable. Warning: Do not try this in summer; it's overwhelming! (See Fern Identification Made Simple, p. 121.)

The common polypody fern, a once-cut fern, favors rocky sites. Rarely more than twelve inches high, the leathery, bright green fronds may have up to twenty pairs of tiny leaflets. Christmas fern, also once-cut, has deep green, leathery fronds up to two feet in length. Its lobed leaflets resemble a Christmas stocking. Marginal wood fern is twice-cut and grows to two feet. Its fruitdots, on the underside of the frond, are conspicuous along the margins of the leaflets—hence its name. The thrice-cut spinulose wood fern has lacy, foot-long fronds, and its fruitdots are clustered near the veins on the underside of the leaflet. It is most easily identified in comparison with the marginal wood fern.

This stretch of road blooms in May with early meadow rue, hepatica, white trillium, spring beauty, and Dutchman's-breeches. A rich mix of deciduous trees includes sugar maple, white ash, paper birch, hop hornbeam, shagbark hickory, black cherry, butternut, and basswood. To the left is the original carriageway, it base on boulders built into the hillside.

Walk about fifty feet into an entrance marked Service Vehicles Only. An open sand pit gapes on the left, the remains of a glacial kame. As glacial ice melted, sand accumulated against the hillside and remained after the ice was gone. This is the origin of many local sand and gravel pits.

The paved road gets steeper. While catching your breath, admire a huge patch of jewelweed on the left flourishing in the damp soil.

Look up at the towering cliff. Notice that the quartzite is layered, the color changing at irregular intervals. This rock was laid down as sedimentary rock, a sandstone, and then subjected to heat or pressure to become the harder, metamorphic quartzite. At the base of the mountain, softer shale crumbles beneath its weight and chunks of quartzite break off. This flank of Mt. Philo is littered with chunks of quartzite. We will see the best exposures of shale on the walk downhill.

Along the last stretch before the summit another sea of spring wildflowers bloom: hepatica, spring beauty, trout lily (or dogtooth violet), white trillium, and sessile bellwort. Pink lady-slipper also flowers in these woods.

Dutchman's-breeches are among the abundant spring blooms on Mt. Philo.

The summit is home to mature northern white cedars in addition to red oak, shagbark hickory, and hop hornbeam—trees at home in the thin, drier soil on the summit. Oaks prefer warm, well-drained sites. In the Champlain Valley they often grow on south- and west-facing slopes. The quartzite bedrock has a calcareous component (see Pease Mountain, p. 111) favored by the cedars.

Walk to the farthest observation point on a rocky outcrop facing west. Notice the quartzite sloping uphill toward the west. In a tumultuous earth-building event about 350 million years ago, the older Monkton quartzite was thrust westward over younger, softer shale. It is this sloping layer of erosion-resistant quartzite that gives the sheep-back mountains their characteristic shape.

Now look south to the similar profiles of Buck and Snake Mountains. They share the same gradual eastern flanks and sharper drop-offs to the west.

The road starts down from the parking lot, next to the sign recognizing the CCC and State Forester Perry Merrill. The more gradual eastern slope has deeper soils and retains more moisture and nutrient runoff than the west-facing cliffs. Trees are taller and plant diversity greater. You will find several indicators of rich or limy soil, including maidenhair fern, herb Robert, and basswood. Large clumps of American beech grow in the woods. They prefer soil that never dries out. There are few oaks.

After a grove of paper birch, the road rises slightly. On the left, just beyond a culvert, three of the evergreen ferns grow together on the left: Christmas fern, marginal wood fern, and spinulose wood fern.

Beyond the lower campground, as the road curves to the left, look for exposed shale. The thin, brittle layers slump visibly beneath the weight of the overriding quartzite.

The roads rejoin at the fork, where another massive patch of jewel-weed flourishes on the left.

✳ FERN IDENTIFICATION MADE SIMPLE

Fronds are divided into four categories of leaf structure. Imagine a flat palm frond and a pair of scissors. If you cut from the edge of the leaf to its mid-vein, you create simple leaflets (once-cut). If you take each resulting leaflet and repeat the procedure, cut it from its edge to its middle, the leaf is twice-cut, into subleaflets. If the subleaflets are cut yet again, a lacy-leaf (thrice-cut) fern results. Thus we have once- twice- , or thrice-cut ferns. The fourth category includes ferns with unusual or nonfernlike leaves.

Next, determine the shape of the frond or leaf. There are three types: broadest at the base, i.e., a triangle; semitapering to base; and tapering to base. These last are pointed at both ends.

With the leaflet type and frond shape established, the spore cases positively identify the species. These organs, also called fruitdots, are usually found on the underside of the leaflets, although they sometimes occur on separate stalks (even easier to identify).

The Vermont Department of Forests, Parks, and Recreation distributes a free booklet, "Common Ferns of Vermont," at state parks. It is clear, simple, and very helpful.

⚓ WHICH WAY TO THE BEACH?

The bodies of water that filled the Champlain Valley at the end of the Ice Age, Lake Vermont and the Champlain Sea, left behind many shore- and lake-level indicators. Mt. Philo was an island in Lake Vermont and near the shore of the Champlain Sea. Which way, you might ask, to the beach?

While vegetation hides much of the surface geology, some evidence is visible. Beach gravel from the Champlain Sea straddles State Park Road where it joins Route 7. Pebbly sand from Lake Vermont begins at the park gate and grades into beach gravel as the access road climbs toward the switchback. On the east side, downhill from the park road, are deposits of lake sand and boulder-strewn lake sediments.

A detailed map is included in a booklet describing the geology of three state parks, D.A.R., Mt. Philo, and Sand Bar. It is available at many state parks or from the office of the state geologist (see bibliography).

Getting There

From the stoplight on Route 7 in Charlotte, drive south on Route 7. Turn left on State Park Road at the blinking light, 2.5 miles. The park gate will be in front of you in 0.6 mile. Park safely off the road and do not block the gate.

For More Information

Mt. Philo State Park
Mt. Philo Road
Charlotte, VT 05445
802-425-2390

Southern Champlain Valley

Kingsland Bay State Park

Nature Trail

Ferrisburg

0.6 mile

45 minutes

easy, but the footing can be uneven

A forested peninsula on Lake Champlain with lovely views of lake and mountains. Beautiful wildflowers.

Not many of Lake Champlain's 587 miles of shoreline are publicly accessible. Much of that public land has a recreational purpose and has been cleared for swimming, boating, or fishing access. A lakeside walk through a quiet forest of old, gnarled trees is thus a rare pleasure indeed.

MacDonough Point has many cool and shady spots from which to enjoy the sights and sounds of the lake. On a quiet day you may hear fish flopping and loons calling. The gnarled northern white cedars paint a picture of survival, their tortured roots and contorted trunks testimony of an ambiance of wind, waves, and ice.

The 264-acre Kingsland Bay State Park was until quite recently a summer camp. The lovely stone Hawley House dates from 1790. The park warden can give you a key to see a newly installed exhibit of maritime history.

The walking trail begins near the shore, to the north of the swimming and picnic areas. It immediately disappears into the woods. In May, thousands of white trillium bob in the breeze. Large-flowered trillium

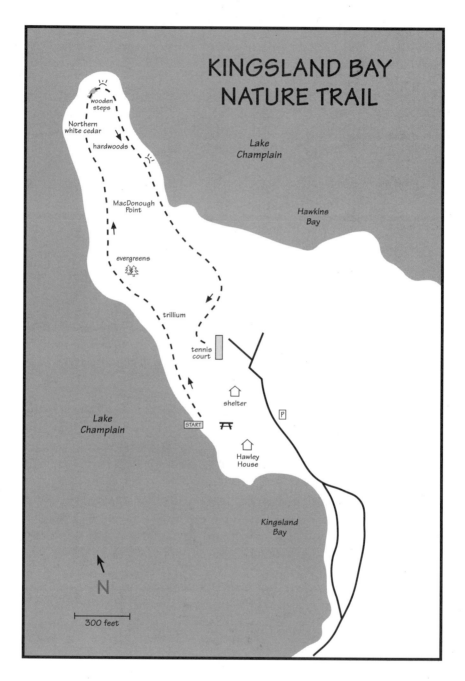

KINGSLAND BAY
NATURE TRAIL

wooden steps

Northern white cedar

hardwoods

Lake Champlain

MacDonough Point

Hawkins Bay

evergreens

trillium

tennis court

shelter

Lake Champlain

START

Hawley House

P

Kingsland Bay

N

300 feet

(*Trillium grandiflorum*) are members of the lily family that prefer deciduous woods with neutral soils. The three-petaled flower, which turns pink before it fades, sits atop a whorl of three leaves. Picking the flower will almost certainly kill the plant because there are no other leaves to manufacture food.

The trail rises and descends gently on a bluff above the water. As the trail approaches the lake you will feel a chill in the spring and warmth off the water in the fall. This shoreline microclimate means that flowers and leaves near the shore are slow to emerge in the spring and the last to succumb to frost at the end of the season.

After a few minutes you will see woodpecker excavations on a white cedar to the left of the trail. Only the pileated woodpecker makes holes of this size while searching for carpenter ants or making a nest cavity for its family. These huge woodpeckers, nearly eighteen inches from beak to tail, are quite shy of humans. You may hear them drumming in the distance or find a heap of wood chunks at the base of a tree. If you see the enormous bird there is no mistaking it: huge red crest on its head, long beak, black body with bold white stripes on the head, and the long, strong tail with which it props itself against trees.

These woods are home to four evergreen conifers, the northern white cedar being dominant. The white cedar (*Thuja occidentalis*) has scales rather than needles, and its bark often shreds in vertical strips. These trees hug the edges of the cliffs, often with dramatic result.

The familiar white pine, with its five long needles (remember w-h-i-t-e), has dark gray bark, which makes it easy to distinguish from the red pine. Red pine needles are longer than those of the white pine and are bunched in twos. You won't be able to see that on tall trees, so look instead at the rosy trunk. The bark of a mature red pine is a beautiful thing, thick rosy plates beneath a layer of brown.

The fourth conifer is the hemlock, with short, flat needles. Its shallow root system enables it to survive on this thin soil. The bedrock, which keeps appearing underfoot, is never far from the surface.

Where evergreens are thick, few plants survive beneath them. The ground is covered with fallen needles, mosses, and the occasional fern.

On the hillside to the right of the trail, in the center of the peninsula, deciduous trees grow, a mixture of shagbark and bitternut hickory, oak, maple, ash, birch, and hop hornbeam. Before these trees leaf out, a riot of wildflowers unfolds beneath them: trillium, trout lilies, false Solomon's seal, and hepatica among them.

A northern white cedar clings to life at Kingsland Bay.

On a quiet May day, a pair of loons paddled nearby (see Loons, below); swallows swooped for insects just above the water's surface, fish splashed, and three Baltimore orioles flitted at the edge of the woods.

The trail turns right and descends a set of wooden stairs built into the hillside before returning on the eastern, or bay side of the peninsula. Immediately you will notice that the trees are taller, protected from the wind and weather of the open lake. Several oak and ash trees have grown to a good height. Above a moss-covered rocky outcropping on the right side of the trail is a remarkable sight: a grapevine must have wound around a paper birch when it was young. The tree has a series of diagonal stripes making it look like a barber's pole.

The trail hugs the shore, which is eroded in places. Across Hawkins Bay you will see Camel's Hump, Vermont's most distinctive mountain. Mt. Philo in Charlotte is on the left in the foreground.

On the right side of the trail are several clumps of American yew or ground hemlock (*Taxus canadensis*), a low, shade-loving plant. Its needles are yellow green in contrast to the darker blue green of the eastern hemlock. In the late summer yew produces an almost translucent red berry with a cylindrical hole right to the seed in its center. These berries are poisonous to humans.

The trail turns away from the shore and returns to the fields near the tennis courts.

✦ LURE OF THE LOONS

Notwithstanding the 6 billion birds summering in the United States, Vermont's 122 (1997 count) black-and-white common loons (*Gavia immer*) have captured a disproportionate number of hearts. Although the state's loon population is slowly growing, pairs abandon their nests when humans venture too close. Please enjoy them from afar.

With their big feet and torpedo-shaped bodies, loons can dive to 100 feet in the water, where they may fish for more than a minute. A specially designed rib cage forms an overlapping lattice, which prevents compression of the loon's lungs under pressure.

Loons cannot walk and, with dense bones, are poorly designed for flight. Their wing-area-to-weight ratio makes it hard for them to soar even after a long run and shallow climb. Remarkably, once airborne, they can fly as fast as 100 mph.

Loon eggs, usually two, hatch one day apart in June. Like most ground-nesting birds, the chicks are sufficiently developed to leave the nest quickly and can soon swim.

If a storm erupts or a predator threatens, parents will lure away the first-born chick and abandon the second. Predators include northern pike, muskellunge, or snapping turtles from below and hawks or eagles from above. Cold is a greater threat than predation, perhaps the reason adults give chicks rides on their backs in the first few weeks of life.

Loons may live to be thirty years old. Perhaps the key to longevity is their shoe size. Extrapolated to humans it would be 45 triple R!

Getting There

From Route 7 in Ferrisburg, turn west on Little Chicago Road—coming from the north this will be a right turn; from the south a left turn. The town clerk's office is on the corner. Follow this road across the river and the railroad track. At 0.9 mile, turn right onto Hawkins Road, which meanders through farmland and along the Otter Creek. The entrance to the state park is on the right at 3.4 miles.

For More Information

Kingsland Bay State Park
Ferrisburg, VT 05456
802-877-3445

In the Area

Rokeby Museum
A stop on the Underground Railroad, Rokeby was the home and sheep farm of Quaker abolitionists. Family home to the Robinsons for nearly two centuries, Rokeby reveals the life and times of this unusual family.
     Rokeby is on Route 7 in Ferrisburg.

Button Bay
State Park

Champlain Nature Trail
Ferrisburg

1.6 miles

1 hour

easy with occasional rough footing

A lakeside walk through an old forest atop some of the oldest fossilized coral in the world. A nature center for all ages. Remember, fossil collecting is not allowed on state lands.

Button Point is a quiet, wooded peninsula with magnificent views. It also has some stately old oaks, hickories, and pines. Button Island, just off the point, is part of the oldest coral reef in the world. Coral formations are visible on the far side of the island.

As the earth's plates shifted over its molten center some 450 million years ago, great pressure converted the organic debris—coral, shells, and ocean sediment—to limestone and shifted it to its current location. The reef surfaces again in the Champlain Islands but on private property.

In more recent geologic time, the Champlain Valley was inundated by a freshwater lake and a saltwater sea. Clay deposited by these waters lies thick across the valley, and in Button Bay it took on some unusual shapes, many like buttons. These flat, doughnutlike disks inspired British soldiers to dub the area Button Mold Bay.

In the late 1800s, Samuel Putnam Avery bought the land from the state in order to build a summer home on Button Island. The property stayed in Avery's family until the 1970s when his niece, Amy Welcher, sold it back to the state of Vermont.

The nature center was Amy Welcher's summer camp. A self-taught naturalist, Welcher built the camp with many windows and doors to bring

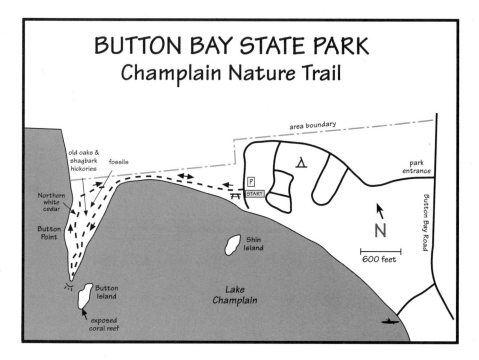

nature indoors. The fireplace is built from local stone, including fossils, concretions, and two brilliantly polished pieces of coral. Look at it carefully when you visit the center.

Begin walking west along the gravel road. Within ten minutes you will come to the nature trail on the right. Stay left on the gravel road toward the nature center. We'll return along the nature trail.

As you enter these woods, look up! You'll miss the majesty of these old trees if you don't. They are a mix of very old hickory, oak, white and red pine, hemlock, and white cedar.

Button Point has exquisite views at nearly every bend. The first vista is to the east. Ship Island, also known as Shin Island, is in the foreground and Snake Mountain rises to the right. The ridge line of the Green Mountains is in the distance. Straight ahead is the Sugarbush Range; its tallest peak, Mount Ellen, is tied with Camel's Hump as the state's third highest mountain at 4,083 feet. To the right, farther south, is the Middlebury Range.

Patches of trout lilies thrive beneath the oaks. Their yellow bells dangle over spotted green leaves that resemble trout.

The trail continues toward the point through a dense understory of white cedar, hemlock, and white pine saplings beneath towering red and white oak, white cedar, and red and white pine. Notice the beautiful patches of rosy bark on the red pines.

The bedrock is exposed at Button Point, and you can see striations scraped onto its surface by glacial ice. Rocks frozen into the massive glacier scraped, from northeast to southwest, over the relatively softer limestone (see Ice Age in the Champlain Valley, below).

Across the lake the Adirondacks rise quite abruptly from the shore, a striking contrast with the wide Champlain Valley of Vermont.

The trail returns along the west, or lake, side of the point. (Don't forget to stop at the nature center.) The trees are scrubbier near the open lake, where they are more exposed to winter winds and year-round storms. The trail continues over rocky ground and many old white cedars cling tenaciously to the shore. Gnarled branches of the oaks tower overhead, and the gray bark of aged sugar maples peels away from the trunks. A few flowering plants and ferns find enough sunlight among the trees: hepatica, false Solomon's seal, trout lilies, polypody fern, and marginal wood fern.

On a prominent limestone outcrop to the left of the trail are several snail-like fossils, *Maclurites magnus*. These appear on the surface of the rock as faint circles several inches in diameter. These snails lived in tropical waters about 500 million years ago. Shells form part of the limestone bedrock and contribute to the highly fertile, limy soil.

The trail bears to the right. There are several large specimen trees, a shagbark hickory, a few hemlocks, and a cluster of white pines. One of these pines has a diameter of more than two and a half feet. As the trail crosses the peninsula back to the trailhead, there is a final patch of trout lilies on the left.

ICE AGE IN THE CHAMPLAIN VALLEY

The Ice Age is a recent blip in geologic history, a science that counts time in millions and billions of years. The last large glacier of the Ice Age, the Wisconsin glacier, flowed over New England between 18,000 and 20,000 years ago. One mile thick in places, the ice sheet covered Vermont's highest mountains, smoothing their peaks and removing soil deposited by earlier glaciers.

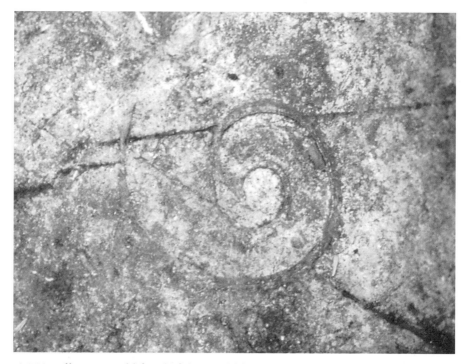

A 500-million-year-old fossil of the snail-like Maclurites magnus.

As the earth's temperature rose between 10,000 and 12,000 years ago, the Wisconsin glacier slowly melted. Thawing ice combined with precipitation and runoff to create a series of lakes dammed to the north by ever-present glacial ice. Many lakes formed, sometimes merging as more ice melted and sometimes separating as dams and shorelines were breached by accumulating water. Glacial lakes reached beyond the Green Mountains, where water followed the fingerlike valleys of the Lamoille, Winooski, and Missisquoi Rivers.

Lake Vermont, the largest of these bodies of water, filled the Champlain Valley far beyond the reaches of the current lake. While the Green Mountains were above lake level, only the highest of the valley hills—Mt. Philo and Pease Mountain in Charlotte and nearby Snake and Buck Mountains—were islands in Lake Vermont.

All bodies of water leave behind evidence of their shorelines. These lake-level indicators may include ridges of sand or gravel left by waves, terraces at the high-water level, and wave cuts and deltas of sediment where streams entered. Lake-level indicators from Lake Vermont remain on each of these mountains. (See Mt. Philo, p. 117)

As the glacier continued to melt, receding to the north, water flowed from Lake Vermont northward into the St. Lawrence valley. The level of Lake Vermont lowered significantly. But the melting glaciers caused the ocean level to rise, and eventually the tide turned. Salt water now poured southward. Freshwater Lake Vermont was turned into the Champlain Sea as icy Arctic waters filled the Champlain Valley. The Champlain Sea never reached the size of its freshwater predecessor, and much of Middlebury, Charlotte, and Hinesburg stood above water.

Fossils of marine life have been found in the clay soils deposited by the Champlain Sea. Along the shoreline of Button Bay, east of the nature trail, layers of clay in the cliff faces occasionally reveal marine artifacts, including clamshells related to contemporary Arctic species. In Charlotte, not far from the present shore, an 11,000-year-old Beluga whale fossil was uncovered during the building of the railroad in 1849. (See Charlotte the Whale, below).

The buttons, for which Button Bay was named, are formed from glacially deposited clays. Because of calcium in the lake water, they solidify like concrete into a variety of interesting shapes, called concretions, about an inch or two in size. Although the process continues, plant growth along the water's edge keeps them from drifting to shore. It is rare to see a button along the shore today.

Hours, Fees, Facilities

The nature center is open from mid-June through August. The center is closed while the resident naturalist leads nature walks and activities. Call in advance for a schedule.

Getting There

From Route 7 in Vergennes, take Route 22A south. After you pass through the town of Vergennes you will cross the Otter Creek. Take a right onto Panton Road 0.3 mile past Otter Creek. Follow Panton Road 1.4 miles to Basin Harbor Road and turn right. After 4.4 miles you will turn left onto Button Bay Road. The entrance to the park is 0.7 mile on the right. Follow signs to the picnic shelter, 0.7 mile. Just beyond the stop sign, park on the left. (Handicapped parking is located at the trailhead.) Continue on foot along the gravel road, following signs to the nature center.

For More Information

Vermont Department of Forests, Parks, and Recreation
Park Ranger
802-475-2377
Nature Center
802-475-2375

In the Area

Lake Champlain Maritime Museum, Basin Harbor

Just minutes from Button Bay, the lake's maritime history unfolds in very tangible ways. Replicas of historic boats are constructed based on underwater archaeology. Maps of shipwrecks, models of historic crafts, and artifacts fill the lake-shore exhibits. Open early May to mid-October; 802-475-2022.

Charlotte the Whale

Charlotte the Whale, Vermont's state fossil, resides at the Perkins Geology Museum at the University of Vermont, Burlington; 802-656-8694.

Dead Creek Wildlife Management Area

Addison

two 1.0 mile walks, plus driving

each walk less than 1 hour

easy

Vermont's largest waterfowl-management area attracts thousands of migrating geese and shorebirds.

The lazy waters of the Dead Creek flow northward to the Otter Creek through the flat agricultural lands of Addison County. The Vermont Department of Fish and Game manages more than 2,800 acres, providing an aquatic habitat for nesting, brood rearing, and stopovers for migratory waterfowl. In addition, the department lowers the water level in impoundment areas to encourage diverse plant growth and to attract migratory wading and shorebirds.

Visit Dead Creek with binoculars and a bird book. Raptors soar overhead, attracted by open fields and thermal currents near Snake Mountain. Each October tens of thousands of Canada and snow geese feed and rest at Dead Creek. Shorebirds wade in the shallows and red-winged blackbirds spend the summer in cattail marshes.

Peak viewing season is generally the first two weeks in October for Canada geese and the third week in October for snow geese. Other waterfowl, birds, and wildlife can be seen from early spring until late fall.

Several locations may be visited. The refuge headquarters, on the north side of Route 17, is home to much of the preserve's infrastructure: grain storage buildings; a garage for boats, trucks, and farm equipment; an incubator; and a brooder house. Please stay in your car.

Continue west on Route 17, passing a seventy-acre refuge on the right where geese nest and are banded. A native breeding population was devel-

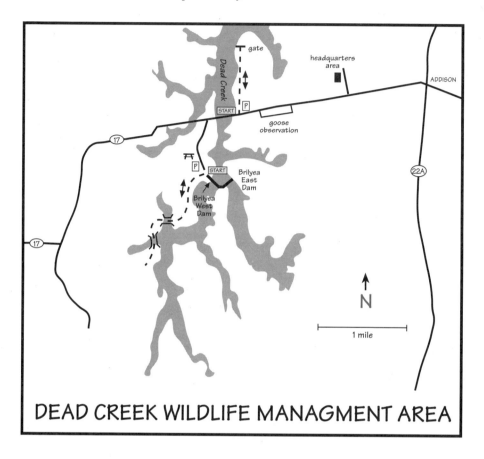

DEAD CREEK WILDLIFE MANAGMENT AREA

oped here in the 1950s, when few Canada geese stopped on their annual migration.

On the south side of the road is a large viewing area, generally packed with photographers on October weekends. Farther west on Route 17, just before the creek, is a boat access on the right. A dirt road parallels the creek to the north for about a half-mile, a particularly good vantage point for spring viewing of waterfowl.

Great blue heron, the largest shorebirds of the region at up to four feet, fish here. With long legs and neck and a yellow, daggerlike beak, the slow motion of their wings in flight defies gravity. These carnivores eat fish, frogs, and insects in the shallows. Otter, muskrat, and mink, as well as ducks, rails, gallinules, and green heron, frequent the creek. Bald eagles, osprey, and peregrine falcons occasionally have been spotted.

Drive west on Route 17 a few hundred feet, cross Dead Creek, and turn immediately left on a dirt road. The creek is on the left and agricultural fields are to the right. Several oaks have been gnawed by beaver along the road.

The parking area for Brilyea East Dam is at 0.8 mile, at the edge of an oak-hickory forest, once commonplace on the clay soils of the Champlain Valley. If left undisturbed these young shagbark hickory and red, white, and swamp white oak trees could grow to great size in this warm, fertile plain. The trees have potential life spans of more than 300 years.

This is a nice spot for waterfowl viewing, lunch, or a walk. Snake Mountain is to the east, with its maroon quartzite cliffs. A farm road leads south along the creek, crossing several more dams. A leisurely stroll to the end of the road and back takes less than an hour.

Walk past the orange gate on the dirt road. Dead Creek is dammed on the left, and there is a small swamp on the right. A row of young, scrubby trees grows along the creek and immature woods are on the right. Raptors often float overhead, riding air currents. In addition to the huge number of raptors seen during spring and fall migrations, kestrels, red-tailed hawks, and marsh hawks spend the summer in the area.

Cattail marshes are home to red-winged blackbirds as well as a host of waterfowl and terrestrials.

Within ten minutes another gate blocks the road at a second dam and a cattle guard keeps livestock in the fields. Buttonbush grows at the water's edge. After passing through another wooded stretch, the path crosses a third dam, with water on both sides. Wood-duck boxes dot the perimeter and a splendid view of Snake Mountain looms to the east, on the left.

The trail rises up a slight slope, passes through woods, meadow, and woods in succession before ending at the boundary of the preserve. Retrace your steps to return.

Be aware: This area is used in the early fall for the training of hunting dogs. Blank shots, shrill whistles, and barks punctuate the tranquillity as dogs are trained to respond to hand and whistle signals.

✖ A BIT ABOUT THE BIRDS

Canada Geese

Canada geese are known for their honking and V-shaped flight formations during spring and fall migrations. Lake Champlain is part of the Atlantic flyway, the eastern route followed by migratory waterfowl as they journey between their summer and winter homes. Tens of thousands of geese stop at here for rest, food, and water.

The Canada goose is a large brown bird with a long black neck and head and a white cheek patch. The male and female look nearly identical, except that the male is larger. Geese mate for life and are very protective of their territory. While there are goslings in the nest, they will chase away other geese or humans who venture too close.

Adult Canada geese molt once each year in midsummer. For several weeks they cannot fly. By the time the adult flight feathers have grown in, the young are also ready to fly. By late summer the geese gather into large flocks for their migration.

Greater Snow Geese

The greater snow goose is also a migratory waterfowl, generally white and in the process of a comeback from reduced numbers.

Twenty years ago, 100,000 snow geese migrated along the Atlantic flyway, generally following the East Coast from the Arctic to the mid-Atlantic region. Now up to 700,000 make the same journey. While this makes for some beautiful October days on Dead Creek, the growing population is taking a toll. Their breeding ground on the Arctic tundra cannot support these numbers and has difficulty recovering because of the harsh

From Dead Creek, the west-facing cliffs of Snake Mountain.

climate and short growing season. In 1996, farmers in Quebec filed $1 million (Canadian) in claims for hay and alfalfa crops lost to snow geese.

While the Vermont Fish and Game Department allows hunting of snow geese, they are difficult to hunt. They always travel in flocks, so it's difficult to place decoys. Adult birds, as old as fifteen, recognize human tricks and will take flight with an entire flock in tow. As one official explained, "It's hard to fool those fifteen-year-old eyes."

Red-winged Blackbirds

One of the first signs of spring is the return of red-winged blackbirds. With bright red epaulets and black feathers, the males return several weeks in advance of the females. They frequent marshes and generally nest in cattails, shrubs, or grasses.

Males are territorial and will scold those who venture too near a nest. Some are polygamous and will defend as many females as have nests in their territory.

Red-wings raise several broods annually, each in a different nest. Toward the end of summer they disappear to a secluded marsh for their annual molt. In September, with new feathers, they flock together to feed and roost before beginning their annual migration.

In the spring red-wings gobble insects by the thousand, but later in the season they may eat crops. When they congregate for winter roosting, by the hundreds of thousands, they can be very destructive.

Getting There

From the north, take Route 22A south from Vergennes (about 6.0 miles). At Addison, turn right on Route 17 west. The headquarters buildings are 1.0 mile on the right. Another 0.4 mile on the right is the refuge, used seasonally. On the left or south side of the road is a long stretch for parking, viewing, and photography.

For More Information

Vermont Department of Fish and Wildlife
(See Organizations: Useful Names and Addresses.)

Snake Mountain Wildlife Management Area

Weybridge and Addison

3.0 miles, round-trip, with a 900-foot elevation gain

2–3 hours

moderate/difficult

One of Vermont's loveliest views and a great spot to see hawk migrations. A gratifying hike for children. Wear hiking boots and bring binoculars.

An abandoned carriage road is the route up Snake Mountain, located in the 999-acre Snake Mountain Wildlife Management Area. The land, including an 80-acre parcel owned by the Nature Conservancy, is managed by the Vermont Department of Fish and Wildlife.

Called Grand View Mountain by locals, Snake has a truly grand view! It was the site of the Grand View House, one of many mountaintop hotels in Vermont at the end of the last century. Imagine, as you pace along in hiking boots, carriages full of women in fancy hats and voluminous petticoats bouncing up the same path!

Snake Mountain takes its name not from an infestation of reptiles but from its shape. Four summits stretch along a serpentine ridge line. One of several sheep-back mountains in the Champlain Valley, Snake has a gently sloping east side and a precipitous western drop. (Picture a sheep munching grass, its head low and its back rising to an abrupt backside.) The sheep-back mountains were smoothed by the flow of glaciers during the Ice Age, but they owe their underlying shape to the durability of the quartzite on their summits. Thrust from east to west over a softer shale, their eastern flanks of quartzite determine their shape. This is very clear on the summit of Mt. Philo (see. p. 117). Nearby Buck and Pease Mountains have similar shapes.

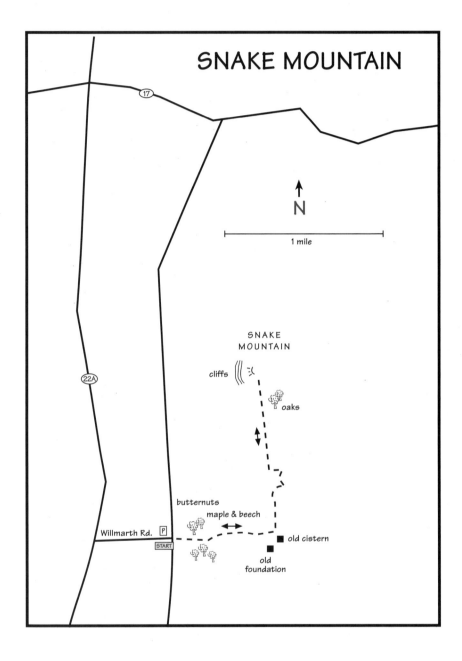

Observers flock to the west-facing cliffs to view spring and fall hawk migrations. On the perfect September day, it is possible to see more than 1,000 migrating hawks. With binoculars walkers can look down on huge flocks of migratory geese at a favorite resting and refueling spot. Dead Creek Wildlife Management Area (DCWMA see p. 135) attracts as many as 14,000 geese each day in October. Snow geese, which outnumber Canada geese three to one at DCWMA, look from a distance like masses of shifting snow.

The blue-blazed trail starts behind an orange gate at the end of Willmarth Road. The roller-coaster trail has been bulldozed to discourage wheeled vehicles. In minutes you are in the woods. Beech trees and sugar maples dominate the long-abandoned farm fields. The smooth gray bark of the beech makes them easy to distinguish in any season. Shagbark hickory are also scattered through the woods, long vertical strips of bark peeling away from their trunks. We once filled our pockets with hundreds of shagbark hickory nuts and then turned to Euell Gibbons's *Stalking the Wild Asparagus* for inspiration. The resulting thick soup tasted rich before a bitter aftertaste nearly choked us. Hats off to the pioneers who used these nuts to sweeten their corncakes and hominy!

Other denizens of this rich soil include ash, hop hornbeam, bitternut hickory, basswood, large-toothed aspen, and paper birch trees. A large red oak on the right side of the trail has a diameter of three and a half feet, and the occasional maple has extensive side branches, indicating it grew in a field rather than the woods.

After about twenty minutes the trail arrives at a T-intersection with the original carriage road, also blue blazed. If your muddy boots haven't already done so, a thick cluster of jewelweed confirms perennially moist soil. These leafy plants with succulent stems can grow to five feet by late summer, and their seedpods are irresistible. When touched, even gently, the ripe pods explode their seeds in every direction, leaving behind only an empty green curlicue (see Seed Dispersal, p. 145).

Turn right for a short detour. About a hundred feet from the intersection, remnants of an old farm peek out from the ever-thickening woods: an open cistern ringed in flat stones is on the left side of the trail; to the right are a collapsing foundation, piles of chimney bricks, rusted farm or household implements, a stone wall and a tree stump that grew around barbed wire.

An expansive view of the agricultural fields of the Champlain Valley from Snake Mountain.

Sheep farms and apple orchards were mainstays of the local economy in the nineteenth century. In 1837 Addison County, home of Snake Mountain, boasted a population of 260,000 sheep. When Australia entered the wool market sheep farming collapsed and small farms like this one failed and were consumed by encroaching woodlands.

Turn back and pass the intersection. A small stream flows on the left as the trail climbs steadily. Deciduous woods like these are host to many flowering herbs. Trillium, false Solomon's seal, large-flowered bellwort, sweet cicely, hepatica, herb Robert, early meadow rue, and bloodroot grow along the trail.

Keep your eyes open for turtles. One late-summer day we were startled by an enormous map turtle (*Graptemys geographica*) nearly a foot in length. It was not startled by us, however, and didn't budge or blink. Of the large native tortoises, only map turtles are known to range far from water during summer.

In late summer and early autumn we have seen large praying mantises and even the elusive walking stick. The latter had found camouflage on a white pine, the ends of its green legs mimicking exactly the tree's needles. Large insects like these, fully mature and ready to lay eggs, are most visible as their summer camouflage dies back.

After about twenty minutes, the trail becomes steeper, leading uphill to the right and then swinging to the left. The carriageway is lined with beech trees across a small plateau, many bearing carved initials. Striped maple, with its candy-striped green and white trunk and huge leaves, is an abundant shrub.

After the plateau, the trail goes steeply uphill to the right and then turns sharply to the left. One more sweeping right turn and the road climbs gently to the summit. Clumps of beautiful moss grow along both sides of the path. Serviceberry trees, with sensuous gray curves on their bark, are common, and a number of red oaks tower overhead. Partridgeberry leaves are thick on the ground. After fifteen minutes the trail leads left to the abrupt edge of the mountain, where it ends at an incongruous cement slab.

Hawks and turkey vultures often float on thermal air currents below the cliffs. It's a powerful feeling to look down on a dozen or more soaring raptors. At your feet is some of the finest farmland in Vermont, a patchwork of corn and hayfields dotted with Holstein cows. Lake Champlain stretches north and south and the voluptuous layers of the Adirondacks provide the western backdrop. There may be more expansive panoramas from the higher peaks, but the scale and scope of this view from Snake Mountain is very special.

Retrace your steps to return. It will take about an hour. Don't miss the right turn onto the spur near the bottom—both the carriage road and the spur are blazed blue, and it is easy to walk beyond this turn.

❋ SEED DISPERSAL: HITCHHIKERS, PARACHUTES OR TASTY TREATS?

While the ultimate mission of a plant is to reproduce, creating viable seeds does not guarantee survival of its offspring. Seeds need to germinate far enough from their parents to avoid competition for water, sunlight, soil, and nutrients.

Since plants can't travel, how do they disperse their seeds?

Coconuts float far from home to give baby palms a distant germination point, and pussy willows drop their seeds into waterways beside which they grow.

Squirrels, birds, and even humans are unwitting participants in another travel scheme as they transport fruit to eat or store. Sometimes edible seeds are left behind; forgetful squirrels and chipmunks bury nuts a perfect distance below ground for safe germination. Birds drop seeds far from where they were consumed, passing berry seeds and cherry pits through their digestive systems intact. Neither apples nor cherries can germinate until the flesh is removed. Humans, too, carry fruit from place to place. Tomatoes did not float to Europe unassisted.

On a blustery day, dandelions, cattails, and milkweed demonstrate their parachutes. Other flyers include the winged carriers of maple, ash, and elm seeds, lightweight with a large surface area to catch the wind. Hitchhiking seeds with hooks or barbs attach themselves to passersby. Have you or your dog brushed up against a burdock lately?

Last but not least are exploding pods, which launch ripe seeds away from the parent plant. This is how jewelweed, also known as touch-me-not, got its nickname.

Getting There

Take Route 22A south from Vergennes. From the crossroads at Route 17 in Addison, continue 3.0 miles farther on Route 22A to Willmarth Road, a dirt road on the left. This road ends in 0.5 mile at Mountain Road. Turn left to the parking area 0.1 mile on the left. The trailhead is at the intersection of Willmarth Road. Don't miss the butternut trees as you walk along Mountain Road. It's rare to see so many in good health.

For More Information

Vermont Department of Fish and Wildlife
(See Organizations: Useful Names and Addresses.)

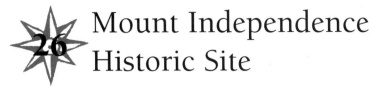

Mount Independence Historic Site

Orwell

3.0 miles, minimal elevation change
1.5–2 hours plus time at the visitor center
easy with occasional rough footing

A National Historic Landmark and the least-disturbed site of the American Revolution. Lovely lake views even for those not impassioned by military history. The strategic location and historic remains are best viewed when the trees are not in full leaf. Pets must be on a leash. Cross-country skiers are welcome.

This rugged peninsula sits across a narrow stretch of Lake Champlain from Fort Ticonderoga. In June of 1776, American troops began clearing trees from this 400-acre site. Surrounded by natural barriers—cliffs, the lake, and a marshy creek—the mount offered several strategic benefits. It has a commanding view to the north, the feared invasion route of British troops coming from Canada. Mount Defiance, another British stronghold, sits just across the lake. And Fort Ticonderoga could easily be reached a few hundred yards over water.

By the fall of 1776, with camps, batteries, and a fort accommodating more than 12,000 soldiers and their families, Mount Independence had nearly as large a population as Boston. When the British general Guy Carleton considered an assault on the position, he quickly abandoned the idea and retreated to Canada for the winter.

Many American troops returned to their homes that winter, and those who remained struggled against cold, hunger, and disease. In July of 1777, as General John Burgoyne's British forces moved into the area, the Americans abandoned the mount and withdrew. That summer witnessed confrontations at nearby Hubbardton, Bennington, and finally the Americans' decisive victory at Saratoga. British and German forces stayed at Mount Independence until November, when they learned of the British surrender at Saratoga. In a parting gesture, they burned and destroyed the site.

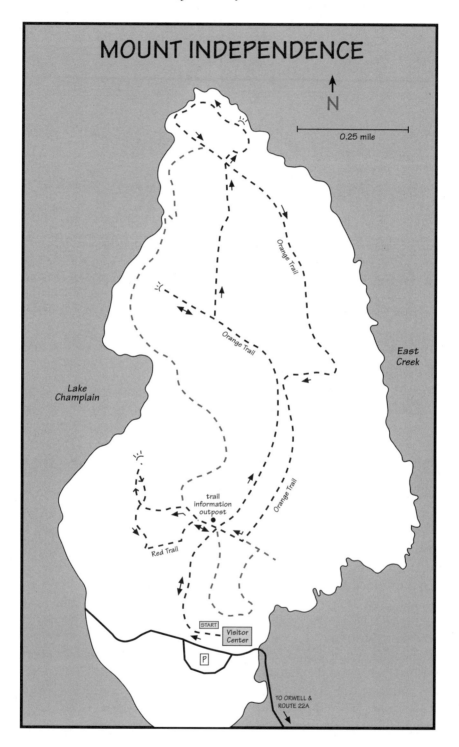

MOUNT INDEPENDENCE

N

0.25 mile

Orange Trail

Orange Trail

Orange Trail

East
Creek

Lake
Champlain

trail
information
outpost

Red Trail

START

Visitor
Center

P

TO ORWELL &
ROUTE 22A

Today archaeologists gently peel back the layers of time. A wide array of artifacts in the visitor center help paint a picture of domestic and military life: a ship's cannon; fishing paraphernalia including hooks, weights and fish vertebrae; pots; bowls; ammunition; medicine vials; knives; hoes; axes; spades; buttons; pipestems; shoe soles; keys; cufflinks; and belt buckles.

No reconstructions have or will be made. Bring your imagination on this walk through history. Make sure to pick up a map.

Walk up the slope behind the visitor center. An information outpost sits at the top of the rise, and all four trails begin here. The red and orange trails make a good combination as they encompass much of the perimeter of the fortress as well as many important remains.

Follow the red and blue trails to the left. Go left again on the red trail.

The Americans clearly anticipated heavy casualties: Remains of the stone foundation of a 600-bed hospital are visible, as well as excavations for an addition. The building was begun in the April mud of 1777, and was still under construction when the Americans evacuated in July. Disease was as much an enemy as the invading armies, taking a high toll on the 2,500 soldiers who wintered here in 1776–77.

The trail turns right and passes a stone foundation, possibly an officer's quarter, as housing for enlisted men did not have foundations. The trail continues to a lookout facing across the lake to Mount Defiance and Fort Ticonderoga. The trail returns to the outpost by way of a nineteenth-century gravestone. There are no marked graves of soldiers on the mount, although 2,000 bodies are presumed to be buried here in unmarked graves.

Back at the outpost, look for the orange trail going left. It passes through woods of mature white cedar, sugar maple, hop hornbeam, and shagbark hickory. Many of the shagbarks and hop hornbeams are large. The invasive buckthorn is thick in the understory (see Williams Woods, p. 106).

A member of the birch family with characteristic lacy branches, the Eastern hop hornbeam (*Ostrya virginiana*) has very hard wood, hence its other common name—ironwood. The fruit of the hop hornbeam are nutlets in a papery brown cover, resembling hops. Its bark is shaggy in narrow vertical strips, and the tree never grows to more than fifty feet.

The barracks of the Star Fort were located on the highest point of land. The earth was so heavily pounded by marching feet that even today trees do not grow. The one exception is the cedar at the presumed location of the whipping post. Legend has it that the tree is nourished by spilled blood!

Fort Ticonderoga from Mount Independence.

Archaeologists unearthed hundreds of musket balls with tooth marks in them, presumably bitten by soldiers as they were being whipped. Records have been found with victims' names, dates, and number of lashes.

The trail goes left to the edge of land, where a crane was used during the Revolutionary era to unload boats 200 feet below.

Retrace your steps until a trail goes left. Several shop foundations are on the right as the trail leads toward the point. At Stop 4, the remains of the horseshoe-shaped battery can be seen, the location from which cannons commanded the lake to the north. With the heavy growth of trees it's difficult to see that these gun placements pointed straight up the lake. The shore battery, at Stop 5, had even heavier firepower.

Along the shore, just beyond the battery, is Stop 6, where the floating bridge once connected to Fort Ticonderoga. The bridge was twelve feet wide and had twenty-two sunken piers. Twenty-one cribs remain in the lake.

The trail goes uphill to the left on the old road. At Stop 7 the ship masts for Benedict Arnold's fleet were stepped, a nautical term for fixing the mast. The foundations here show traces of mortar, the only such evidence on the mount. Mortar was used by the French occupiers of Fort Ticonderoga.

Cross the battery again and enter the woods. Imagine this entire plateau devoid of trees. Stop 8, an L-shaped foundation, overlooks East Creek, another important component of the mount's defenses. Many broken wine bottles were excavated from three-sided watch huts, the sentry outposts just down this bank.

The final stop along the trail, also close to the creek, is a rectangular foundation, perhaps a blockhouse. A large area of black chert, a low-quality flint, is nearby. It was used by Native Americans for tools and weapons and during the Revolution for gun flints.

Turn right and follow the trail back to the information outpost.

Hours, Fees, and Facilities
The visitor center is open daily, Memorial Day weekend through Columbus Day weekend, 9:30 A.M. to 5:30 P.M. Admission $2, ages fifteen and older.

Getting There
From the intersection of Routes 22A and 73 in Orwell, take Route 73 west. In 0.4 mile the road forks. Go straight while Route 73 goes right. After 3.0 miles you will fork right. After 1.8 miles take a sharp left uphill. The visitor center and parking are at 0.1 mile.

For More Information
Mount Independence State Historic Site
Orwell, VT 05760
802-759-2412

In the Area
Fort Ticonderoga
Across the lake in Ticonderoga, New York, the reconstructed fort has daily reenactments of eighteenth-century events. Built by the French in 1755, Fort Ti was later controlled by the British and eventually taken by the Americans.

Fort Ticonderoga Ferry
Crossing on an irregular basis as early as 1759 and in scheduled operation since 1799, the Fort Ti Ferry is one of the oldest in the country. It crosses the lake using underwater cables. Don't miss "The Incomplete History of the Fort Ticonderoga Ferry," available on-board.

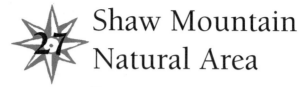

Shaw Mountain Natural Area

Benson

2.0 miles

1.5–2 hours

moderate

Shaw Mountain is a natural treasure and a beautiful place to walk. Located on limy bedrock near the lake and in close proximity to southern species, it hosts some unusual plants for central Vermont. The 275 acres include seven natural communities and twenty-five rare plant species. These plants in turn attract diverse wildlife. Amphibians breed in temporary spring or vernal pools, wild turkeys roam throughout the preserve, and bobcats den amongst the rocky slopes and ledges.

A carpet of fine, grasslike sedge lies beneath a forest of oak, hickory, and hop hornbeam. With few shrubs or saplings, the woods present a striking visual sensation, a bit like a winter walk with leaves on the trees. In addition to this unusual savanna, a vast swamp, marsh, and limestone outcrops are visible along the walk.

At the beginning of the trail, along both sides, are at least a dozen small blue beech trees, also called musclewood or ironwood. Smooth-barked with blotchy patches of bluish gray, the trunks are sinuous like a muscle and their wood very hard. (See Robert Frost, p. 170). Its seeds are eaten by birds and squirrels.

Also on the left within the first few yards are sizable patches of bloodroot, an indicator of fertile soil. Ferns; yellow, white, and purple asters; and hepatica nestle among the outcrops of whitish limestone.

The trail is blazed white and climbs without delay through mixed woods of hop hornbeam, oak, sugar maple, hickory, ash, birch, and beech. Plantain-leaved sedge (*Carex plantaginea*) is very conspicuous, growing in rosettes of ribbonlike leaves with long parallel veins. The lance-shaped leaves are a blotchy gray green. Christmas fern is common here and throughout the walk.

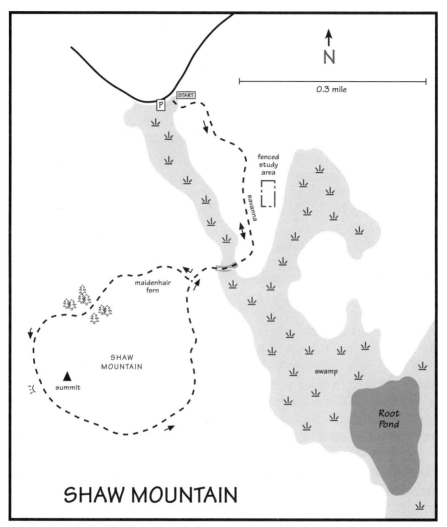

Base map information courtesy of The Nature Conservancy—Vermont Chapter.

Rocky outcroppings make the footing uneven. The trail switches back and forth, making several well-marked turns. Changes in direction are marked either with arrows or two blazes, one above the other. There is a beech tree with bear claw marks on the right.

One of the most common wildflowers on this walk is hepatica. Its evergreen leaves, sometimes red rather than green, are round-lobed and were once thought to look like the liver. One of the earliest of spring blooms, its simple flowers range from white to deep purple.

Within ten minutes the trail rises past a stone wall and arrives at the sign-in box.

Take a sweeping look around. This doesn't look like most New England woodlands. Lofty shagbark hickory, hop hornbeam, black birch, beech, and maple trees rise over a low, pale green carpet of sedge. The ground cover is Pennsylvania sedge (*Carex pennsylvanica*), which looks like long, thin grass. This sedge is well suited to the dry habitat and enjoys a competitive advantage in that it spreads by rhizomes as well as seeds. This underground network makes it difficult for other plants to gain a foothold.

Beechdrops (saprophytes which grow off the roots of beech trees), a few ferns, and some flowering herbs are all that stand between the sedge and the canopy. Be on the lookout for two spectacular plants, the fringed polygala and the walking fern.

Fringed polygala, also called gaywings, is a tiny but vivid spring wildflower. The bright pink-purple, orchidlike blossoms resemble tiny airplanes or the caricature of a moose. With two lateral sepals which look like wings, or ears, the petal ends in a burst of pink or yellow fringe. All this in a flower smaller than an inch on a plant less than seven inches high.

When ferns are categorized as once-, twice-, or thrice-cut, walking fern is categorized instead as nonfernlike, or unusual. Walking fern is as uncommon as it is unusual, and if you are lucky you will find it on limestone outcrops. It is an evergreen fern with long, narrow, arching fine-pointed leaves. When these tips touch the ground, the fern "walks," rerooting and sprouting new plants. The leaves reach a foot in length and prefer shaded, mossy limestone outcroppings.

The trail dips and crosses an old road before rising again. On the left a swamp stretches to Root Pond in the distance. Waterlilies, cattails, sumac, red osier dogwood, and stumps of dead trees populate the swamp. In early October it is a patchwork of reds: the orange red of sumac and the brown red of red osier dogwood. Look for a keyhole tree on the left, the hole where a branch once grew.

About ten minutes from the sign-in, a bridge crosses the swamp. Redosier dogwood, cattail, purple loosestrife, orange jewelweed, willow, and elm form a chaotic thicket of color and texture.

The trail rises uphill to the right and climbs through a shrubby section of young saplings, ferns, asters, and goldenrod. As the trail switches back and forth, rising slightly, maidenhair fern appears in large clumps. This is another unusual fern, its fronds circular or horseshoe shaped with black, forked stalks, and its leaflets shaped like fans. Maidenhair ferns prefer limy soil and generally grow beneath mature hardwood trees.

The swamp at the base of Shaw Mountain through a keyhole tree.

The trail forks within five minutes. Look for logs bordering the trail. Follow the right fork and blazes, which are now blue on white. (The trail loops and you will return from the left.) As the trail rises toward a plateau, the understory diminishes, again leaving towering trees, an assortment of ferns and herbs, and a mat of sedge. Three-leaved hog peanut creeps along the ground and meadow rue, herb Robert, and sweet cecily bloom.

Several rock walls crisscross the woods, the moss-covered limestone light in color. Maidenhair and Christmas fern are abundant; marginal wood fern also grows here. A rainy August day brought dozens of red salamanders onto the path, and Indian pipes poked through the leaf litter. Occasional butternut trees, also indicators of rich soil, look unhealthy. Butternut often falls victim to a fungus, butternut canker, which is devastating the species across the country.

Double blazes mark the few turns along the plateau. The trail meanders along the summit ridge, crossing limy outcrops and stone walls. To the right the land drops off precipitously and hemlocks grow on the shady northwest slope. The trail stays left on the ridge line near the 715-foot summit. The Adirondacks are visible to the west through the trees.

The trail turns left, crossing a rocky outcrop, and begins to descend into a moister, darker hollow. Sedge is replaced by maple seedlings, asters, false Solomon's seal, and ground cedar as the trail passes through a damp slump. Maple, oak, basswood, hickory, beech, hop hornbeam, and ash share the canopy. Shagbarks are the largest-diameter trees, approaching two feet, and hop hornbeams, with their vertical strips of shreddy bark, the most common.

Numerous dead or dying white ash are testimony to another forest pathogen as well as the sensitivity of the species. Like the sugar maple, which shows decline through much of the Northeast, the white ash is vulnerable to general environmental stress. A discussion of these threats to the forest can be found in Tom Wessels's book *Reading the Forested Landscape*.

The trail continues to bear left, completing its circular route within an hour. The swamp is visible downhill to the right, a splash of red in early October. The trail continues its gradual descent until it reaches the bridge.

CALCAREOUS BEDROCK (AND WHY WE CARE)

Why do different plants grow on different bedrock? Plants survive in a given location because of a number of factors: extremes of temperature, moisture, sunlight, wind, favorable sites for seed germination, and available nutrients.

The limestone bedrock at Shaw Mountain has a high pH, an important factor in soil fertility. The presence of lime, or calcium carbonate, keeps the pH high, making the necessary elements, especially calcium and magnesium, available to plants.

Water constantly leaches away nutrients needed for healthy plant growth. Thus soil becomes more and more acidic over time, making fewer nutrients accessible to plants. Limestone hillsides, located over a long-term source of calcium carbonate, do not become as acidic as other locations The fertile soil is home to such environmental indicators as maidenhair and walking fern, bloodroot, and basswood and butternut trees, in addition to the usual array of less particular plants.

Getting There

From Route 22A, nearly 1.0 mile south of Route 144, follow signs to Benson on an unnamed road to the west. At the stop sign, 0.8 mile, go straight. Turn left on Parkhill Road, 1.1 miles, and drive for 0.5 mile. Go right on Money Hole Road until you see the Nature Conservancy sign at a pullout, 1.7 miles on the left.

For More Information

The Nature Conservancy
Vermont Chapter
(See Organizations: Useful Names and Addresses.)

Central Green Mountains and Valleys

Green Mountain Audubon Nature Center
27

Sensory Trail, Fern Trail, Brook Trail, and Hemlock Swamp Trail

Huntington

1.5 miles

1.5–2 hours

moderate

A variety of hillside and valley habitats with views of Mount Mansfield and Camel's Hump. The Sensory Trail is roped for the visually impaired, with Braille signs and an optional audiotape.

Two hundred and fifty-five acres of the Green Mountain Audubon Nature Center are tucked in the Huntington River valley six miles upstream from the Winooski River. Rich soils attracted farmers to this fertile kame terrace left by melting glaciers of the Ice Age. Until the 1940s, much of this land was a working farm with open, hilly pastures.

In 1966 the nature center was established on land donated by Christine L. Hires (after whom the Hires Trail is named). More than five miles of trails weave through forest, field, swamp, and marsh, past ponds,

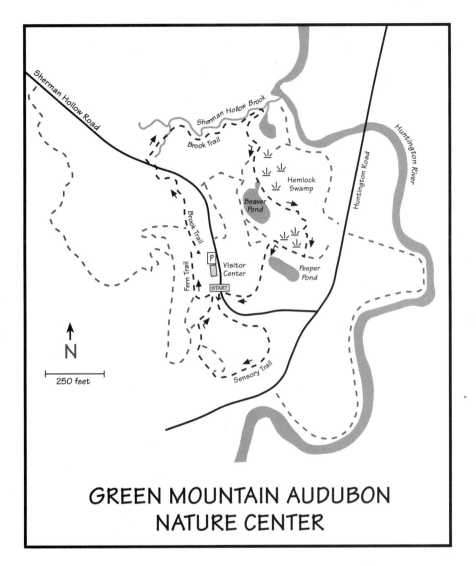

GREEN MOUNTAIN AUDUBON NATURE CENTER

streams, and river. A working sugarbush has 800 taps and produces hundreds of gallons of maple syrup each spring. Visitors are welcome on Sundays in March for sugaring. Tasting is, of course, part of the process.

Year-round workshops, classes, and programs explore environmental and nature topics. Day and overnight camp programs are offered for children in summer. The staff is active in bird research and monitoring projects. The Audubon chapter is expanding its outreach to local high schools and court-diversion programs as well as the general public.

Signage is better on some trails than on others. Make sure to pick up a map and get oriented before setting out.

I did my best to appreciate the Sensory Trail as it is intended. Roped along its entire 0.7 mile, the path crosses several habitats, allowing visually impaired visitors to touch, smell, taste, and hear the sounds of fields and woodlands. Twenty Braille and large-print interpretation signs line the trail.

The woven rope starts at the bottom of the steps at the visitor center and leads to a raised herb garden. Touch these plants and smell your fingers. I was surprised at how many scents were unmistakable, many etched in childhood memory: marigold, basil, parsley, oregano, chives, and bee balm. One plant has sticky stems, another long trumpet flowers, and a third fuzzy leaves.

Pick up the rope again on the left. Young mixed woods are on the left, and a backyard habitat on the right includes raspberry and blueberry plants, lilacs, and fruits trees.

Stop and listen for a moment. In the spring dozens of migrating birds sing in the early morning hours, while the ovenbird and American redstart sing all day long. The wind rustles the nearby white pines and the valley echoes the sounds on nearby Huntington Road.

Tactile sensations at the edge of the woods include thorns on hawthorn and black locust trees; small, woody alder cones; and beady fertile fronds of sensitive ferns. Raspberry and blackberry canes are prickly.

Raspberry, blackberry, and thimbleberry are brambles, members of the rose family whose stalks or canes live for two seasons until they produce their fruit. (The rose family also includes apple, pear, plum, cherry, strawberry, almond, and spirea.) Blackberry can be distinguished by angular stems with stout prickles. Red raspberry has round, bristling stems, and purple-flowering raspberry, often called thimbleberry, has hairy stems. Thimbleberry leaves resemble those of maples, while other brambles have compound leaves with three to seven elliptical leaflets. The fruit of the thimbleberry is not as sweet and succulent as its cousins, but it is a favorite of wildlife.

The trail enters the woods, old pastures planted in white pine. The overgrown woodlot wasn't previously managed, and the center is now thinning the pines as fuel for sugaring. If too many trees are cut at once the remaining ones will be vulnerable to wind. Listen for chickadees, which nest in the snags.

The conspicuous spores of the marginal wood fern, one of many types along the Fern Trail.

Close your eyes again. Needles are soft underfoot and the cool, dark woods are damp and smell of pine. If you touch a tree it may be sticky with resin.

The trail climbs to a ridge through mixed woods and descends through more white pines before bending right and returning to the open meadow. A final right turn brings us to the beginning of the trail.

Look behind the visitor center for the Hires Trail. Within two minutes it climbs to the Fern Trail on the right. Follow this sylvan path along the hillside through lush, thick, and varied ferns. The woods are a mixture of paper and yellow birch, maple, and hop hornbeam. A rocky cliff on the left is covered with moss, ferns, and young hemlocks. Partridgeberry, Clintonia, and club moss are underfoot.

The Fern Trail goes steeply downhill to join the Hires and Brook Trails. Turn left on the trail and then stay right on the Brook Trail when the Hires Trail forks left. The trail makes several ups and downs for about ten minutes before reaching the road.

Turn left and walk 100 feet on road. Take the Brook Trail right, into the woods. The trail winds downhill through mixed northern woods of maple, poplar, yellow birch, hop hornbeam, hemlock, white pine, and basswood. The herb layer is rich with Canada Mayflower or wild lily of the valley, Clintonia, red trillium, twisted stalk, Solomon's seal, wood sorrel, ferns, and hobblebush. The hobblebush has been nibbled by deer and moose. The footing can be slippery and there are many superficial roots.

The trail bears right over a small stream and the larger Sherman Hollow Brook is on the left.

The trail wanders next to the brook, over a wooden bridge, and onto a sandy bed of spring overflow. This oxbow is now separated from the brook except during high water. The trail rises to higher ground along the edge of the brook and crosses it. Note the erosion of its banks and the piles of sediment, sorted by size. As the flow of water slows, the river has less carrying capacity. It drops bigger stones first, then smaller ones, and finally sand. Fine silt usually settles at the mouth of a river.

A boardwalk crosses the river and the trail climbs out of the riverbed.

Look at the map to get your bearings within the maze of trails. Take the first right at a backward fork, then a right again at the next fork. You are walking toward the visitor center and the Hemlock Swamp on a flat, wide trail through mixed deciduous woods. At a fork follow signs left toward the Sugar House and Hemlock Swamp.

The trail crosses a small stream on a raised boardwalk near an open swamp of cattails. Follow signs right toward the Sugar House. The trail rises slightly through sugar maple woods.

A sign points right, to the Hemlock Swamp over a wide grassy roadway. Cross a dirt road and continue straight ahead toward the Hemlock Swamp. At an intersection of several trails, go straight, and at the next set of signs turn right, at last, into the Hemlock Swamp. This zigzagging should take about ten minutes.

A boardwalk about sixty feet long leads through the spring-fed swamp. Uprooted trees covered with moss, ferns, and young saplings lean across the swamp and duckweed coats the open pools. Hemlock, swamp maple, green ash, and yellow birch are numerous. Look for both yellow birch and hemlock growing on stilts. These trees can germinate on nearly any moist surface and often do so on stumps. When the stump rots away the tree roots support a tree several feet off the ground.

The trail crosses a peninsula of drier ground where several shrubs adapted to cool, damp conditions thrive. Both hobblebush and winterberry produce a bonanza of red berries. Striped maple, like hobblebush, has been heavily browsed by deer. Look for painted trillium, which prefers a cool, acidic environment. It more often produces two flowers per plant than either red or white trillium.

Cold-climate plants like to grow on mounds of sphagnum moss: goldthread, wood sorrel, Clintonia, partridgeberry, red and painted trillium, starflower, and wintergreen. The five-petaled yellow blooms of marsh marigolds dot the swamp in May.

The trail crosses another section of boardwalk. Hummocks of sphagnum moss and tree roots elevate less water tolerant trees, like the birches, above water level.

Stairs climb to a plateau. Follow signs right, along the edge of a field, toward the visitor center. Peeper Pond is on the left. As the trail enters the white pine woods, turn left. The trail rises to a set of steps, which lead to the visitor center.

🌿 KNOWING THE TREES

To begin identifying trees, start with one you already know, perhaps a sugar maple, and describe it: simple leaves with five pointed lobes, branches opposite each other, paired seeds with wings, and, on old trees, gray, furrowed bark. You will make similar observations as you identify other trees.

There are about thirty different hardwood species in this area, many of these in families like the oaks, maples, poplars, and birches. If you learn one new tree on each walk in this book, the job will be done!

Most local trees exhibit alternate branching, where leaves and branches sprout alternately, first on one side then on the other, along a branch. For those with opposite branching, an acronym helps: MADCapHorse, for maple, ash, dogwood, Caprifoliaceae (the family including viburnum, honeysuckle, and elderberry), and horse chestnut.

Leaves are simple or compound. A compound leaf is divided into many leaflets. Ash, hickory, locust, butternut, and horse chestnut have multiple leaflets, whereas maple, oak, and poplar trees, among others, have a single, undivided leaf. The shapes of many of these leaves are familiar: the lobed leaf of oaks and maples, the oval of birch and elm leaves, and lance-shaped willow leaves.

A tree guide points out further distinctions: bark, flower, and seed descriptions; thickness of twigs (a great winter guide); habitat (sugar maples do not grow in swamps); size. Shape can be misleading if a tree grows in the woods, where it develops only a few side branches.

Hours, Fees, Facilities

Trails open from dawn until dusk daily. No admission fee but donations are welcome. Restrooms in the visitor center open Monday to Friday, 9:00 A.M. to 4:30 P.M. Dog policy varies: no dogs on the unimproved woods trails; dogs on leash in the sugarbush; dogs off leash but controlled on the east side of the Huntington Road.

Getting There

From the stoplight on Route 2 in the village of Richmond, turn south on Bridge Street. Pass the historic Round Church on the left and follow the main road, which bears right. You will travel 5.2 miles to Sherman Hollow Road, a dirt road, on the right. Turn right and follow signs toward the Audubon Nature Center and the Birds of Vermont Museum. The parking area is 0.3 mile on the left.

For More Information

Green Mountain Audubon Nature Center
255 Sherman Hollow Road
Huntington, VT 05462
802-434-3068

In the Area

The Birds of Vermont Museum is located 0.6 mile beyond the visitors center on Sherman Hollow Road. Open May 1 through October 31.

Lifelike carvings of hundreds of birds are presented in their native habitat with nests and eggs. Founded by artist and carver Bob Spear, the nonprofit museum informs and enchants through the beauty of nature's creatures and the skill of the artist.

Mad River Greenway

Waitsfield

5.5 miles

3 hours

easy

*Dairy farms, a meandering river, and mountain views in a
river valley. Great for cross-country skiing or snowshoeing.
Dogs must be leashed.*

The nonprofit Mad River Path Association (MRPA) has created a network of trails linking the towns of the Mad River valley. The Mad River
Greenway wends its way through lush agricultural land along the banks of
the Mad River.

Today the river provides a scenic venue for walking, kayaking, or
trout fishing. Not long ago, the river defined life in the valley, providing
water, fish, gravel, ice, recreation, and power. Gravel was removed, bucket
by bucket, for use on the roads, and ice, a cash crop, was cut several times
each winter. The Mad River's steep grade was well suited to mills and many
were built: cider, grist, and sawmills. Recreation centered on the river as
well: skating in winter, swimming in summer, and fishing between times.
Removal of gravel made for better swimming holes, too!

The river dictated the rhythm of life. Many farmers worked subsistence hill farms and then put in hours at the mills. When water filled the
pond behind the dam, work began at the mill and lasted several hours until
the water was depleted. Then back to the farm while the pond filled again.

Not always beneficent, the Mad River occasionally spills over the valley. The flood of 1927 destroyed bridges, mills, houses, and cattle, and the
1938 hurricane flooded many homes and farms. As recently as the 1990s,
the river has risen beyond its usual flood plain during heavy rains.

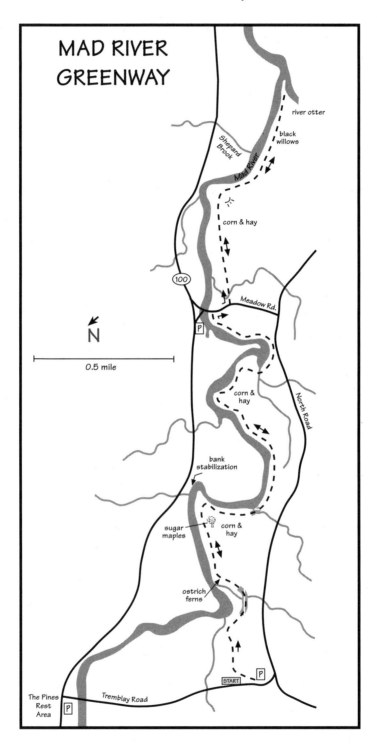

MAD RIVER
GREENWAY

river otter

black
willows

Shepard
Brook

Mad River

corn & hay

100

Meadow Rd.

N

0.5 mile

P

corn &
hay

North Road

bank
stabilization

sugar
maples

corn &
hay

ostrich
ferns

START

P

The Pines
Rest
Area

P

Tremblay Road

Reminder: This is not public land! Don't forget as you walk, snow-shoe, or ski, that private landowners have generously allowed nonmotor-ized use of their properties. Yield to farm equipment and please be careful.

The trail begins to the left of the parking area. White, plastic-covered rolls of hay, like giant marshmallows, dot the farm fields, which stretch to the river. Beyond them farmhouses, barns, and ski trails rise into the mountains.

A thicket borders a stream on the right. Several paper birch line its banks entwined with wild grape, virgin's-bower (*Clematis virginiana*), and wild cucumber. With leaves like a maple, the wild cucumber (*Echinocystis lobata*) produces an inedible fruit covered with weak spines. The hollow, fibrous shells remain on the vine into winter. Speckled alder, sensitive fern, box elder, and willow are all indicators of damp soils, while basswood and common elderberry prefer both wet and rich soil.

Within ten minutes the trail reaches the end of the field and goes right across a wooden bridge into woods dominated by yellow birches. The trail crosses another wooden bridge and immediately turns left. Hay and corn fields stretch to the right and young woods border the stream on the left, a mix of sugar maples, speckled alder, ash, linden, and some scraggly butternut. (Butternut trees across the Northeast are dying from a fungus.) Ostrich ferns and jewelweed are big and lush in the damp, fertile soil. Ostrich ferns can grow to six feet in river bottoms and open, wet wood-lands. The twice-cut fronds taper to both the base and tip and may have as many as forty pairs of narrow, pointed leaflets.

The trail approaches the slow-flowing Mad River on the left. On the bank, a hawthorn tree is a parasol of vines as it struggles for survival against a wild grapevine, its diameter about half that of the tree.

After about thirty minutes of walking, a sign of the Lake Champlain Basin Commission and Friends of the Mad River explains efforts to stabilize the riverbanks. Dormant willow posts are interspersed with saplings. In the wet soil the willows sprout and their roots add to the anchoring power of the saplings. Live stabilization, more aesthetic and less expensive than stone rip-rap, has additional benefits. Shade cools the river and insects fall from the trees to feed fish. While in geological time the river will ultimately prevail, meandering back and forth across valley floor, these efforts protect farmland and buildings important to the current economic health of the valley.

Detour left into the riverbed, across sand and onto the gravel bar. We are on the inside of the curve, the shortest distance water must travel. As the river slows, it drops its sediment, depositing sand and gravel. On the

Eroded bedrock of the Mad River.

opposite, outer bank, erosion takes place as fast moving currents cut into the bank.

Return to the trail and turn left to continue. The river has turned almost ninety degrees. Corn and hayfields are on the right. Farmers rotate their crops from year to year to prevent soil depletion. The river soon meanders left again.

In a few minutes an arrow marks a left turn and the trail crosses a wooden bridge. A stone bench is on the right. In winter this is the intersection of two major snowmobile routes. Signs indicate distances, directions, and amenities on the network of trails. The local snowmobile club, the Mad River Ridge Runners, works in concert with the MRPA in routing trails and building bridges.

We continue to walk at the edge of hay- and cornfields. In summer, the corn is "as high as an elephant's eye"—eight to ten feet. A bench overlooks eroded bedrock in the river before the trail arrives at Meadow Road, about an hour into the walk. Another parking area is across the river.

The path continues north through a thicket of young trees until it meets a farm road, where it turns left. Several basswood, or linden, trees have dropped their fall load of thousands of gray, pea-sized nuts. Continue following the river as agricultural fields stretch to the right.

Stately trees shade a grassy stopping place. Its back to the water, a bench faces the mountains over the fertile fields, houses, and barns.

Several huge, gangly black willows preside over the last stretch of trail. Deeply ridged and furrowed bark covers their Medusa-like trunks and limbs. Across the Mad River, Shepard Brook enters from the west.

The mowed path enters young woods, where it ends at the tip of a peninsula. Look for otters frolicking here.

At a leisurely pace, the outbound walk takes about an hour and a half to two hours. The return, with fewer stops, takes about an hour.

🐟 MEANDERING RIVER

The slightest obstruction can shift a river's current against one of its banks. The current is then deflected to the opposite bank. Erosion takes place on the outside of each bend and deposition usually occurs on the inside of the next bend, where the water moves most slowly.

As the river makes bigger and bigger swings, the difference in the water's rate of flow (between the inner and outer curves of the meander) increases, which in turn increases the erosion and deposition. This process continues for hundreds or thousands of years until the curves meet. The channel then flows again along a straight path and the meander—now called an oxbow—is abandoned.

Getting There

From Waitsfield take Route 100 north from Bridge Street for 1.2 miles. At a rest area, the Pines, turn right onto Tremblay Road. A small parking area is on the left at 0.7 mile.

From the north, take Route 100 south. Tremblay Road is on the left, 3.1 miles south of the junction of Routes 100 and 100-B.

For More Information

Mad River Path Association
P. O. Box 683
Waitsfield, VT 05673-0683
802-496-PATH (7284)

In the Area

Two other trails of the Mad River Path Association are located nearby, the Village Path and the Millbrook Trail.

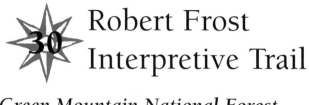

Robert Frost
Interpretive Trail

Green Mountain National Forest
Ripton

1.0 mile, minimal elevation gain

1 hour

easy

A walk through Robert Frost country enhanced by his poetry.
Great on snowshoes and with children. Pets must be leashed.

Part of the 335,000-acre Green Mountain National Forest, this unusual trail unites the poetry of Robert Frost with the landscape that inspired it. Frost spent twenty-three summers in a small cabin less than a mile from here. Many of his poems are posted along the trail.

The forest service actively maintains the open areas to keep them from reverting to forest. Logging, brush cutting, and prescribed fires are used to maintain the fields, blueberry bushes, and views. Many plants are identified along this walk, even a few obscure ones. There are lots of benches in settings that tempt you to stay awhile.

The trail has a figure-eight shape, the near loop being wheelchair accessible.

Begin to the right. Many black cherry trees line the path. You can recognize them by their curled plates of dark, peeling, and bitter-tasting bark. The trail leads to a bench at the edge of a swampy area and the poem "The Pasture."

We cross the swamp on a wooden bridge. A wood-duck box is on the right. The path turns left and passes through a thicket of red raspberries and speckled alder, which is identified. The alder is a shrub that thrives at the edge of streams and in swamps. Its strong, matted roots help to stabi-

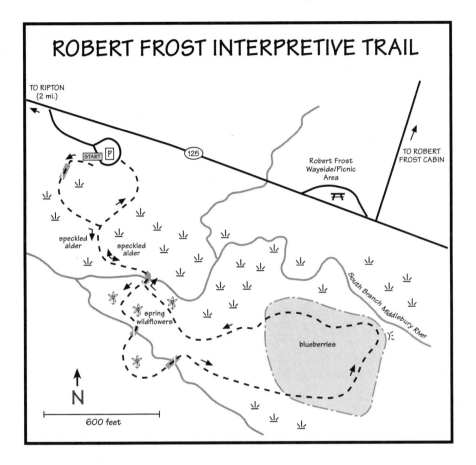

lize banks along waterways. Tiny, woody cones cling to the branches through winter and can be seen in the company of its catkins and leaves the following spring. The bark has conspicuous white lenticels, horizontal lines across the bark which admit air into the branches. The poem "A Winter Eden" is about a winter garden in an alder swamp.

Very shortly we come to a T-intersection and turn right. The trail crosses the river on a wooden bridge and is no longer wheelchair accessible. Hemlocks hug the riverbank. The poem "Come In" welcomes us to the deeper woods. As the trails diverge we turn right by the poem "The Road Not Taken." The trail climbs slightly as we pass an identified red spruce. Red and black spruce are easier to tell apart by their location than their looks. Black spruce is a smaller tree usually found in bogs, swamps, and high latitudes. In drier, mountainous habitats, red spruce grows to seventy feet.

The trail meanders to the left, past a wooden bench and a large yellow birch. Hobblebush is identified, an easy shrub to recognize. In winter its huge yellow buds look ready to burst open and in summer its opposite, heart-shaped leaves lie nearly horizontal along the stem, like a row of saucers. Partial to cool woods, this viburnum family member reroots when its branches touch the ground, hobbling the unsuspecting passerby. Also known as witch-hobble, it is a favorite food of deer and moose.

The trail makes a right turn, crossing a stream on a small bridge. The poem "Spring Comes First" reminds us that spring comes to the forest floor first and works its way toward the canopy. The understory here is thick with spring-flowering plants—Canada mayflower, Clintonia, bunchberry, wild sarsaparilla, trillium, and wood sorrel.

The trail rises slightly and the American beech tree is identified on the right. This is one of the easiest trees to recognize by its smooth gray bark. Beech trees sprout from existing roots, and here you can see a circle of beech saplings around an older tree. Sugar maple trees are dominant as we rise toward an intersection with the Watertower Trails on the right. We bear left. Hay-scented fern is identified on the left. When crushed, this fern smells like freshly mown hay.

There's a bench on the right and the poem "In Hardwood Groves." The trail slopes gently down toward the brook. On the left is a hospitable glacial erratic, home to a striped maple sapling, ferns, grasses, and moss.

The trail crosses the bridge and turns right. Bracken fern is identified on the left but was in short supply when I visited. Sometimes called the laid-back fern, its three nearly horizontal fronds arch backward. Its leaflets are quite lacy and delicate. Unlike most ferns, which prefer damp, rich locations, bracken fern thrives in full sun on poor, barren, or burned-over soil.

On the left is an unusual tree, the blue beech (*Carpinus caroliniana*), with its rather splotchy colored but smooth bark, thin twigs and buds, and alternate branching. It never grows over thirty feet in height. A member of the birch rather than the beech family, this tree has many names and is often confused as a result. It is also known as water beech (perhaps because it looks watermarked), musclewood, ironwood, or American hornbeam.

Here's the confusing part. Also in the birch family is the American hop hornbeam (*Ostrya virginiana*), with shreddy, shaggy bark. It is also known as leverwood or ironwood. Although the trees look very different, their names are used interchangeably.

A hobblebush bud already swelling in early October.

The trail soon leaves the woods and crosses a meadow. Lowbush blueberries and meadowsweet are low shrubs, the latter a spirea with a reddish stalk of flowers at the end of each stem.

The trail turns left when it arrives at the South Branch of the Middlebury River. A sign explains the U.S. Forest Service burn policy, used to perpetuate lowbush blueberries. Another panel offers a good explanation of why fields are temporary, describing the fate of pioneer plants, which alter the environment for their offspring. It's hard to imagine most of the Green Mountain National Forest as open fields.

At the edge of the meadow the trail enters a tunnel of trees. On the right, black cherry is identified. There's a good example of its deeply curled, mature bark on a tree several feet into the woods.

A mix of red spruce, hemlock, birch, and red maple thrives on the bluff over the river. We turn right and cross the bridge. Once again a thicket of speckled alder borders the gravel path. We bear right at the final intersection, and the poem "Stopping by Woods," to complete the loop. The poem "Reluctance" appropriately ends the trail.

BIRCHES

(Don't miss Frost's poem "Birches.")

Four types of birches grow in northern Vermont, and their names, if not the trees themselves, are often confused.

There's no mistaking the sweet birch (*Betula lenta*), also called the black or cherry birch, with its dark brown to black bark. The crushed twigs and leaves are fragrant and taste of wintergreen.

The other three birches, all with whitish bark, have overlapping characteristics and names. Bark characteristics are used, not always precisely, to describe them.

The paper, or canoe, birch (*Betula papyrifera*), often called white birch, was used by Native Americans to make canoes. The creamy bark peels off in large sheets like paper. The tall, single-trunked tree favors rich, moist soils and ample sunlight and can live as long as 200 years.

The gray birch (*Betula populifolia*), also dubbed white, is a short-lived tree that usually grows in clusters. It rarely exceeds thirty feet; prefers full sun; and will grow on poor, sandy, or overgrazed soil. Its flexible limbs bend to the ground under the weight of ice, often snapping. While its bark is a grayish white, it does not peel like the bark of paper birch. There is often a dark triangular scar beneath the branches. Gray birch, also called wire or old field birch, is a pioneer of old, depleted fields.

The last of this trio is the yellow birch, occasionally called gray or silver birch (*Betula alleghaniensis*). It's bark has a rich bronze cast and peels into narrow strips. Yellow birch is a big tree, growing as tall as 100 feet. It may live more than 300 years. Like black birch, its mature bark becomes reddish brown and fissures into scaly plates, and its twigs and foliage may have a slight aroma of wintergreen.

Hours, Fees, Facilities

The near loop of the trail is gravel and is wheelchair accessible. There is a year-round toilet at the trailhead.

Getting There

From Middlebury, drive south on Route 7 to the intersection of Route 125 east, about 4.0 miles on the left. Take Route 125 through East Middlebury and Ripton, past the Breadloaf campus of Middlebury College, to the Robert Frost Interpretive Trail on the right, 6.3 miles from Route 7.

For More Information

Green Mountain National Forest
Middlebury Ranger District
(See Organizations: Useful Names and Addresses.)

In the Area

An impressive cooperative effort has established the twelve-mile Trail Around Middlebury (TAM), a recreation path crossing parks, Middlebury College, public preserves, and an assortment of public and private lands. Although not yet complete, this circuit promises to be a remarkable asset to the Middlebury community. For information contact the Middlebury Land Trust. (See Organizations: Useful Names and Addresses.)

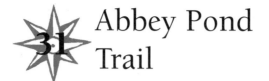

Abbey Pond Trail

Green Mountain National Forest
Ripton

3.8 miles, round-trip, 1,160-foot elevation gain

2.5–3 hours

moderate/difficult

Abbey Pond is in a wilderness where bear, moose, deer, and bobcat freely roam. Great blue heron nest at Abbey Pond. In years when they nest, the trail is closed from May to July— call the Middlebury Ranger Station before setting out. Great on snowshoes.

The trail begins on an unmarked logging road bordered by sprouting stumps. Within five minutes the road enters the woods, a mixed northern forest of yellow, paper, and black birch; hemlock; American beech; maple; ash; hop hornbeam; and cherry. The first blue blaze is at the edge of the woods.

In the spring mud I followed moose tracks along this road, the stride more than two feet in length, the print four inches wide and six long. Deer tracks, similar rounded troughs, are tiny by comparison, about three inches long.

The trail rises and turns left, passing over Roaring Branch at the sign-in ledger. Be careful of slippery and rotting wood on the bridge. The rushing water spills over picturesque falls to the right.

The trail makes a right turn and climbs, sometimes steeply, before leveling off. The rocks underfoot can be slick as the trail passes beneath a thick tunnel of hemlocks. Hemlocks preclude most other growth in their deep shade. In winter, evergreen ferns peek through a cascade of icicles on a rocky outcrop to the left of the trail.

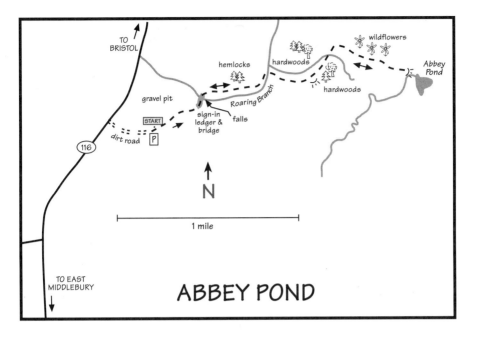

TO
BRISTOL

TO EAST
MIDDLEBURY

wildflowers

hemlocks

hardwoods

Abbey
Pond

gravel pit

Roaring Branch

hardwoods

sign-in
ledger &
bridge

falls

START

dirt road

116

P

N

1 mile

ABBEY POND

We cross Roaring Branch again on a bridge of boulders and turn left. A logging road rises quite steeply. Pale jewelweed thrives on the damp banks along with asters, nettles, jack-in-the-pulpit, and bloodroot.

Hobblebush and striped maple, called she-moosewood and he-moosewood, respectively, thrive in the cool, dark woods and are heavily browsed in winter. Striped maple has the largest leaves of the family, usually from five to seven inches long and four to five inches wide. This is characteristic of understory trees, which receive less light as it is filtered through the canopy. They need disproportionately large leaves to capture adequate sunlight. These striped maple, with bright green and white striped trunks, are unusually large with diameters of five inches.

A mossy outcropping on the right is covered with club moss, bright green even in winter. Its tiny branches resemble spruce, with pointed leaves in a spiral around the entire three-inch stem.

Spikenard flourishes along the trail. Growing to five feet, the shrub-like member of the ginseng family has heart-shaped leaflets, as many as twenty-one on a branch. Its fruit resembles a bunch of tiny grapes, turning from green to dark purple in September.

The trail climbs moderately but steadily. On the right, when the leaves are off the trees, you can glimpse Lake Champlain and the Adirondacks.

The trail bends right, then left. A beech tree on the left shows scars of bear claw marks. Beechnuts are high in protein and are a favorite food of bears as they bulk up for winter. Other inhabitants of these woods include chipmunks, red and gray squirrels, and the lumbering porcupine. This clumsy rodent is generally nocturnal, girdling trees to dine on their bark. While spruce and hemlock are preferred, birch is another favorite. Black birch grows along the trail, its leaves, twigs, and smooth, dark bark tasting of wintergreen.

The trail continues to rise very gradually past many herbs of the northern forest: starflower, partridgeberry, trillium, jack-in-the-pulpit, wild sarsaparilla, and Clintonia.

The tail crosses Roaring Branch for the third and last time on large rocks in the stream bed. There are several large white ash and an increasing number of red maple as we walk over soggy ground. A few of the older

Tranquil Abbey Pond.

specimens have very shaggy bark. Several old paper birch dot the hard-wood forest. There is scarcely a conifer to be seen.

These woods were once half spruce but were logged repeatedly over the centuries for softwoods. A sawmill on Roaring Branch made shingles and, in the late 1800s, hardwoods were taken for charcoal. The last landowner continued to log birch, ash, basswood, and poplar into this century. Most of the land along the trail was purchased by the federal government in 1935.

In November 1950, a nonhurricane windstorm ripped through Vermont with gale-force winds. South of Abbey Pond the devastation was great, and these blowdowns are the most recent cause of widespread forest upheaval.

Hobblebush grows profusely along the last section of trail, as well as a riot of spring wildflowers: starflower, Indian cucumber-root, wood sorrel, goldthread, and jack-in-the-pulpit. Patches of princess pine provide year-round greenery and sensitive fern attests to the high level of moisture.

Abbey Pond is a tranquil sanctuary in the woods, a nice place for a picnic before returning on the same trail. The twin peaks of Robert Frost Mountain rise to the south. Bracken fern and heaths prosper in the sunshine. A dam and lodge are evidence of beaver activity.

BUSY BEAVER

For all of the evidence they create—dams, lodges, ponds, and pencil-sharp stumps—beaver are not easy to spot. A nocturnal laborer, the beaver (*Castor canadensis*) works at night and sleeps all day. Your best chance is in summer, very early or late in the day, as their construction spills over into daylight hours.

Like all rodents, the beaver has incisors that never stop growing. If a rodent doesn't gnaw, it will die, as its teeth grow into the opposite jaw. Poplar, willow, and birch are preferred before the harder oak and maple. Evergreens are rarely gnawed. Family groups work together, chewing a groove around a trunk until it falls. They drag their quarry to a dam site, adding smaller sticks, mud, and rocks to complete construction.

As the dam backs up water into a pond, the beaver build their lodge next, a platform of sticks and saplings covered with a dome-shaped mound. Shredded and chewed plants make a soft carpet and water drains out through the floor. Underwater entrances keep the beaver's home safe from predators. Winter food rafts, leafy branches anchored to the pond bottom, are also protected by water and ice.

Winter confinement suits beaver. They can be heard chatting in the lodge while they groom each other's fur with special waterproofing oil. A beaver may occasionally gnaw a hole in the ice near the dam, allowing water to escape. With the lower water level beaver can enjoy meals at the raft without returning to the lodge to breathe.

Beaver have some remarkable adaptations: lots of body fat for warmth, nose and ears with special valves to keep water out, a special protective eyelid for seeing in water, and huge cheeks which close behind the teeth so they can work underwater without choking. Five-fingered front feet are dexterous, like those of a raccoon, and the rear feet are webbed paddles for swimming. The leathery, flat, oval tail is used as a balancing prop when gnawing, a sculling oar for swimming, and for slapping the water to warn of danger.

Beaver have a dramatic effect on their neighborhood. A dammed stream creates a pond, which in turn attracts frogs, deer, fox, otters, bobcats, ducks, and turtles. As sediment fills the pond it becomes swamp and no longer provides protection to beaver. When they move upstream to build another dam, the swamp fills with plants and begins its passage through wetland succession (see Ethan Allen Homestead, p. 42).

Beaver pelts were the currency of early Dutch settlers, and beaver fur was a fashion statement in Europe for years. Trapped nearly to extinction, first in Europe and later in the States, the animals were endangered everywhere at the end of the nineteenth century. They were reintroduced and have successfully colonized in every state but Hawaii. They are no longer endangered.

Getting There

From the intersection of Routes 17 and 116 west of Bristol, take Route 116 south. Just beyond the entrance to a gravel pit, look for a brown Forest Service sign to Abbey Pond on the left at 7.3 miles. The dirt road forks immediately but the forks rejoin. The right fork is better maintained. Follow it 0.4 mile until several dirt tracks intersect. Park off the road and do not block it. The trail begins on the logging road, the continuation of the road you have driven.

For More Information

Green Mountain National Forest
Middlebury Ranger Station
(See Organizations: Useful Names and Addresses.)

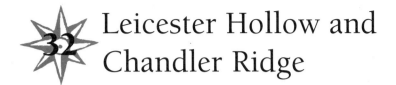

Leicester Hollow and Chandler Ridge

Green Mountain National Forest
Brandon

| 3.0–4.0 miles |
| 2–3 hours |
| moderate |

This is an unconventional itinerary for a beautiful and interesting walk. Leicester Hollow is a cool, damp limestone valley where a rich variety of moisture- and lime-loving plants flourish. A few hundred feet to the west, on a quartzite ridge running parallel to the hollow, a completely different cast of acid-loving plants thrives in drier conditions. The contrast between these two trails speaks volumes about habitat.

While a circuit of trails makes a seven-mile loop, that walk is longer than the parameters of this book. It is possible to see the areas of greatest contrast by walking north on each trail less than a mile and then returning.

Leicester Hollow, a shady valley nestled between two ridges, is cool and damp at all times. Chandler Ridge, three hundred feet above the hollow, has sweeping views east to the Green Mountains and west to the Adirondacks. The ridge of Cheshire quartzite is sunny, dry, and quite open.

Depending on the type of day and time of year, you might choose to take this walk in reverse order.

Walk around the gate, which marks the beginning of the Leicester Hollow Trail. This dirt road once led to the Silver Lake Hotel. Be alert for beech trees with bear claw marks. The smooth, gray bark scars readily when bears climb to their favorite fat- and protein-rich nuts. The scars grow with the tree, leaving the impression of very large bears!

A glacial erratic on the right is home to a sizable yellow birch with three trunks. Within five minutes the Minnie Baker Trail (to Route 53) is on the left. Shortly thereafter a cross-country ski trail climbs to the right.

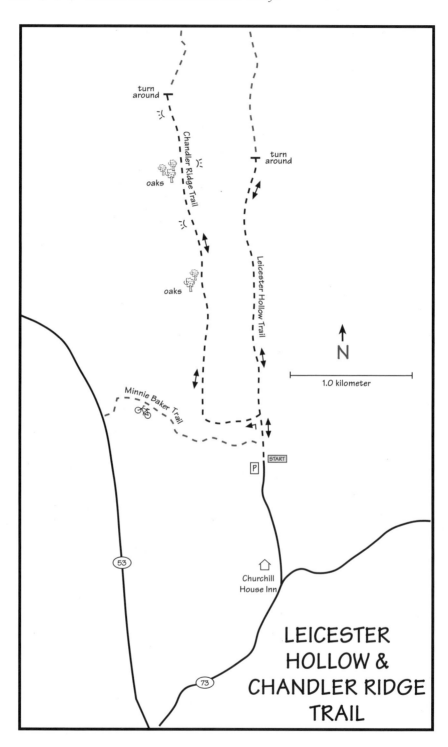

turn
around

Chandler Ridge Trail

oaks

oaks

turn
around

Leicester Hollow Trail

N

1.0 kilometer

Minnie Baker Trail

START

P

53

Churchill
House Inn

73

LEICESTER
HOLLOW &
CHANDLER RIDGE
TRAIL

Within ten minutes of the parking area, the trail crosses Leicester Hollow Brook. Immediately, the Chandler Ridge Trail goes left, stone steps rising steeply up a blue-blazed trail.

The trail heads south initially and after five minutes bears right to continue westward up onto the ridge. Finally it turns northward. Red and white oaks share the canopy with hop hornbeam, the occasional basswood, elm, ash, sugar and red maple, yellow and paper birch, and beech. Beech saplings sprout from the roots of larger trees.

Many of the herbs and shrubs tolerate dry or acidic conditions: Canada mayflower, starflower, Clintonia, partridgeberry, trailing arbutus, and wintergreen. The dominant fern is bracken fern, which generally grows in sunny, dry conditions on poor soil. Lowbush blueberry, huckleberry, and witch hazel are among the shrubs.

The woods are peppered with moss-covered glacial erratics hosting a giddy array of plants: reindeer moss, ferns, club moss, blueberry, mountain maple, and trailing arbutus, among others.

The canopy thins and a vista opens to the west. Red and white oaks dominate, but the thin, dry soil atop the ridge keeps them from reaching great size. Many red oaks have double trunks, reminders of a logging past. The footing is quite rocky. Witch hazel (*Hamamelis virginiana*), a shrub or small tree with wavy-toothed, uneven-based leaves, flourishes. A favorite of dowsers, or water witches, the shade-tolerant plant grows to twenty-five feet. Only after its leaves fall in autumn do spidery yellow flowers appear, four long, crinkly, narrow petals about three-quarters of an inch long. The petals curl back into a bud when the temperature drops and open again in warm weather. Its small, orange-brown fruit explodes to send seeds up to thirty feet. Extract of the bark and leaves is used as a topical astringent, while its seeds, buds, and twigs are eaten by pheasant, bobwhite, ruffed grouse, white-tailed deer, cottontail rabbit, and beaver.

Extravagant in the fall are Indian cucumber-root, whose deep blue berries sit atop of a whorl of red leaves. Purple and white asters bloom luxuriantly, pink lady-slipper hides its seed in a brittle leaflike hood, and false Solomon's seal produces a cascade of pink or red berries. Look for the pendulous red berries of wintergreen and tiny, bright orange-red partridgeberries.

A ridge rises on the right—the east. The soil is deeper and there are fewer rock outcroppings along the trail. The understory is thicker with saplings, especially striped and red maple, but there is still a splendid view to the west of the Champlain Valley and the Adirondacks.

An uncommon and unusual fern, maidenhair fern is prolific at limy Leicester Hollow.

When the trail makes a right turn and descends into a damp ravine, turn around. The return to the trailhead is a gradual descent and will take thirty to forty-five minutes. Blue blazes are frequent in both directions.

As you descend the ridge you meet the cool of the hollow. Turn left on the Leicester Hollow Trail.

The hollow was created over thousands of years as erosion and naturally acidic rainwater dissolved the soft limestone. The alkalinity of the bedrock produces fertile, limy soil that supports an unusual assortment of plants (see Shaw Mountain, p. 152).

Maple, yellow and paper birch, basswood, ash, and beech grow tall in the hollow, thriving in deeper, fertile soil with more moisture. In late May or early June, this is a wildflower paradise. Moisture-loving plants include jewelweed, ferns, nettles, and Indian pokeweed, its long, thin leaves growing sheathlike around a central stalk. Plants partial to limy soil abound, including maidenhair fern, blue cohosh, herb Robert, and bulblet fern. Despite its fernlike leaves, herb Robert is a flowering plant with a delicate pink-purple bloom. Red trillium and jack-in-the-pulpit, both partial to rich soils, grow to great size.

Look for Clintonia and Canada violet with a pansylike flower, its petals white on the inside and purple outside. Ramps, or wild leek, are fragrant. Virginia waterleaf, named for the mottles on its leaves, produces a cascade of purple or white bell-like flowers on tall stalks towering above the five- to seven-lobed leaves.

The stream bed and boulders on the valley floor are pale-colored limestone or marble. The trail crosses the brook a total of six times while

Bear claw marks grow with the tree, leaving this beech with some impressive prints.

rising gently. Two of the bridges are wooden and can be very slippery. Tread carefully!

The 800-foot elevation and cool temperatures are hospitable to hobblebush, a prolific shrub of the northern forest. Its large, heart-shaped, opposite leaves lie nearly horizontal along the stems, which often reroot, "hobbling" the unsuspecting.

Stinging nettles are a fact of life in the hollow. Late in the season, when the plants are huge, stick to the center of the road to avoid them. Heart-shaped, opposite leaves grow on plants up to four feet. Stinging bristles on both the leaves and stems deliver an acid that causes a burning skin irritation. Flowers are tight white clusters that appear in the leaf axils.

You will cross the sixth and final bridge in less than an hour. From here the valley between the ridges widens and the hollow is less pronounced. The land was once farmed, and you may see apple trees, day lilies and other evidence of civilization.

Retrace your steps to return to the trailhead.

Getting There

Routes 53 and 73 meet about 3.0 miles east of Brandon. Take Route 53 east for 0.8 mile. Immediately past the Churchill House Inn, take the unmarked dirt road that forks left. Follow this narrow road, Brandon Town Road 40, 0.6 mile to a small parking area, where the trail begins.

For More Information

Green Mountain National Forest
Middlebury Ranger District
(See Organizations: Useful Names and Addresses.)

Moosalamoo Partnership
c/o Brandon Area Chamber of Commerce
P. O. Box 267
Brandon, VT 05733
802-247-6401

Texas Falls

Green Mountain National Forest
Hancock

1.2 miles

1 hour or slightly more

moderate

A pretty, plunging river in woods with luxuriant spring wild-flowers. An interesting walk for children. Pets must be leashed.

This is a beautiful spot to enjoy the northern woods. We have left the warmer Champlain Valley for the slopes of the Green Mountains. Trees, shrubs, and wildflowers of the northern forest thrive here. Gone are the oaks, hickory, and white trillium of the lowlands.

This trail has the feel of the mountains and is an accessible way to enjoy the sights, sounds, and smells of more-remote locations.

The trail begins across the road. Stop to admire the beautifully sculpted bedrock of Hancock Branch. Thrust up at an angle, its different layers have eroded unevenly over the years. Potholes have been scoured by the abrasive action of whirling water and stones. At one time the water level was higher, leaving potholes above the current flow of the river. Notice the isolated pool on the near shore filled by seasonal high water.

Several trees cling perilously to the opposite bank. The river has eroded soil from around their tenacious roots.

The trail goes down some steps to the right and crosses a bridge. The water is aquamarine in color. Look upstream at the deep cut made by the water over time.

Be careful not to trip over tree roots. Hemlocks and yellow birch, both with wide-spreading, shallow root systems, anchor themselves horizontal-

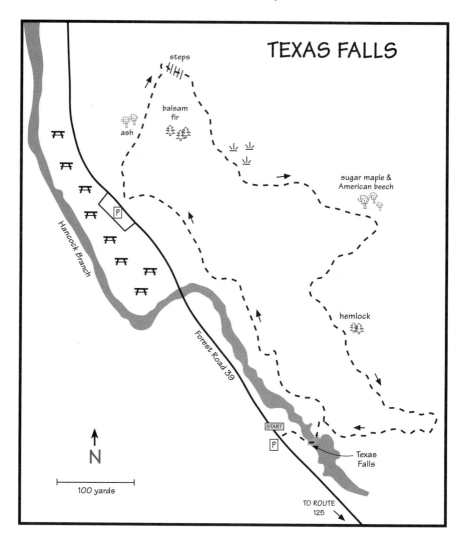

ly on this shallow soil. Their seeds can germinate in nearly any moist place and saplings often begin life on such unlikely places as boulders and stumps.

Follow signs to the Nature Trail, although it is no longer maintained as such. Turn left to walk upstream with the river on your left. A shaded bench overlooks the falls, a nice perch for admiring spring wildflowers. Both painted and red trillium grow here in addition to wood anemone and Clintonia. Clintonia has a pair of thick oval leaves. A cluster of yellow bell-like lilies, turning to deep blue berries, is at the end of a single stem.

Shrubs that prefer cool or shady locations flourish here, including American yew, hobblebush, and striped maple. These last two have been heavily browsed by moose or deer.

Less than ten minutes into the walk the trail becomes a wide gravel path and climbs away from the river. The woods are dominated by yellow and paper birch, beech, maples, and white ash. The river disappears across the road and the woods are quiet except for birds and chipmunks. Within five minutes the trail slopes down and approaches the river again. A picnic area is across the road with covered picnic tables.

The trail, well marked with blue blazes, turns right and climbs easily but steadily. There is a large ash on the left with a triple trunk; the diamond pattern of its bark makes it easy to recognize. Water bars have been built to prevent erosion. The entire trail has been unobtrusively but aggressively maintained against the onslaught of wear and weather.

We pass more red trillium, jack-in-the-pulpit, tall meadow rue, false Solomon's seal, wild sarsaparilla, and more heavily browsed hobblebush. Many beech saplings are sprouting from the roots of more mature trees.

A ten-minute climb brings us to a right turn and steps built into the hillside. The understory is lush with deciduous saplings, striped maple, hobblebush, and young hemlock. The trail is very easy to follow. On the inside of a right turn is a huge black cherry tree with characteristic "burnt potato chip" bark, one of the largest I've seen on my walks. There are occasional red spruce as we gain elevation, with short, spiky gray-green needles. The other boreal, or northern, tree making an appearance is the fragrant balsam fir. If you remember the adage that fir is friendly and spruce is spiky, you won't have trouble distinguishing the trees. Particularly in the spring, the new, yellow-green growth of the balsam fir feels like feathers. Later in the year balsam distinguishes itself with upright cones like candles.

Spring flowers are everywhere: painted trillium, Clintonia, wild lily of the valley, Indian cucumber-root, starflower, and Solomon's seal. In May I saw pink twisted stalk in bloom, a delicate pink bell dangling from each axil. The plant resembles Solomon's seal but is much smaller.

The trail crosses a series of small rivulets in a swampy stretch with many blowdowns. Waterlogged soil forces a tree to extend its roots along the surface to get adequate oxygen. Trees with shallow root systems are more easily uprooted. Some shaggy-barked, old sugar maples prevail in the company of smooth-barked American beech with distinctive blue-gray coloring. Although shallow, the beech's root system is extensive, which may enable it to endure strong winds.

Bunchberry resembles its relative the dogwood, producing a four-petaled white flower (actually bracts) and red berries.

On the right side of the trail is a nurse log. Seeds often germinate on the moist, rich surface provided by rotting stumps. This log is home to moss, ferns, and jack-in-the-pulpit.

The trail bends to the right and begins a gentle descent. A small stream rushes in the distance. Many small, round holes dot the earth, leading to chipmunk burrows. Their complicated tunnels can be thirty feet long yet may reemerge only a short distance from another entrance. Food is stored there, and a leafy nest is fit for winter slumbers and spring litters of young. Its most-feared predator, the slim weasel, can pursue the chipmunk throughout its burrow.

Three wooden bridges cross small streams in rapid succession. Ash trees are frequent again and the hemlocks begin to thicken. Not much grows beneath the hemlocks except the occasional fern.

Walk carefully down a stairway built into the hillside. The trail continues on the level for a few minutes, then crosses another bridge before bending to the left and descending again.

The hillside and trail are reinforced against erosion as the descent becomes steeper. We pass a beech tree on the left with beech blister, a canker disease killing large numbers of the trees. A few more turns and steps bring us to a final vista of the falls and its pools. The trail returns to the parking area.

* TRILLIUM THREE

There are three types of trillium in our area. The name of the plant tells much of the story: three leaves, three petals, three sepals.

Near Lake Champlain the large-flowered trillium (*Trillium grandiflorum*) flourishes. Its large, white flower stands above a whorl of three broad leaves. The plant can be as tall as eighteen inches. The blossom lingers for several weeks and turns pink before fading. In rich woodlands with neutral or basic soil, trillium bloom before the trees leaf out.

Beech leaves unfurling in the spring.

Growing in cooler hills and mountains, purple trillium (*Trillium erectum*) are a deep red or maroon. The flowers and leaves are generally smaller than those of the white trillium and the leaves are net veined rather than parallel veined.

Least common in our area is the painted trillium (*Trillium undulatum*). Its blossom has a central V of deep pink, which bleeds slightly toward the tips of the petals. Painted trillium favor moist, acidic woods and swamps.

Trillium have a symbiotic relationship with ants. The red, berrylike covering of the trillium seed is delectable to ants. The ants drag the seed to their underground colony, where they devour only its covering. They leave the bare seed to germinate in this ideal location. It still takes seven years from germination until a trillium produces a flower.

Getting There

From Route 7 south of Middlebury (about 4.0 miles) turn left onto Route 125 east toward Ripton. You will pass the Breadloaf campus of Middlebury College and the Middlebury Snow Bowl. After cresting the Green Mountains the road descends. At 13.1 miles turn left at a sign for Texas Falls Recreation Area, National Forest Road 39. The parking area is 0.4 mile on the left. Additional parking is available at the picnic area, another 0.2 mile.

From Route 100 in Hancock, take Route 125 west for 3.0 miles. Turn right at the sign for Texas Falls, Forest Road 39.

For More Information

Green Mountain National Forest
Middlebury Ranger District
(See Organizations: Useful Names and Addresses.)

Montpelier Area

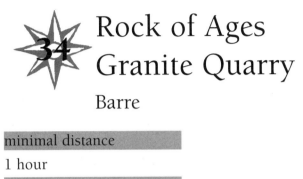

Rock of Ages Granite Quarry

Barre

minimal distance

1 hour

very easy

Home of Vermont's two-century-old granite industry.
Fascinating for kids.

The granite quarries are too interesting and awe inspiring to overlook even if there's really no walk here. The quarries also provide an excuse to look at geologic history—in case you fell asleep during that class. How did such an impressive quantity of granite find its way to Vermont?

Barre granite has been quarried since shortly after the War of 1812, although surface stone was used in the late 1790s for fence posts, doorsteps, and boundary markers. The state capitol in Montpelier was built of Barre granite in the 1830s, unfortunately a money-losing project for the quarry owners. It cost more to transport the stone twelve miles using horses and rollers than the suppliers were paid! It was only with the arrival of the railroad to Barre in 1775 that the granite industry began to flourish.

The hardest rock known to man, granite is very durable. The local stone has a uniform color and medium-grained texture. Granite is an igneous rock whose main components are quartz, contributing hardness; feldspar, determining its color; and mica, allowing finished stone to take a high polish.

Rock of Ages quarry.

The majority of the granite from these quarries is used for monuments. Huge rollers, used in the manufacture of paper and for grinding cocoa nuts, are cut from unusually large pieces of stone weighing about 200 tons. Granite is also used in scientific work, including space missions.

Scraps and imperfect pieces are crushed as a bed for road pavement or cut into curbstones.

Gray granite is quarried elsewhere in Vermont, in Hardwick and Woodsbury, while white granite is found in Bethel. Elsewhere in the world granite exists in shades of pink, green, black, and red.

Behind the visitor center is an abandoned quarry. The water is 200 feet deep, indicating the depth to which stone was removed.

A bus takes visitors to an active quarry during working hours. Grout (the Scottish word for waste) piles cover the hillsides en route. Today unused pieces are returned to old quarries to reclaim them. Before mechanized transportation, debris was dumped as close as possible to the source.

This active quarry, opened in 1880, covers five acres and is 500 feet deep. There are about thirty workers in the quarry each day. Because the pit is so deep, crane operators on the rim cannot see their cargo and signalers must communicate between granite workers and the cranes.

In recent years, 150-foot Douglas fir derricks from Oregon have been replaced with steel, and their fifty-ton capacity has been increased fivefold. Other strides have been made in productivity and worker safety. Jet torches, burning at 4,200° Fahrenheit, have replaced explosives for most of the cutting, and stone dust, cause of the lung disease silicosis, has been eliminated with wet drilling. Yet dangers still exist. The quarried stones, averaging ten by ten by five feet, weigh twenty-five to thirty tons each.

This granite massif has been measured sonically at two by four miles on the surface and ten miles deep. At the current rate it can be quarried for 4,500 years!

GEOLOGY OVERSIMPLIFIED

Geology is very complicated. Scientists examine our landscape and try to reconstruct billions of years of history. Geological theories continue to evolve with advances in technology, new means of dating, continued archaeological excavations, and even space exploration.

This simplified geologic history breezes through the millennia in an effort to make the very basics clear. Several references are listed in the bibliography and I encourage you to explore them. Like recognizing birds, ferns, leaves, or animal tracks, knowing about rocks adds to the enjoyment of being outdoors.

The earth was once a mass of molten materials. As this liquid cooled, a crust formed on the surface, not unlike the skin on hot milk. The crust broke into pieces as it floated over the liquid center. These pieces are called plates and their movement, plate tectonics.

These plates moved (and still do) back and forth over the earth's molten core. In bumping into one another, they pushed up mountain ranges. One of the oldest exposed mountain ranges on earth is the Adirondacks, believed to be 2 billion years old. The Adirondacks were on the east coast of a major plate, ancestral North America, and over millions of years the mountains eroded and their sediment built up along the east coast of the continent.

Meanwhile the plates of North America and the European/African continent, separated by an early Atlantic Ocean, were drifting apart. Then, around 445 million years ago, the plates reversed direction and began to drift toward one another. A chain of volcanic islands, a bit like today's Hawaiian Islands chain, had been building beneath the Atlantic Ocean. These volcanoes, called the Bronson Hill volcanic arc, got pushed against the coast of North America.

As the plates closed against each other, these volcanoes were subjected to great pressure. The magma, or liquid rock, in these volcanoes couldn't reach the surface and cooled slowly beneath the earth's surface. The resulting rock is granite, but we'll get back to that later.

The continents continued to move closer together until they collided about 350 million years ago. The Bronson Hill volcanoes were no longer on the east coast of the North American continent but in the middle of a huge land mass called Pangea.

Around 200 million years ago the tides turned and the continents drifted apart. When the land masses separated, some of the European continent remained attached to North America. This European fragment is now much of New Hampshire and Maine. The remains of the volcanic arc are the White Mountains and the mass of granite seen at the quarries around Barre.

With this information we can visualize, from west to east, the ancient Adirondacks, sediment from ancient seas which constitutes much of Vermont's western valleys, the Green and White Mountains, and the foreign appendage of New Hampshire and Maine.

Hours, Fees, Facilities

The visitor center is open May through October, from 8:30 A.M. to 5:00 P.M. Monday to Saturday, and noon until 5:00 P.M. on Sunday. Quarry tours are conducted between 9:30 A.M. and 3:00 P.M., Monday through Friday. Tour cost is $4.00 for adults, with reductions for children and seniors. Water, restrooms, and a snack bar are located at the visitor center.

Getting There

Take I-89 Exit 7. The exit road becomes Route 62, which you follow to the fifth light at 4.9 miles. Turn right onto Route 14 south. Bear right at a fork in 0.5 mile, staying on Route 14, or South Main Street. Look for Quarry Street at 0.9 mile and turn left. Follow this road uphill. At 2.5 miles turn left onto Graniteville Road. Stay left at a fork in 0.3 mile. The visitor center is on the right in 0.7 mile.

For More Information

Rock of Ages Corporation
P. O. Box 482
Barre, VT 05641
802-476-3115

In the Area

Rock of Ages Industries

One mile from the visitor center, the Rock of Ages Manufacturing Division handcrafts the monuments that have made Barre granite famous. A free, self-guided tour allows visitors to watch the cutting, sculpting, and polishing from an observation deck above the work areas.

Hope Cemetery

Just north of Barre on Route 14, Hope Cemetery is a monument to monuments. From the early days of local stonecutting, immigrant sculptors carved statuary to remember their loved ones. Hope Cemetery has dozens of remarkable carvings from local granite.

Hubbard Park

Montpelier

1.5 miles

1.5–2 hours

easy/moderate

A wide range of habitats within the city limits of Vermont's capital. Cross-country ski trails are groomed in winter.

The city of Montpelier is blessed with two significant natural areas, Hubbard Park and North Branch River Park. While the two parks are connected by a right of way open much of the year, each merits a visit.

Hubbard Park, 185 acres of meadow, swamp, and woodland, was established in 1899 by a gift from the estate of John E. Hubbard. A winter cross-country ski destination, the park bustles with summer activity on its trails, softball diamond, recreation fields, the tower, and picnic shelters.

Various benefactors have contributed additional land or funds for improvement over the years. In 1915, work began on a fifty-foot stone observation tower, constructed from nearby crumbling stone walls. The tower, completed in 1930, has stunning mountain views.

During the Depression, the Civilian Conservation Corps built and improved roads, buildings, and fireplaces throughout the park. In the 1960s a nature trail was added, refurbished in 1997. A fitness trail was threaded through the sylvan setting in the 1980s. Hubbard Park has nearly seven miles of trails.

We will walk a figure-eight through the woodlands and climb the tower for a spectacular view.

From the parking area at the hairpin turn, look across the road for a sign to the self-guided nature trail. A history display shows the park, once pastureland, without trees and then, thirty years ago, growing up in forest. Seasonal displays feature autumn leaves and wildflowers.

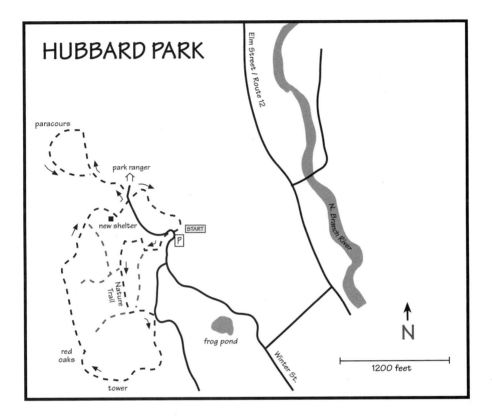

Sugar maple mix with hemlock and white pine, the thick canopy allowing minimal ground cover of wild lily-of-the valley, goldthread, partridgeberry, sensitive fern, and spinulose wood fern. At a fork the trail rises. Alternate-leaved dogwood, starflower, and interrupted and Christmas fern grow in the understory beneath maple, beech, hemlock, paper birch, red oak, and black cherry. Notice the characteristic curls of black bark, like burned potato chips, on the cherry trees.

Turn left. The trail rises slightly beneath red pines. Go left at a fork beneath thick hemlocks. At Stop 5, this dead red maple was originally damaged when it was split by frost. This significant threat to deciduous trees is little appreciated. With no leaves to protect it from the low winter sun, the trunk absorbs the sun's heat and expands. The darker the color of the bark, the greater the absorption. When the sun dips below the horizon, frigid air contracts the wood. The outer bark cools more quickly than the insulated pulpwood. The bark cracks to relieve pressure, creating an opening in the tree's protective layer. Organisms enter the wood and the tree begins to rot. This tree shows attempts to heal around the wound before it succumbed. Insects and diseases kill more trees each year than spectacular forest fires.

The trail crosses a small brook on a boardwalk. On damp ground, spirea grows in the only available sunlight.

The trail turns right before passing through an evergreen plantation dating from 1937. It includes the droopy-boughed Norwegian spruce and red pines. A glacial erratic sparkles with mica beneath a cover of moss.

The trail dips downhill and the beautiful golden bark of yellow birch glows in the sunshine. The trail turns right, around a large red oak with three trunks, then bends right, around a large white pine. At a T-intersection, turn right and then to the left shortly thereafter. When the trail reaches the dirt road, go right. When the road forks, go right to climb the dirt road, with red oaks towering overhead, to the tower.

A steep five-to-ten-minute climb brings us to the tower. Sixty-five steps climb past beautiful stones with varied colors, textures, and striations. On a clear day the views stretch west to Camel's Hump, east to New Hampshire's White Mountains, and slightly west of north to Hunger Mountain in the Worcester Range. A plantation of red pines blocks the view of the golden capitol dome.

When you come out of the tower turn left on the dirt road. Huge red oaks share the woods with both red and sugar maple. Red maple leaves tend to have three lobes and a V between the central and side lobes. Sugar maples have five-lobed leaves and the angle between the central and side lobes is rounded, like an old sap bucket. Sugar maple leaves have smooth edges, while reds are serrated or toothed.

The road passes an old stone gatepost. Go left on a small trail that leaves the dirt road at a picnic table. In this moist ground there are beech and many birch, maple, and oak with multiple trunks. Pass a stone wall with very large rocks. The understory is lush with ferns, goldthread, wild lily of the valley, partridgeberry, Clintonia, and wintergreen, its white flowers like tiny bells. Indian pipes are abundant in the dead leaf litter on both sides of trail.

When the trail arrives at a dirt road, go left. Just before the park gate take the dirt road on the right. Hemlock, oak, and Norway spruce are dominant, and box elder and birch mix in. Do not take the trail that crosses the road; continue straight. The road leads slightly downhill, crosses a bridge,

On a clear day the tower at Hubbard Park has views of several mountain ranges but not the golden dome of the capitol building at its feet, which is obscured by trees.

and approaches the new picnic shelter. Bear left to cross the open area. Turn left at the dirt road.

Along the dirt road, young basswood sprout from the base of a parent tree on the left. Hemlocks dominate the canopy. Several log benches are scattered and a bank on the right is covered with luxuriant moss.

In the swamp on the left hobblebush is abundant beneath black ash, birch, and maple. The road curves left and rises. Several ski trails go off to the right.

Turn left at the Paracours fitness trail marked by green arrows on white squares. These are rich northern woods, a mix of yellow birch, ash, hemlock, black cherry, hobblebush, and striped and sugar maple. The herb layer is a combination of ferns, jewelweed, trillium, jack-in-the-pulpit, and sassafras.

The bark path is silent and soft underfoot. The trail turns left at Stop 15. Hobblebush is solid in the understory, its heart-shaped leaves lying parallel to the ground. A large hemlock is peppered with rows of sapsucker holes. With its brushlike tongue, this woodpecker laps at the sap that oozes from the holes and also consumes the insects attracted to it.

The path crosses a stream on a bridge. At Stop 18 a rotting trunk on the right, a nurse log, is home to tendriled moss, goldthread, wood sorrel, starflower, and spinulose wood fern. The trail crosses another wooden bridge. Follow the green arrows for the Paracours along the road briefly and then into the woods again.

The trail goes uphill and to the left, past Stops 13, 20, and 21. (The trail is going in both directions here.) Follow the path to the right. When the trail forks, go right or straight (not left) past Stops 12 and 22 on a plateau. A beech tree on the left has sprouted lots of saplings from its roots near Stops 11, 23, and 24. Past Stops 10, 25, and 26, the trail leads to a picnic table and fireplace overlooking the open meadow at the parking area.

🌰 CONIFERS, IN BRIEF

Conifers are trees with woody cones (hence the name) and needles or scalelike leaves. Pollen and seed cones are generally found on the same plant and rely on wind for pollination.

The tamarack, or eastern larch, is the region's only deciduous conifer, losing its leaves each fall. Its bright green, one-inch needles occur either singly or in large bunches.

The pines, four native and two introduced species, have bunches of needles. Red and gray, or jack, pine have clusters of two needles; pitch pine, three per cluster; and white pine, five. The two nonnative pines, Scotch and Austrian, each have two needles per cluster. Needle length and bark coloration aid in identification.

Vermont has four common spruces, three native and one introduced, plus one native fir. Red, white, and black, or swamp, are the native spruces; Norway, the introduced species; balsam, the fir. If you grip a branch of these trees, the spruce will feel "spiky" and the fir "friendly."

Hours, Fee, and Facilities

Hubbard Park is open daily year-round from 7:00 A.M. to 9:00 P.M. Gates open to cars at 9:00 A.M. There are no fees. Restrooms and water are available seasonally. Cars may drive to the tower on Wednesdays and Sundays from May through September.

Getting There

From I-89 take Exit 8 and follow the exit road to the first stoplight, 1.3 miles. Turn left on Bailey Avenue. Just over the bridge turn right onto State Street, 0.1 mile. Beyond the capitol building turn left at 0.4 mile on Elm Street. Turn left on Winter Street at 0.4 mile. Winter Street enters Hubbard Park at 0.1 mile. Drive up the dirt road, bear right at the fork, and park in a designated area on the right 0.3 mile from park entrance.

For More Information

Montpelier Park Commission
39 Main Street
Montpelier, VT 05602
802-223-5141

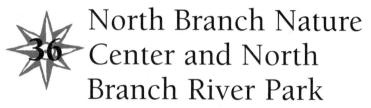

North Branch Nature Center and North Branch River Park

Montpelier

North Branch Nature Center

0.6 mile

45 minutes

easy

North Branch River Park

1.5 miles

1.5 hours

moderate

River and hillside with a variety of habitats and a connection to Hubbard Park. Good wildlife viewing. Dogs must be leashed.

Two riverside preserves in northern Montpelier soon will become one destination for walking, skiing, and snowshoeing. On the west side of the North Branch of the Winooski River is the North Branch Nature Center (NBNC), a satellite of the Woodstock-based Vermont Institute of Natural Science (VINS). On the eastern bank and extending into the hills is North Branch River Park, a municipal park of the city of Montpelier. A bridge is scheduled to connect these resources by the spring of 1998. With or without the bridge, each property merits a visit. We will walk them separately with the knowledge that the link is not far away.

Both properties have access to a lovely, lazy stretch of the river. Otter, beaver, and muskrat make their homes here and deer, moose, and bobcat venture down from the hills. The north Montpelier properties are seasonally connected to Hubbard Park (see p. 198). The connecting trail passes through a deer yard and is closed in winter.

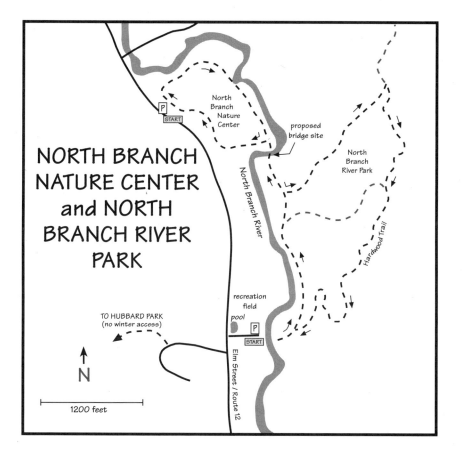

The NBNC was opened by VINS in 1996 on an old sheep farm. For a quarter-century VINS has pursued its mission of environmental education. Through its ELF (Environmental Learning for the Future) program alone, VINS reaches more than 13,000 Vermont schoolchildren each year. Its new NBNC facility offers year-round programs for the public and school groups, including summer day camps. Beginning in the summer of 1998, the NBNC will rent backpacks to visitors with equipment for field and river exploration. The nature center houses nature displays and a gift shop.

North Branch Nature Center

Take the old farm road from the north side of the parking lot. It approaches the river as it loops clockwise around the fields.

In the fertile soil of the riverbank, butternut, black ash, maple, and many large black willow trees grow. Beneath them wild grapevines entangle hawthorn and apple trees, red osier dogwood, and honeysuckle. Bluebird boxes, in pairs, face away from each other, one to accommodate tree swallows, the other for bluebirds. Community gardens are on the right.

VINS actively manages the fields to create a range of habitats. Ragweed, bird's-foot trefoil, black-eyed Susan, cow and crown vetch, red clover, Queen Anne's lace, wild sunflowers, and sensitive ferns create a colorful meadow. This is a great spot to see bobolinks and displaying woodcock in the spring. Part of the field is actively hayed. In another area hay is cut and left to lie, providing food and shelter for meadow moles, voles, and migrating geese. VINS monitors this patch to see if these small mammals attract more raptors. Snipe and the occasional duck visit a wet area in the middle of the field.

Spur trails lead through a forest of ostrich ferns to the river. Huge black willows dominate the riverbank along with a number of black cherry and butternut.

The river is lazy here. Look for erosion patterns on the riverbank from when the river flowed at a higher level. Harder rocks, like quartz, have resisted erosion. Several potholes are visible. Great blue heron come to dine in the river, and otter scat is often found on the banks.

The trail continues along the edge of the field, with detours to the river. The exposed bedrock at the turn in the river is beautiful. Paper birch and hemlock roots cling to the rock face where high water has eroded the soil.

Japanese knotweed, an introduced pest, grows to twelve feet along the bank. Its jointed red stems produce alternate round leaves and clusters of greenish white flowers at each axil (where the leaf grows out of the stem). Resembling bamboo, Japanese knotweed spreads aggressively and is difficult to eradicate.

Another denizen of these wet banks is spotted joe-pye weed, often growing to six feet and topped with a flat cluster of purple-pink fuzzy flowers. Its coarsely toothed, lance-shaped leaves grow in whorls of three to five.

The evergreen Christmas fern has leaflets which resemble a Christmas stocking.

The trail follows the meanders, where black willows continue to tower over the river. The trail returns along the fence line to the nature center.

Hours, Fees, Facilities

NBNC is handicapped accessible, including part of the trail. There is no admission charge. Restroom is in the nature center, which is open Wednesday through Saturday from 10:00 A.M. to 3:00 P.M. Call for updated hours. A limited number of snowshoes, donated by Tubbs, are available to borrow on a first-come, first-served basis.

North Branch River Park

From the pool area, cross the bridge and walk right, diagonally across the mowed field. A path climbs the hillside and joins a dirt road that parallels the river. Turn left on the dirt road and head north. Almost immediately a trail forks uphill to the right. Stay left. We will return from the right.

The river flows on the left and a tangle of shrubs, young trees, and vines grow on its banks: speckled alder; red raspberry; Japanese knotweed; gray, paper and yellow birch; vines; butternut; poplar; cherry; willow; ash; elm; and box elder.

The trail rises to an open meadow where goldenrod, chicory, fleabane, milkweed, raspberry, and butter-and-eggs add color, texture, and variety to the grasses attracting birds and insects. Speckled alder and willow saplings are establishing themselves.

It's about ten minutes to the first junction of mowed grass trails. Go straight, not right. Stay on the main grass path until it comes to the river edge, about twenty minutes from the trailhead. Take the left fork, down a set of wooden steps to a peaceful setting along the North Branch. Sensitive fern are lush, hemlocks cling to exposed bedrock, and lichen and moss have pioneered on rocky outcroppings.

Return up the steps and detour left. The path wanders through a waist-high thicket of bracken fern, ragweed, purple asters, speckled alder, paper birch, and virgin's-bower (*Clematis virginiana*), a wild relative of the domestic vine. The trail ends at the edge of the beaver pond.

Follow the trail back to the meadow and at the first junction turn left, away from the river. The trail passes through shrubs and young saplings as it starts to climb: honeysuckle, hawthorn, speckled alder, sumac, box elder, willow, red maple, and basswood. Leaves of the Virginia creeper are already bright red in early September.

The trail levels off between steep sections. Spruce and occasional balsam fir begin to mix with the hemlock and hardwoods. There are lots of saplings and some ferns in the understory.

After the second steep section the trail levels off and the woods are dominated by hardwoods. Within fifteen minutes the serious climbing is over and the Hardwood Trail goes to the right.

Despite its name, the Hardwood Trail is also home to many conifers. The trail rises gently through the northern forest of yellow birch, ash, maple, beech, balsam fir, black cherry, spruce, and hemlock; the more hemlock, the sparser the vegetation in the understory. The wide, well-groomed trail rises and falls. It crosses a stream on a log bridge and then over several more newly constructed bridges past some jack-in-the-pulpit and Christmas fern as the trail bears to the left and starts gradually downhill.

A stone causeway crosses another stream where logs and large rocks are used to retain the hillside. As the trail descends there are fewer evergreens.

The Hardwood Trail crosses another brook and forks after about twenty minutes. Go left through more hardwood forest with only ferns in the understory. Traffic noise tells us that Route 12 is not far away. The butternut and cherry trees are unhealthy. Follow the trail to the right.

Within five minutes a wider dirt trail comes in from the right and leads to the original path along the river. The return to the parking area takes less than five minutes.

 OTTER

If you are lucky enough to catch a glimpse of the river otter (*Lutra canadensis*), it will probably make you smile. Its broad, flat head with tiny eyes peers from a hole in melting ice or pops out of the water at ever-changing locations, like gophers at a carnival game. A relative of the weasel, the web-toed otter lives on fish, frogs, and other small animals and has rich, glossy brown fur.

Otters are shy and not easy to spot—unless you find them sliding. Otters use earthen hillsides or snowbanks like toboggan runs. They must forget themselves with the fun of it all as they whiz down their slick slides.

For More Information

VINS North Branch Nature Center
713 Elm Street, Route 12
Montpelier, VT 05602
802-229-6206

North Branch River Park
City of Montpelier
Montpelier Park Commission
39 Main Street
Montpelier, VT 05602
802-223-5141

Getting There

Take I-89 to Exit 8 to Montpelier. Follow the ramp, which joins Route 2 east, to the junction of Route 12 in Montpelier. Turn left onto Main Street, Route 12. At the rotary, 0.5 mile, go left to stay on Route 12. Immediately jog right. Route 12 is now Elm Street. The distance to the Recreation Field access to North Branch River Park is 1.1 miles. Drive an additional 0.4 mile beyond to the North Branch Nature Center. Parking is just beyond the NBNC on the right.

Waterbury/Stowe Area

Tundra Trail, Mount Mansfield (via the Toll Road)

Stowe

0.75 mile (extension possible)

40 minutes

easy

A walk across the top of Vermont through a unique Arctic-alpine environment. Bring warm clothes and, if you plan to walk beyond the Tundra Trail, wear hiking boots. A great place for children old enough to respect the fragility of the plants.

To borrow a phrase from Michelin, the Tundra Trail is worth the voyage. The Summit House, a hotel that burned down in 1964, welcomed overnight guests for more than a hundred years. As early as 1922, the Toll Road accommodated their automobiles over its 4.5-mile distance. Rising to an elevation of 3,850 feet, the road is by far the easiest way to reach the Tundra Trail.

There are dozens of hiking trails to the summit of Mount Mansfield, but most are not for the novice. They require strength, stamina, and a certain mountain savvy. The Green Mountain Club's *Guide Book of the Long Trail* describes the options and includes a trail map of the area. Stowe's gondola also climbs to within a short distance of the Tundra Trail. The Cliff Trail from the gondola to the trail is difficult and not for the inexperienced.

The Arctic-alpine zone on the summit of Mount Mansfield is a remnant of the Ice Age. When the last glaciers receded about 10,000 years ago,

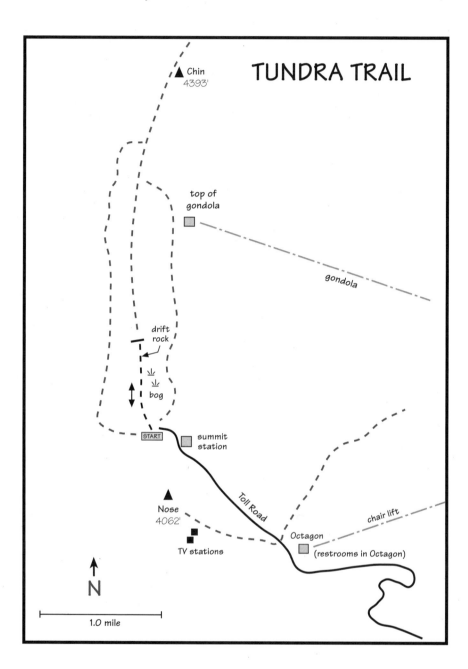

TUNDRA TRAIL

▲ Chin
4393'

top of
gondola

gondola

drift
rock

bog

START summit
station

Toll Road

▲
Nose
4062'

chair lift

■
■
TV stations

Octagon
(restrooms in Octagon)

↑
N

1.0 mile

plants adapted to severe conditions began to grow in their wake. As the climate warmed, these plants perished, except for those on the summits of a few eastern mountains. Similar communities exist in Vermont on Camel's Hump and Smuggler's Notch, on Katahdin in Maine, and in the highest reaches of New York's Adirondacks and New Hampshire's White Mountains.

These plants survive despite shallow soils, high winds, low temperatures, a short growing season, and high precipitation. (Mount Mansfield receives the equivalent of 100 inches of rain each year.) The small population and low diversity of plants conspire to limit the animal population as well.

Only six species of birds are common in this habitat. You are likely to hear two of them, the loud scolding of ravens and the mournful whistle of the white-throated sparrow.

Many of the tundra plants are in jeopardy. (In decreasing order of peril, the categories used for plants and animals are: endangered, threatened, and rare.) Most of the plants are also very small. You will need to look and tread carefully. Walk only on rocks and do not stray from the marked trail. Painted markings and cairns, pyramidal piles of rocks, indicate the route.

Don't forget to admire the view!

The Summit Station houses a small exhibit that is worth a visit. You will also find trail maps and guides. A Green Mountain Club ranger is available in the summer to answer questions.

Look for the trail to the north of the Summit Station. You will see a Long Trail sign where the trail enters the trees. The Long Trail is a 265-mile footpath running the length of Vermont, mostly along the spine of the Green Mountains. Despite the sobering distances on the sign, many through-hikers walk the distance each summer.

For the first few minutes the trail cuts through a forest dominated by balsam fir and red spruce. Balsam needles are flat, unlike the many-sided spruce needles, and the pale bottom of each has a conspicuous green midrib. The smell of balsam needles is sweet and may evoke memories of childhood Christmas. Notice that the trees aren't very tall as we approach the timberline.

The trail crosses a maintenance road and reenters the trees. A scattering of birch and mountain ash grow among the conifers, with the occasional Clintonia and bunchberry along the trail. The bedrock, here and

Hare's cotton grass is one of the bog plants atop Mount Mansfield.

elsewhere on the summit ridge, is a voluptuous whirl of colors and textures. It is a metamorphic schist, sedimentary rock which changed form
under intense heat or pressure beneath the surface of the earth. The rock
is about 400 million years old.

Shortly we rise to the treeline and the upright trees disappear. The
transitional area between the fir-spruce forest and the tundra is called the
krummholz, an area where wind and harsh growing conditions combine to
stunt the trees. You will see many contorted spruce trees with dead or
dying branches. On a clear day you can also see the Champlain Valley at
your feet with New York and Quebec beyond.

Be alert for the flowering alpine plants. The growing season is very
short, with July being the only frost-free month. The tiny yet beautiful
flowers on these diminutive plants appear from mid-June into July. You
may recognize the familiar blueberry, in a miniature version, and a similar
plant, the bog bilberry. Blueberries have narrower, more pointed leaves
than the more oval, bluish green leaves of the bilberry. Blueberries grow in
a clump at the end of the stalk, while bilberries are scattered along the

stem. You will also see mountain cranberry, with its very small, shiny leaves and red fruit.

The trail rises past a huge cairn called Frenchman's Pile and continues north past a radio tower on the right. This area is called the Alpine Meadow, with stunted balsam fir, red spruce, and the occasional heartleaved paper birch. The predominant ground cover here is Bigelow's sedge, a grasslike plant which, although it may not look unusual, is rare in Vermont. The showier blueberry, bilberry, and cranberry are interspersed. More conspicuous because of its height and large white blooms is Labrador tea. Its thick leaves roll downward, partially concealing a brown, fuzzy underside. The plant itself may be a foot tall, and its white umbrellalike blooms are abundant in late June or early July. A pleasant tea can be made from its leaves and was drunk during the American Revolution.

In just a few minutes you can make out a depression on the right. The precipitation that collects here has formed a bog. Sphagnum moss thrives in the acidic environment of bogs and over thousands of years forms a peat mat across the surface of the water. Growing on this mat are acid-loving plants. Several northern, or boreal, bog plants grow here. They are most conspicuous when in bloom: leather leaf, pale laurel, creeping snowberry, and hare's tail cotton grass. The latter looks just as you'd expect, its seeds forming a fluffy white tuft atop an eighteen-inch stem. Similar to dandelion seeds but whiter and denser, they were abundant on my late-June visit.

The Tundra Trail ends at Drift Rock, an enormous glacial erratic carried from the north by glaciers of the Ice Age. Look on the bedrock for striations caused by the scraping of this and other rocks embedded in the mile-thick mass of ice. The glacier crossed Mount Mansfield on a diagonal, from northwest to southeast.

You may turn around here or continue walking. The footing becomes more challenging as the trail continues north.

🌿 HEATHS

Heaths are shrubs, or woody perennials, most of which are found on acid soils. Worldwide they favor temperate regions, but we find many heaths in the cool bogs of northern New England.

Life is stressful for plants in a bog. It is difficult for them to absorb moisture in acid conditions. In addition, these plants endure a short growing season, high winds, and cold temperatures.

Many heaths have evergreen leaves, which enable them to utilize any available sunshine. On the first spring day an evergreen leaf uses sunlight to make sugar, while a deciduous plant is using its stored energy to produce new leaves. The stiff, often leathery texture of heath leaves (not unlike the waxy coating of spruce needles) helps them to retain moisture in the unfiltered sunlight and strong winds.

Among the heaths on Mount Mansfield are Labrador tea, pale laurel, blueberry, mountain cranberry, and bog bilberry.

Hours, Fees, and Facilities

The summit of Mount Mansfield is cooperatively protected by the Green Mountain Club; Vermont Department of Forests, Parks, and Recreation; Mount Mansfield Company; and University of Vermont. The Tundra Trail is a University of Vermont Natural Area. The Toll Road is managed by Stowe Mountain Resort of the Mount Mansfield Company.

There is no admission charge for the Tundra Trail. The Toll Road costs $12 per car and includes up to six passengers. Restrooms are available at the Octagon. Dogs must be leashed and keep to the rocks in the Arctic-alpine zone.

The Toll Road is open from 10:00 A.M. to 5:00 P.M. from mid-May until mid-October, weather permitting. After 5:00 P.M. you will need to get a gate key at the adjacent inn when you descend.

Getting There

From Route 100 in the village of Stowe, take Route 108, the Mountain Road. The Toll Road is 5.9 miles on the left. The Toll Road is 4.5 miles and very steep.

For More Information

Stowe Mountain Resort
5781 Mountain Road (Route 108)
Stowe, VT 05672
802-253-3000
http://www.stowe.com/smr

Sterling Falls Gorge Natural Area

Stowe

0.3 mile

45 minutes

easy

A spectacular river gorge in a boreal setting with waterfalls, cascades, pools, and potholes. Probably the most beautiful walk in this book. Stay on the trail and don't let children walk unattended! Bring insect repellent or, better yet, visit on snowshoes. The ice formations are spectacular.

This scenic section of Sterling Brook was set aside by the Anderson family so that the public could enjoy the beautiful setting and unusual natural features of the gorge. Sterling Falls Gorge Natural Area Trust is a public nonprofit trust. The eight acres at the gorge adjoin four acres of the Stowe Conservation Area to the west, and the protected 2,150-acre Watson Forest lies to the north. The Catamount Trail, a cross-country ski trail that runs the length of Vermont, also crosses the preserve.

Sterling Falls Gorge has three waterfalls, six cascades, and eight pools. (See Water Words, p. 221.) The total drop of the brook within the gorge is 105 vertical feet, making it one of the greatest drops of any gorge in the state.

At the end of the Ice Age, about 10,000 years ago, a series of lakes formed in western Vermont. At various times, with ice blocking the Lamoille River valley to the north, lakes filled the Stowe valley. A beach deposit of pebbly sand lies to the east of the gorge. It is assumed that ice and water combined to create the gorge.

Over the years Sterling Brook was also known as Bingham Branch, Shaw Brook, Mill Brook, and East Branch. Here, in the now defunct town of Sterling, a large sawmill operated from 1860 until 1920. In the early twentieth century nearly eighty people lived and worked in Sterling. A foundation remains from one of four mills located on Sterling Brook. A history and photographs are displayed near the parking area.

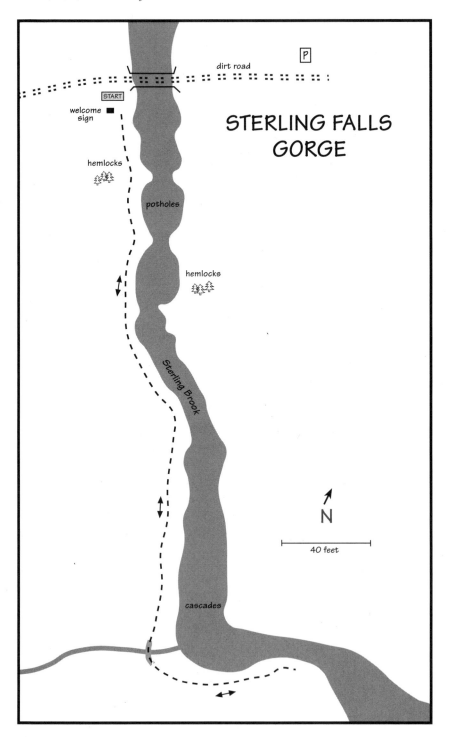

dirt road

P

START

welcome
sign

**STERLING FALLS
GORGE**

hemlocks

potholes

hemlocks

Sterling Brook

N

40 feet

cascades

Walk across the wooden bridge just down the dirt road from the parking area. Some classic Christmas-tree-shaped balsam firs are on both sides of the road, along with several peeling paper birches. The yellow and green triangular marker of Sterling Falls Gorge joins the blue blaze of the Catamount Trail on the right railing of the bridge. Beyond the bridge a set of steps goes down to the left. A sign welcomes visitors and highlights the natural features. The trail begins to the left of the sign.

Enormous hemlocks dominate the shady banks of the gorge and a number of wildflowers bloom here in June: Clintonia; Canada mayflower, or wild lily of the valley; wild sarsaparilla; pink lady-slipper; and trillium. The trillium in this location are red and painted, not the white trillium of the Champlain Valley. Spinulose wood fern are the dominant fern. The shrub layer is dominated by hobblebush with some striped maple, both favorites of deer and moose. There are young balsam fir and hemlock, too. A carpet of wood sorrel, with bright green, shamrock-shaped leaves, blooms in July with dainty pink-and-white-striped flowers. The plant is only a few inches tall.

Stop 1 overlooks the brook. The smooth bedrock and potholes have been worn over thousands of years by the friction of water and rocks. Several potholes, including a few to the right, are above the current water level. These were formed when the brook followed a different course or flowed at a higher level.

Potholes are created by the abrasive grinding of stones in a circular motion. If you look straight down, keeping safely away from the edge, you can see the circular movement of water in a pothole.

As you continue walking, notice that the thicker the canopy of hemlocks, the fewer plants in the understory. There aren't as many wildflowers here.

Stop 2 is at a bend in the brook. On the inside of the turn is a pile of medium-sized rocks. These were dropped by the stream as it lost momentum on the inside of the turn. The faster water flows, the greater its carrying capacity. Wide, slow-flowing river deltas fill with silt because the water loses its ability to carry even the tiniest particles. Sterling Brook, a narrow, rushing stream swelled by seasonal flooding and snowmelt, is able to carry large rocks until either the flow decreases, the water spreads out as the banks widen, or the brook slows down at a curve.

Huge boulders are scattered about the stream bed, larger than anything Sterling Brook could carry. These are glacial erratics, a common sight throughout New England. As glaciers moved south during the Ice Age, they accumulated chunks of rock. After scraping over the landscape, some-

Goldthread, one of the herbs of the northern forest that flourish at Sterling Falls Gorge.

times leaving telltale striations, the glaciers dropped many erratics along the way. They usually have no relationship to the bedrock of the area.

The trail jogs left to Stop 3, where we have a good view both up- and downstream. Water flowing at a much higher level has smoothed the surfaces of the bedrock over the millennia.

Across the gorge is a high wall of exposed rock with lines of erosion running nearly vertical. The bedrock is metamorphic rock, sedimentary rock exposed to heat or pressure causing some recrystallization. The result is the layered schist that makes up the bedrock of the gorge. Different minerals erode at different rates, causing the wavy pattern, called schistosity, we see here and elsewhere in the Green Mountains.

Above the rocks many large hemlocks cling to the edge of the gorge. Their shallow but tenacious root systems allow them to survive on shallow soil and in precarious locations. You would never see an oak of similar size living like this.

En route to Stop 4, about twenty feet into the woods on the right, is a remarkably tenacious hemlock growing on a glacial erratic. Hemlocks can germinate on nearly any moist surface. Moss is growing on the hemlock's roots, and at least one red spruce has germinated in the moss!

At Stop 4 look back up the stream to see the schistosity, or erosion, of the vertical layers of bedrock.

There are more deciduous trees along the trail, and more wildflowers as a result. This upland forest is composed of maple, white and yellow birch, white ash, beech, and black cherry, in addition to the conifers.

At Stop 5 there is a bench. From here we can see a tranquil pool before the water flows down a series of cascades.

The trail goes left onto a bridge, where Stop 6 encourages us to sit over the small stream. The schistosities in the stream are textbook examples.

The trail turns left and the wood sorrel is thick again. Indian cucumber-root flowers here, its tiny, yellowish green flower atop two whorls of leaves. The lower whorl is larger, with six to ten leaves; the upper whorl, just below the flowers, has three leaves. The brittle root, tasting somewhat like cucumber, was eaten by Indians. Birds are attracted to its purple-blue berries.

Stop 7 overlooks waterfalls, cascades, potholes, and the ever-deepening gorge.

The trail continues a few hundred feet to Stop 8 at the end of the gorge. The brook is no longer contained and flows downstream along a wider bed.

Retrace your steps to the trailhead.

 ## WATER WORDS

A gorge is a section of stream channel with rock walls on both sides at least ten feet high. The walls at Sterling Falls Gorge range from eleven to fifty feet high at the southern end.

The distinction between a waterfall and a cascade is in how the water flows. Water must fall nearly vertically at least three feet without touching the underlying rock to create a waterfall. In a cascade the water remains in contact with the bedrock.

Getting There

From Stowe, drive north 0.8 mile on Route 100. Turn left on West Hill Road. At 1.9 miles West Hill Road bends nearly 90° to the left (the dirt road straight ahead is a dead end). After 0.3 mile, turn right onto a dirt road. This is still West Hill Road. The road climbs steadily if not steeply. When you reach a T-intersection at 2.2 miles, turn left. After 0.4 mile you will see a sign for Sterling Valley Road. Another 1.5 miles brings you to a marked parking area for the Catamount (ski) Trail and Sterling Falls Gorge. Walk across the wooden bridge to the trailhead.

For More Information

Sterling Falls Gorge Natural Area Trust
91 Sterling Gorge Road
Stowe, VT 05672
802-253-9035
e-mail: gander07@realtor.com

History Hike

Little River State Park
Waterbury

4.0 miles, 800-foot elevation gain

4–5 hours

moderate

A walk through the remains of a nineteenth-century hill-farm community.

This walk is a journey through time, past foundations, stone walls, and cemeteries—all that remain of a community once filled with life. Subsistence farms dotted these hills in the 1800s, where a few pigs, sheep, chickens, and cows were cared for in addition to gardens and apple orchards. Timber was cut and milled at local sawmills and maple sap was boiled to sugar each spring.

Unlike the flat, rich flood plain of the Winooski River valley, these rocky hillsides were difficult to cultivate and their yield meager. Free homesteads tempted many Vermonters west in the late nineteenth century. These farms had already been abandoned when the great flood of 1927 inundated the valley. A second flood in 1934 spurred construction of the Waterbury Dam. Beneath the reservoir lie the remains of several similar villages.

Take your imagination on this walk, and don't miss the photos of these farms in the park's museum.

The Dallet Loop Trail begins on a dirt road behind a red gate. Pick up a trail guide on the right. It describes each of the sites en route.

Within minutes the Hedgehog Hill Loop Trail forks to the right. Bear left to stay on the Dalley Loop Trail.

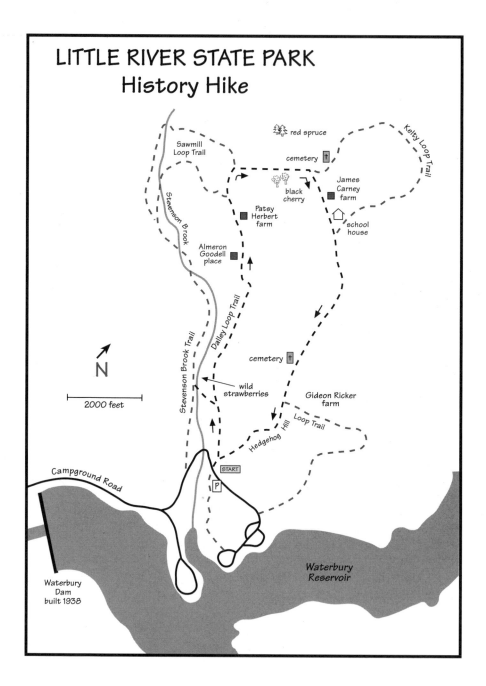

LITTLE RIVER STATE PARK
History Hike

red spruce

Sawmill
Loop Trail

cemetery

Kelty Loop Trail

black
cherry

James
Carney
farm

Stevenson Brook

Patsey
Herbert
farm

school
house

Almeron
Goodell
place

Dalley Loop Trail

Stevenson Brook Trail

N

2000 feet

cemetery

wild
strawberries

Gideon Ricker
farm

Hedgehog Hill Loop Trail

START

P

Campground Road

Waterbury
Reservoir

Waterbury
Dam
built 1938

As the road climbs and crosses a brook far below, most of the trees are northern hardwoods—maple, white and yellow birch, beech, and black cherry—with a few hemlocks mixing in. You are likely to hear ovenbirds, one of the few birds which sings throughout the day.

Keep your eyes open for animal tracks. On two separate visits I found moose tracks and scat. Moose prints are cloven and shaped much like deer tracks but larger, as long as seven inches. Oval moose droppings, resembling those of deer, may be an inch long.

The largest member of the deer family, the moose weighs as much as 1,400 pounds. It has high, humped shoulders, a broad muzzle, large ears, and the prominent hairy dewlap on the throat. The male has broad, palmate antlers, the tines radiating from the center like fingers from a palm. The moose travels, usually alone, in spruce forests (we'll see spruce as we climb along this trail), swamps, and aspen thickets. Striped maple is heavily browsed by moose in winter. In recent years the moose population has swelled in Vermont and a limited hunting season has been reintroduced.

After ten to fifteen minutes you'll find Stop 2 well camouflaged on the right. (Stop 1 is on the Nature Trail.) Clamber up the dirt path to a stone foundation, the remains of the farmhouse of David Hill. Butternut trees often were planted in the dooryard of old farms, and the one in the foundation must be an offspring of that tree. A few lilacs and scraggly apple trees struggle with little sunlight.

Continue up the road. In a clearing on the left lush with wild strawberries, the blue-blazed Stevenson Brook Trail begins its route to the site of a sawmill.

At Stop 3, on the right, the remaining cornerstones of Bert Goodell's foundations still hold firm against the earth. You may find wild ginger, an indicator of rich soils, with its two hairy, kidney-shaped leaves low to the ground. The single reddish brown, three-lobed flower grows in the crotch between the leaves and its roots have a strong fragrance of ginger.

Local legend places the Johnson farm nearby. Although its remains have never been found, the farm was purportedly used as a sanitarium for Civil War veterans with syphilis.

Along a sunny curve in the road are many June-flowering plants: yellow and orange hawkweed, devil's flower, bladder campion, and yarrow. On the left there's a huge patch of horsetail.

The Almeron Goodell house, Stop 4, still stands. Until the state recently asserted its claim, descendants rented the house as a deer camp. I hiked this trail with a man whose father had stayed here for many years

A red maple in flower. It has something red in every season: buds, flowers, stems, and autumn leaves.

during hunting season. The original post-and-beam construction is still visible. Day lilies and lilacs crowd the dooryard and rose plants bloom near the road.

A few minutes up the road on the right is a field cleared for wildlife. Apple trees need sunlight, and local bears need apples. One of the trees has many broken branches. Bears climb the trees, snap the branches, and toss them to the ground to strip later.

A clearing across the road is intended to encourage ruffed grouse. Grouse browse on buds and twigs of young trees. Few of Vermont's 323 wildlife species thrive in middle-aged or mature forests, the natural state of the land. These fields will produce a tangle of berry plants and tender shoots providing food, shelter, and camouflage.

Gaze across the valley to the Worcester Range. Each of these farms once had a similar view.

Foundation stones and rock walls are all that remain of the Patsy Herbert farm, Stop 5, on the right. Herbert was the last resident in 1910. The Sawmill Loop Trail goes left to the site of the sawmill.

Beyond the Herbert farm the Dalley Loop Trail bears right. A spur trail forks left, but we continue on the old town road. Mature maples arch overhead and stone walls line the roadway. Red spruce, a northern tree, appears as we gain elevation and there are many mature black cherries along the roadside. Ferns and blackberries are thick and striped maple is abundant in the understory. You can recognize its green-striped bark and large, three-lobed leaves.

If time is a concern, stay right, on the main road, and look for a basin of rocks in a tiny stream on the left (it may be dry in summer). This was probably a watering trough for animals. (A detour left leads to the well-preserved Joseph Ricker farm.)

The next stop is the Upper Cemetery, an early burial site in use from 1840 to 1860. Mary Cole's headstone tells a common story: she died at the age of twenty five most likely in childbirth.

The Dalley Loop Trail goes right, while the less-maintained Kelty Loop Trail departs to the left. Stop 10, the James Carney farm, was a prosperous one with 700 maples and a sugarhouse in addition to farm animals. The solid house foundation is well preserved, in contrast to some we've seen.

A road forks to the left shortly. On the left beneath leaf litter, about seventy five feet up this road, are stones marking the outlines of the schoolhouse, which would not have had a foundation. Each district offered room and board and a small salary to attract a teacher to its one-room schoolhouse.

Stone walls and foundations mark the William Clossey farm, Stop 12. From the house foundation, on the left side of the road, a well-worn path leads to the grave of onetime owner Jack Cameron. He was unable to eke a living from this hardscrabble land.

Stop 13 has succumbed to beaver activity, and we pass through a soggy area before returning to the woods. Substantial stone walls line the road as we begin to descend. Sensitive ferns like this damp ground, and wild lily of the valley and sessile-leaved bellwort are abundant. We pass through an area thick with spruce trees.

Tom Herbert's house is on the right side of the road at Stop 14. A healthy butternut tree stands in the dooryard. With as many as seventeen leaflets, butternut leaves can be thirty inches long. Farmers planted butternut trees for their beautiful wood, colorful dyes, and rich nuts.

Just a few steps away, to the left and downhill from the house, is a covered well. If you lift the lid (carefully) you will see a stone well shaft. Digging a well by hand was not easy work. A huge hole would be dug until water was found. Then a stone shaft was painstakingly built and soil

Spring beauties, early wildflowers.

returned, bucket by bucket, to support the structure until it reached ground level. No wonder so many farms located near naturally occurring springs!

As the road continues downhill there is another stone watering trough on the left. The Ricker Cemetery is on the right. White cedar trees, their Latin name *arbor vitae* meaning the "tree of life," are a startling sight. Common in the Champlain lowlands, white cedars are not native here. On the far side of the cemetery is a huge double-trunked black cherry. There are several legible headstones.

The last farm on this loop trail, Stop 16, is the Gideon Ricker farm. Portions of a barn foundation can be seen on the left side of the road, the remnants of a 120-foot cow barn, with an 84-foot spruce ridgepole. There is a stone foundation for a silo as well. Across the road the house foundation is the biggest in the neighborhood. (Don't miss the pictures in the museum.) Thick slabs of granite, from a small quarry up the road, added a touch of class to the visible parts of the foundation.

Go right on the Hedgehog Hill Loop Trail to return to the trailhead. The trail slopes downhill, crossing a stream on a very old stone bridge. You can step down on either side of the bridge to see the massive boulders supporting the angular slabs of rock. Characteristically, an old yellow birch with crusty bark and contorted roots clings to a rock next to the bridge.

The trail rejoins the Dalley Loop in a few minutes just a short distance from the parking area.

Hours, Fees, and Facilities

Daily admission entitles you to hiking but not to the recreation facilities. See In the Area, below.

The caretaker can let you into the small museum. There are pictures of the homes, barns, and farm families.

Getting There

From the west, take I-89 Exit 11 in Richmond and follow Route 2 east. From the stoplight in Richmond at Bridge Street, drive east for 11.8 miles. Turn left on Little River Road. You will pass the dam and Waterbury Reservoir on the right before arriving at the park gate 3.4 miles from Route 2.

From the east, take I-89 Exit 10 in Waterbury and follow Route 100 south to Route 2. Turn right onto Route 2 west and drive 1.4 miles to Little River Road on your right.

From the park gate turn right (you will have no choice) and then take two immediate lefts following signs to the dumpsters. This road will bear right, passing the dumpsters, before crossing a bridge at 0.4 mile. Parking for the history trails is on the right in 0.2 mile.

For More Information

Vermont Department of Forests, Parks, and Recreation
(See Organizations: Useful Names and Addresses.)

Park Ranger
Little River State Park
R.D. 1, Box 3180
Waterbury, VT 05676
802-244-7103

In the Area

Waterbury Center Day-Use Park
Admission to Little River State Park allows same-day use of the beach and boat launch at Waterbury Center Park. From Waterbury, take Route 100 north, 5.8 miles from the I-89 overpass. Turn left on Old River Road. The park entrance is 0.1 mile.

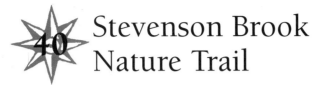

Stevenson Brook Nature Trail

Little River State Park
Waterbury

0.75 mile

1 hour

easy to moderate

A rushing mountain stream in woods grown up on old farmland.

This land was once part of a village of fifty families. Their lives unfold on the nearby History Hike. Nature has since reclaimed the banks of the Stevenson Brook.

Little River State Park is the most heavily used park in the state system and, with more than 100 sites, central Vermont's largest campground. In addition to miles of hiking trails, the park offers swimming beaches and a boat launch to campers.

Stevenson Brook is picturesque, and the woods host a rich diversity of trees, shrubs, and wildflowers.

The loop trail begins and ends next to the parking area. Look for a box with trail guides.

Several small black, or sweet, birch (*Betula lenta*) cluster at the trailhead, their leaves and bark tasting of wintergreen. Within a few yards you will see interrupted, sensitive, and Christmas ferns thriving in the rich soil.

Mountain maple is abundant here. A bushy tree that never grows taller than twenty feet, mountain maple loves cool, damp woods and ravines, always growing in the shade of other trees. Its leaves are maplelike, three-lobed with serrated edges. Its habitat is similar to that of striped maple but its bark is reddish brown (not green like striped maple).

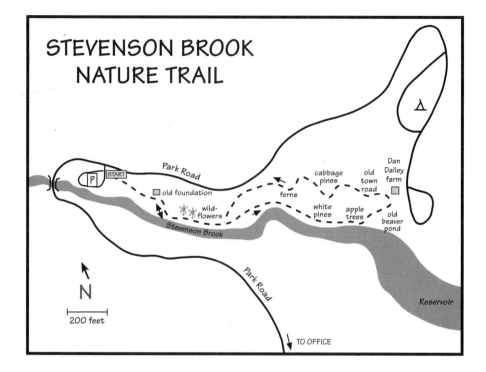

Stop 1 is the stone foundation of an old farm and a good opportunity to compare barks of paper birch and yellow birch. A yellow birch is immediately on the left, its bronze bark peeling in narrow shreds. The paper birch is a chalkier white and peels in wide strips.

The trail continues toward the brook. At Stop 2, tree roots are cantilevered over the opposite bank. Each spring high water and ice rip at the shore, and only the most tenacious trees survive along the banks.

Alternate-leaved dogwood (*Cornus alternifolia*) is at eye level. Dogwood leaves have a characteristic shape, tapering to points at both ends, and the veins follow the leaf edges to the tips. Its green twigs are often browsed by deer and rabbits, and its blue-black berries are eaten by many birds, including the ruffed grouse.

A mixture of northern hardwoods grow in this cool valley, including American beech, maple, birch, basswood, and white ash, with a number of hemlocks and red spruce. Beneath them purple trillium, jack-in-the-pulpit, and false Solomon's seal bloom in late May or early June.

We cross a sandy, U-shaped depression where the brook overflows in the spring. At Stop 5, look around to see several terraces of land rising away from the brook. Over millions of years, the stream has eroded its bed only to have it lifted again by forces inside the earth. The most recent uplift occurred when the last glaciers receded about 10,000 years ago. With the heavy weight of mile-thick ice removed, the land decompressed.

At Stop 6, look for Indian pipe (*Monotropa uniflora*), also known as corpse plant or convulsion root. White and looking like a cluster of upturned pipes, the plant is a saprophyte which gets its nutrients from decaying organic matter rather than from photosynthesis. The absence of chlorophyll accounts for its color.

As the trail leaves the brook, look for wood nettles. Remember wood nettles have alternate leaves, while stinging nettles have opposite leaves. Wood nettle leaves are also longer and narrower than the heart-shaped leaves of the stinging nettle.

The trail bears left onto a higher terrace. Notice the beautiful old bark on a huge yellow birch with two trunks. Stop 7 is in a dense stand of white pines in sandy soil. White pines do not like wet feet and need sunshine.

Near Stop 8, there's a huge double-trunked basswood, or linden, tree on the left. Its bark somewhat resembles an ash and it has heart-shaped leaves as big as six inches across. Also called the bee tree, it is a favorite of woodcarvers because it can be easily worked. Its July flowers attract bees, which produce delicious honey. Basswoods are indicator trees and grow only in rich soil.

Several dead apple trees and a stone wall to the left are signs of an old farmstead.

Stop 9 looks down on an old beaver pond. As plant growth thickens over what was once a pond, the water level lowers and more plants move in. Someday this will be woods again.

The trail turns left, uphill, and then left again at an arrow. There is a detour to an old farm site. Up a short, narrow trail, is the stone foundation of the Dan Dalley farmhouse. Dalley was a Civil War veteran who survived sixteen battles and one capture. With his pension of $12.00 per month he bought this sixty-eight-acre farm in 1878. Picture, if you can, the house in the midst of fields with a vast view across the valley. Notice the big, rectangular foundation stones, quite different from the more randomly shaped stones in the rock walls.

Return to the trail, which follows an old road for a few minutes before bearing left into the woods. The multitrunked white pines at Stop 11 are called cabbage trees. Because of their misshapen trunks they were unsuitable for timber. They may have been attacked by the white pine weevil.

Red maple leafing out, with keys already dangling.

We pass a few apple trees dying for lack of sunlight. The trail turns left and then jogs right without markings. We are on the highest of the three terraces overlooking the brook. There is a huge, peeling paper birch on the left, as well as a red maple with five trunks. The bark shows a bull's-eye pattern characteristic of red maple. There is a large, triple-trunked basswood on the left side with large, nearly round leaves. Basswood trees can sprout from the trunk even if the parent tree is alive.

We come to another stone wall and Stop 12. Downhill to the left is an old butternut tree, its bark deeply grooved. Butternuts are late to leaf out in the spring.

Be careful as the trail descends steps without a railing. At the base of the steps turn right along the next terrace. Indian pokeweed, or false helle-bore, grows in the moist soil, its enormous leaves with parallel veins grow-ing around a central stem. The plant may reach seven feet before the leaves wither in July.

The trail descends a ramp built into the hillside and rejoins the loop at Stop 3. Turn right to follow the path back to the parking area.

Getting There

From the west, take I-89 Exit 11 in Richmond and follow Route 2 east. From the stoplight in Richmond at Bridge Street, drive east for 11.8 miles. Turn left on Little River Road. You will pass the dam and Waterbury Reservoir on the right before arriving at the park gate 3.4 miles from Route 2.

From the east, take I-89 Exit 10 in Waterbury and follow Route 100 south to the intersection of Route 2. Turn right onto Route 2 west. It's 1.4 miles to Little River Road on your right.

From the park gate turn right (you will have no choice) and then take two immediate lefts following signs to the dumpsters. This road will bear right, passing the dumpsters, before crossing a bridge at 0.4 mile. Just over the bridge, signs indicate the Nature Trail and its parking on the right.

For More Information

Vermont Department of Forests, Parks, and Recreation
(See Organizations: Useful Names and Addresses.)

Park Ranger

Little River State Park
R.D. 1, Box 3180
Waterbury, VT 05676
802-244-7103

In the Area

Waterbury Center Day-Use Park

Admission to Little River State Park allows same-day use of the beach and boat launch at Waterbury Center Park. From Waterbury, take Route 100 north, 5.8 miles from the I-89 overpass. Turn left on Old River Road. The park entrance is 0.1 mile.

New York

Point au Roche State Park

Long Point Trail
Plattsburgh

3.0 miles

2 hours

easy/moderate

Nonstop lake views and a wide range of habitats on Lake Champlain. Cross-country skiing is encouraged on twelve miles of trails.

Point au Roche State Park opened in 1986 after several previous incarnations. At various times the lakeside property included a fantasy kingdom, an amusement park, children's camps, summer homes, a campground, farms, and the infrastructure for a subdivision. The 850-acre park was purchased in 1974 after New York voters passed the Environment Quality Bond Act of 1972.

The park incorporates a wildlife preserve, swimming beach and amenities, boat launch, nature center, and 12.5 miles of trails. Habitats include open lake and protected bays, marsh, pond, shoreline, old farm fields and meadows, young woods, lakeside northern white cedar forest, and a mature northern forest.

At the nature center, take a few minutes to look at the collection of fossils and taxidermic mounts of hawks and owls. A white-tailed deer skeleton and owl pellets are among the exhibits.

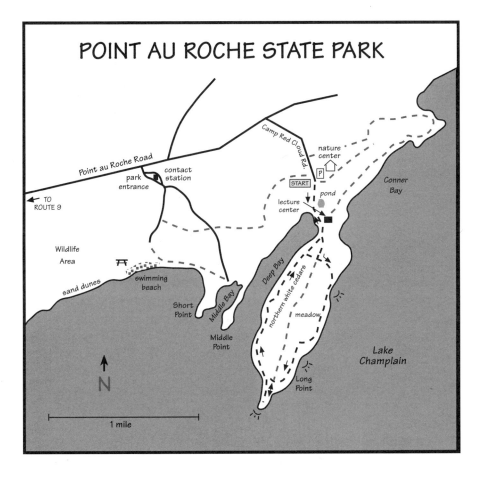

POINT AU ROCHE STATE PARK

The trails of the Eastern Loops, Long and Middle Points, and Ram's Head all traverse a mixture of meadow, wetlands, and forest. The Western Loops include a paved section of bicycle path. All of the trails have panoramic lake views.

To walk to Long Point from the nature center, continue down the dirt road toward the lake. A marsh on the left is used extensively by park naturalists for teaching. Buttonbush, red osier dogwood, willow, red maple, cattails, elm, ash, and cottonwood surround the open water. Great blue heron, belted kingfishers, and ducks come and go in the company of muskrat, otter, deer, and beaver from a nearby lodge.

Waterlilies and bladderwort grow on the water's surface. Bladderwort is a floating carnivorous plant with a small yellow flower. Bladders scattered among submerged leaves have trigger hairs. When swimming prey, such as a larva or minute crustacean, touch the trigger hairs near the mouth of one of the bladders, a flap of tissue opens. The expansion of the bladder sucks the victim inside, where it is digested by enzymes.

Walk toward the lecture center and, as you reach it, turn right on a grassy path. You are now heading south onto Long Point on the Dr. Philip C. Walker Memorial Botanical Trail, passing through meadows along a ridge with splendid lake views to the east. Selective cutting and pruning attract wildlife, woodcock, and ruffed grouse. Old apple trees grow on this former farmland along with young poplars, red and northern white cedars, and pasture juniper. The few large shagbark hickory and white ash may have been left for shade when this was pasture. Look to the east where tall white pines cluster near the shore. The upper branches grow toward the northeast, shaped by the strong, prevailing southwest wind. This is called the *krummholz*, German for "crooked wood," or flag tree effect. The tree tops look like flags stretched by the wind. This phenomenon is common and more pronounced near mountaintops.

Wild thyme is fragrant underfoot and milkweed attracts monarch butterflies. Butter-and-eggs, a tiny member of the snapdragon family, and bedstraw grow among the grasses. The sweet smell of its foliage once made bedstraw the mattress stuffing of choice. Its leaves in whorls of four are lance shaped and up to two inches long. The flowers grow in tiny white clusters at the end of the stems.

Follow a grassy path left across the peninsula to its eastern shore. Northern white cedars cling to the shoreline, and the trail turns south again (right) through a middle-aged forest. Red and white trillium, jack-in-the-pulpit, violets, hepatica, bloodroot, false Solomon's seal, and red-berried elder grow beneath the mostly deciduous trees. A member of the honeysuckle family and a favorite of birds, the elder grows from two to ten feet tall with opposite, compound leaves and clusters of tiny white flowers which become bright red berries.

Hemlocks thicken and the understory decreases. Yellow birch are characteristic of this type of northern forest, but they are few at Point au Roche. A remarkable one, on spindly four-foot stilts, grows along the right side of the trail. It germinated on a stump that has since rotted away.

Ferns are lush in several swampy areas. To the east a pretty view opens up as the trail comes to the shaly shoreline. A small beach of black cobbles, eroded from the shale, harbors little vegetation. Several mullein

White trillium, a spectacular spring flower, can reach eighteen inches in height.

plants grow on the beach. The biennial, velvet-leaved plant sends up a stalk of tiny yellow flowers which can reach six feet. It has a long history of varied uses. The Romans dipped the stalks in grease to be used as torches, and Abenaki used it to start traditional fires. Native Americans and colonists used the leaves to insulate their feet.

The trail turns inland and passes through a more mature forest of American beech, white pine, hemlock, birch, red and white oak, hickory, and maple. Before it was settled, this land was covered with red oak and white pine. White pine trunks were used as ship masts, and red oak was stamped with the king's insignia, shipped to Canada, and used for the interior of ships. Red oak reaches the northern limit of its range here and can be found locally only at elevations below 1,400 feet.

The trail jogs right and meets the road coming from the north of the peninsula. We turn left toward the tip of Long Point and its expansive views. To the northwest are Deep Bay, Middle Point, and Short Point. The park's swimming beach and bathhouse are on the far shore. South of the beach is the park's wildlife preserve, where vestigial sand dunes line the shore. The state hopes that if the dunes remain undisturbed, wind- and wave-driven sand will rebuild them.

Even in late September birds are still active: chickadees, nuthatches, blue jays, and woodpeckers. Loons can be spotted here also; one day in 1997, twenty were seen in the area. Look for cormorants, black-backed gulls, mallards, terns, Canada and snow geese, and common mergansers.

Summer residents lived on Long Point until recently. Several buildings have been demolished but a few still stand. A cement boat ramp leads to the lake and apple trees and day lilies speak of sunlight and human habitation.

Return along the dirt road. Red pine and hop hornbeam join the mixed forest. The road continues, cool and shady, along the western shore of the point with occasional vistas to the west. Mature white cedars, oaks, and maples are dominant on the clay soil. If you prefer open views, turn right and then left to return through the fields and meadows along the top of the ridge.

The grassy path and wooded road meet near the lecture center. Turn left to follow the road back to the nature center.

🦌 WHITE-TAILED DEER

Without traditional predators, particularly wolves and cougars, white-tailed deer (*Odocoileus virginianus*) thrive in the woods of the Northeast. Limited winter food supplies and hunting seasons are the only population controls, as deer inflict damage on gardens, orchards, and forests. Excellent swimmers, deer are found even on islands in lakes. They have keen senses of hearing and smell which allow them to tiptoe away from humans before they are detected. Initially, a deer freezes when it detects motion, even the blinking of a human eye. Then it flees if it senses danger. Tiny hoofs make for silent getaways and fast travel. They can run up to 35 mph, leap thirty feet in one bound, and jump over obstacles as high as eight feet.

Unlike caribou, elk, and mule deer, white-tailed deer are nonmigratory. Despite an insulating coat of hollow hairs, deer are not well adapted to harsh winters. They have no fat reserves like bears, raccoons, and skunks. Their tiny, cloven hooves are at their worst in deep snow. Deer cluster in yards where conifers protect them from the wind and deep snowdrifts, but if their movement is hampered by snow they will deplete the buds, twigs, and nuts in their yard. Rather than relocate, they will starve. Deer are also doomed on ice, as they slip and fall and may die of exhaustion trying to stand again.

The deer has a four-chambered stomach, meaning it can eat now and digest later in safety. A ruminant, the deer eats its required ten to twelve pounds of browse each day and then withdraws to the cover of the woods to regurgitate and chew its cud. Their preferred summer diet includes budding maple, oak, and willow trees and blackberry, blueberry, and sumac bushes.

Hours, Fees, Facilities

There is no admission charge, although one may be instituted in the future. The nature center is open in season when the naturalists are not leading walks or classes. It is closed in winter. Trails are open daily from sunrise to sunset, and restrooms are available at the nature center.

Dogs must be leashed at all times. Point au Roche is a carry-in, carry-out park.

Getting There

From the Grand Isle–Cumberland Head ferry, take Route 314 straight ahead to Route 9, 3.9 miles. Turn right and drive north for 3.8 miles to Point au Roche Road on the right. Follow it past the main park entrance to Camp Red Cloud Road, 2.2 miles. Turn right. The road shortly becomes dirt and ends at the nature center on the left, 0.4 mile.

From I-87 take exit 40. Drive east 0.5 mile on Route 456. Turn right on Route 9, south to Point au Roche Road, 0.4 mile.

Ausable Chasm

Ausable Chasm

less than 1.0 mile

1 hour for the walk, plus an additional hour for the raft ride

easy with lots of steps (down)

A deep canyon carved by glacial ice and the Ausable River.

If you can't make it to the Grand Canyon this year, take a day trip to Ausable Chasm. While there is no confusing Arizona's mile-deep canyon with the local item, Ausable mimics the sheer, rosy riverside cliffs of its western cousin. Eastern in scale and flavor, Ausable Chasm is spectacular in its own right.

As deep as 175 feet from rim to river, the narrow passage through multicolored sandstone and quartzite was sculpted by glacial ice and the waters of the Ausable River about 14,000 years ago. Opened to tourists in 1870, the chasm has been attracting visitors ever since.

Two 1996 events demonstrated once again nature's preeminence as raging water rearranged the chasm's natural and man-made features.

Heavy rains fell during a January thaw, and six feet of accumulated snow melted within hours as the temperature rose to 75° Fahrenheit. The tributaries of the Ausable River unleashed huge quantities of water and ice into the chasm. High water under pressure uprooted sixty-foot trees, ripped out metal handrails, and tore seventy-foot steel bridges from their foundations. Some came to rest at the bottom of the chasm; others have never been found.

New bridges with thirty-inch steel beams were built and walkways reestablished. Ausable Chasm had survived a once-in-a-lifetime event and opened on schedule for the 1996 season.

On November 9, nature struck again. Heavy rains fell on already saturated ground, causing unprecedented flooding. Nearby roads and bridges were destroyed and the chasm fared no better. Two bridges that had survived the January onslaught succumbed, as did the three new bridges. The volume of water raging through the chasm was the greatest ever recorded.

242

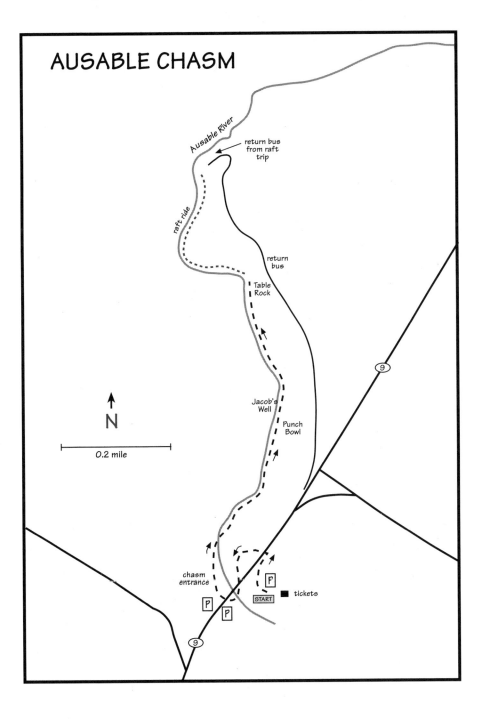

AUSABLE CHASM

Ausable River

return bus from raft trip

raft ride

return bus

Table Rock

Jacob's Well

Punch Bowl

9

N

0.2 mile

chasm entrance

P P

F

START ■ tickets

9

Trails and bridges were rebuilt yet again, this time farther from the river, and the chasm opened to visitors in 1997. Within the chasm, piles of debris, barren rock faces, and scarred trees attest to the events of 1996.

The chasm and 823 acres are owned by the Ausable Chasm Company, a private corporation incorporated in 1896. Several stockholders are descendants of the original owners.

There is a two-tiered admission structure: a fee for the walk only, with a return bus from Table Rock, and a higher charge for a raft ride through the lower portion of the chasm. The lower chasm is a stunning natural feature, unique in the East, and I recommend it.

Use the door to the right of the ticket desk to begin the walk. Several displays are on the right, including a fossil of ripple marks from the riverbed. These were left by the Cambrian Sea more than 500 million years ago. Another item on exhibit is the 1996 wreckage of a chasm bridge.

Cross under the road. You will pass a vantage point into the chasm where the visitors' walkway once descended. Walk across the highway bridge and turn right to the chasm entrance. The walk begins on a bark trail on the west bank high above the Ausable River. Only a few ferns grow beneath a thick canopy of red and white pines and hemlocks.

A wooden walkway leads to Rainbow Vista, a view back up the river to Horseshoe and Rainbow Falls. Several times the path comes close to the edge overlooking the rushing cascades. From Rocky Point Vista you can see, far below on the opposite bank, the railing of an old walkway.

The trail meanders over occasional stretches of boardwalk through the woods. Lichen, reindeer moss (really a lichen), and polypody fern grow on rocky outcroppings. Wintergreen, huckleberry, and lowbush blueberry, all members of the heath family, grow beneath openings in the canopy on the sandy, acidic soil. Northern white cedar, the occasional white oak, and a few paper birch join the pines and hemlock.

On the right is a cleft thirty to forty feet across and as deep as the chasm, called a tension joint, one of many along the route. (See How the Chasm Came to Be, p. 246.)

The trail descends several stairways, at one point passing through a bank of dainty polypody ferns. It then snakes along the chasm wall, so close at times you must mind your head and shoulders. In tiny soil pockets, tenacious plants anchor themselves on the rock face: herb Robert, ferns, violets, bedstraw, mullein, and asters. An extravagant yellow birch grows on almost no soil, with a fantastic web of surface roots.

Sedementary and metamorphic rock form the walls of Ausable Chasm. Photo courtesy of Ausable Chasm Company.

Close to the river, many feet below, the twisted remnants of metal railings poke into the air at odd angles.

The trail descends to Punch Bowl Vista. This large pothole was eroded by the abrasive action of swirling rocks and stones. It takes thousands of years for a pothole to form. Jacob's Well is an unusual pothole, now well above water level. A strong localized current formed this cylindrical hole, six feet in diameter and twenty feet deep.

The trail gets closer and closer to water level. We cross the 1996 flood line. Lush vegetation—mosses, ferns, saplings, and abundant northern white cedar—grows above this line. Below, only a few plants have reestablished themselves next to the few surviving trees.

A yellow birch perches over the trail, its roots growing up, down, and sideways in search of anchor and sustenance. Bark was scoured off the tree and heaps of rocks, sticks, and stumps, are wedged behind it up the hillside.

On the left is the Cathedral, another lateral fault, or tension joint, the height of the chasm. Sunlight filters through its apse of arched hemlocks.

The walls of the chasm get closer together and rise high as the trail descends. Look at the layers of sandstone and quartzite, their relative durability, changes in color and texture, and vulnerability to erosion. Don't forget to look up, too, to appreciate the height of the chasm walls.

At the end of the walkway, stairs go up to the left for the return by bus. Steps down to the right lead to a removable aluminum bridge across the river to Table Rock, departure point for the rafts.

The raft glides through the twelve-foot-wide Grand Flume. It then floats past two clefts in the chasm wall, the Sentry Box on the right and the Broken Needle on the left, the latter with a massive chunk of leaning rock. At the Whirlpool Basin the river appears to flow uphill as the striations on the rock walls play tricks with our eyes. Some gentle rapids speed the raft into a basin, where the walls of the canyon disappear and the river widens. The Ausable looks like any sleepy river as it flows gently out of sight.

HOW THE CHASM CAME TO BE

More than 500 million years ago the ancient Adirondack Mountains were on the east coast of an early North American continent. Over the years, 100 million more or less, wind and weather eroded these mountains into sediment, which ran down the flanks and accumulated along the ocean shore. This sediment, combined with vestiges of marine life, eventually compressed to form sandstone, layer upon layer of minerals and organic debris. Through subsequent mountain-building events, this sandstone came to the surface.

As rocks go, sandstone is relatively soft. During the Ice Age glaciers covered the area and scraped off much of the sandstone. As the glaciers melted and the Ausable River formed, it found a channel in the soft sandstone and began to erode it. The release of pressure as the weight of the ice was removed caused tension joints. These irregularities, minor faults, and differences in texture and hardness produced uneven erosion and account for the clefts along the sides of the gorge.

Hours, Fees, Facilities

Ausable Chasm is open from mid-May until early October; the exact dates are weather dependent. The walking tour is self-guided and available from 9:30 A.M. to 4:30 P.M. The raft trips depart about every ten minutes.

Admission for the walk and return bus, $9 for adults and children twelve and older. Seniors and children five through eleven, $7. Admission for the walk, raft ride, and return bus is $19 for adults and $17 for seniors and children.

Getting There

Take I-87 Exit 35 and follow Route 442 east for 3.0 miles. Turn right on Route 9 south. You cross the wide, slow-flowing Ausable River after 1.4 miles. Continue until you cross it again as it enters the chasm at 3.8 miles. Parking is on both sides of the bridge.

From the intersection of Route 9, 9N, and 22 in Ausable Chasm, take Route 9 north for 1.4 miles to the parking area.

For More Information

Ausable Chasm
P. O. Box 390
Ausable Chasm, NY 12911
800-537-1211

In the Area

Clintonville Pine Barrens, Ausable Forks

This unusual pitch pine–heath barrens is maintained naturally by fire. The Adirondack Nature Conservancy and Adirondack Land Trust plan to manage the property using prescribed burns, on which the community's survival depends.

Contact the Adirondack Nature Conservancy for further information. (See Organizations: Useful Names and Addresses.)

Coon Mountain Preserve

Westport

2.0 miles round-trip, 500-foot elevation gain

1.5 hours

moderate with a rocky section

A short and sweet mountain to conquer, with wildflowers,
wild blueberries, and sensational lake and mountain views.
Wear hiking boots.

This monadnock is a compact knob at the edge of the Champlain Valley. Expansive views stretch southeast to Lake Champlain and west across agricultural valleys to the Adirondack peaks. The trail passes some impressive rock faces. Outcroppings at the summit are great for a picnic, and in season you'll find wild blueberries. You may even see kettles of migrating hawks in spring and fall.

Vegetation is lush and diverse on Coon Mountain. A number of calciphiles, plants that prefer limy soil, grow on the lower slopes, while the summit hosts acid-loving trees and shrubs. This is a northern outpost of red and white oak and shagbark hickory, trees that reach the limit of their range in the Champlain Valley.

A legend tells of the Coon Mountain panther that cried like a maiden in distress, luring local men into the deep woods. Many did not return from these forays. The panther was allegedly shot but its body was never found. The last stronghold of the panther or mountain lion (*Felis concolor*) in the Northeast was in the Adirondacks; the most recent credible record is from 1903. East of the Mississippi the large, pale brown, unspotted cat lives only in the swamps of Florida.

Coon Mountain is a joint project of the Adirondack Land Trust (ALT) and the Adirondack Chapter of the Nature Conservancy. The ALT protects working lands with a goal of protecting productive forests, agricultural land, and natural areas. The Nature Conservancy manages the property.

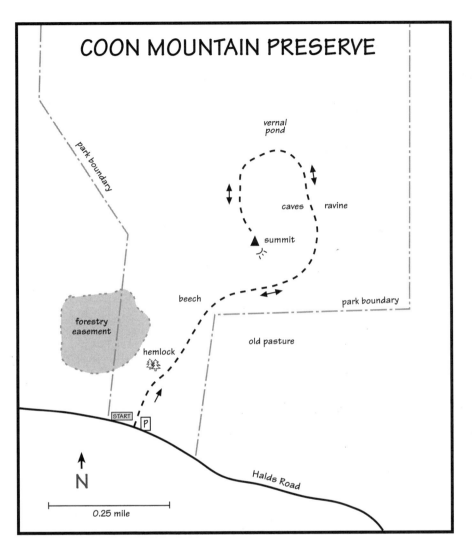

COON MOUNTAIN PRESERVE

vernal
pond

caves   ravine

▲ summit

beech

park boundary

forestry
easement

hemlock

old pasture

START P

N

Halds Road

0.25 mile

The walk begins in young woods where none of the trees is very large or mature. Jewelweed and ferns are abundant in the damp soil. The adjoining 73 acres to the west are privately owned but conserved with the ALT for preservation and forestry. Selective logging is intended to allow the land to reseed naturally.

The woods thicken as hemlocks dominate briefly. We then pass into woods of hickory, oak, beech, and maple. The red and white oaks and shag-bark hickories grow only at lower elevations on Coon Mountain. Other than in the warm Champlain Valley, these trees are not found in the north country. The low elevation, southern exposure, and warming influence of the lake combine to make this a hospitable location.

On the left, pale gray beech trunks stand out against the dramatic backdrop of a cliff. Look carefully at the beech bark for bear claw marks. Beechnuts, high in fat and protein, are a favorite food of bears as they bulk up for winter sleep. (See Surviving Winter, p. 251.)

A large red oak on the right, bristling with barbed wire, tells us that this was once pastureland. Some fast-growing large-toothed aspen are among the tallest trees. These trees don't grow beyond fifty feet but they do grow quickly.

As we start up a rocky scramble, jewelweed tells us the soil is damp, and herb Robert and basswood trees confirm its fertility. Maidenhair fern prefers limy soil and we will see several patches of this unusual fern. Its fronds are lacy and grow in a near-circle.

View to the southeast over Lake Champlain from Coon Mountain.

When you come face to face with a rock cliff, the trail goes right. Detour just a few feet to the left for a shimmering view of Lake Champlain.

The trail is very rocky as it continues. Lichen, like peeling paint, clings to the rocky overhang, and moss is thick on the wetter sections. Many of the moss-covered rocks are home to ferns, wildflowers, and saplings. The rocky caves are home to porcupines. Look for the neatly gnawed, irregular patches of tree bark they have eaten.

Flowering plants are thick on both sides of the trail: false Solomon's seal, trillium, twisted stalk, perfoliate bellwort, sweet cecily, and blue cohosh. You can recognize blue cohosh by its cluster of bright blue berries and compound leaves with twenty seven leaflets.

The trail levels out and the footing is effortless. Striped maple and hobblebush are thick in the understory. Next year's yellow hobblebush buds are already swelling in August.

With snowmelt and abundant spring rains, vernal pools develop in several hollows here. The water evaporates later in the season, but not before providing an important breeding place for frogs and salamanders.

The trail rises gradually toward the summit, always bending to the left in a near-circle. The vegetation changes to more acid loving plants. The thin layer of soil over the igneous bedrock anchors red and white pines, juniper, and lowbush blueberries. Wild lily of the valley and pink lady's slipper are among the few wildflowers.

Don't miss the two summit areas, one facing west to the Adirondacks and the other looking south over Lake Champlain.

❖ SURVIVING WINTER (WITHOUT A WOOD STOVE)

How do animals survive the rigors of a northern winter? Some birds and butterflies migrate; animals may become dormant or hibernate; others simply persevere, searching for food and shelter in the snow, your stone wall, or the compost heap.

Warm-blooded mammals have little temperature flexibility. They must maintain a narrow range of body temperature in extraordinary swings of outdoor temperature. Few animals actually hibernate, a deep, long-lasting sleep in which the body temperature lowers and heart rate plummets. Bats, the jumping mouse, and the woodchuck are among the hibernators. Come spring, the animals' heartbeats accelerate and their body temperatures rise until they become alert again.

Dormant animals are more active, sleeping and waking intermittently in burrows, tree cavities, caves, and other shelters from wind and cold. On warm days they may venture out in search of food. The raccoon, skunk, and chipmunk may experience some lowering of body temperature but not to the degree of the hibernators. Black bears are also dormant.

The majority of local mammals do what too many humans do—they accumulate an extra layer of fat and do their best. Fur coats thicken. Deer grow hollow hairs to retain additional body heat. Snowshoe hares and weasels turn white for camouflage against the snow. Grouse grow comblike bristles on their toes, which serve as snowshoes, while extra fur serves a similar purpose for the snowshoe hare.

What becomes of pond dwellers? Unable to regulate their body temperatures, cold-blooded animals slow down, their activities and metabolism virtually stopping, as they slumber through the cold with minimal needs. They generally survive if they are not encased in solid ice. Protected beneath the ice in water that never freezes, these creatures are insulated from temperatures that may plunge well below zero.

Amphibians, such as frogs and toads, may sleep through winter on land. Other amphibians lay eggs in the fall before dying. The eggs will hatch in the spring.

Getting There

From the intersection of Routes 9N and 22 in the village of Westport, take Route 22. Turn right on Lake Shore Road at 0.4 mile. At Halds Road, in 2.5 miles, turn left. The parking area is on the right in 0.6 mile.

For More Information

Adirondack Nature Conservancy
P.O. Box 65
Keene Valley, NY 12943
518-576-2082

Organizations:
Useful Names and
Addresses

Addison County Chamber of
Commerce
2 Court Street
Middlebury, VT 05753
802-388-7951

Appalachian Mountain Club
5 Joy Street
Boston, MA 02108
617-523-0655

Birds of Vermont Museum
900 Sherman Hollow Road
Huntington, VT 05462
802-434-2167

Bluebirds Across Vermont
c/o Green Mountain Audubon Society
255 Sherman Hollow Road
Huntington, VT 05462
802-434-3068

Catamount Trail Association
P. O. Box 1235
Burlington, VT 05402
802-864-5794

Central Vermont Chamber of
Commerce
P. O. Box 336G
Barre, VT 05642
802-229-5711

Town of Colchester
Recreation Department
Blakely Road
Colchester, VT 05446
802-655-0811

Ethan Allen Homestead Trust
1 Ethan Allen Homestead, Suite 2
Burlington, VT 05401-1141
802-865-4556

Green Mountain Audubon Nature
Center
255 Sherman Hollow Road
Huntington, VT 05462
802-434-3068

Green Mountain Club
R.R. 1, Box 650
Waterbury Center, VT 05677
802-244-7037

Green Mountain National Forest
Middlebury Ranger District
R.D. 4, Box 1260
Middlebury, VT 05753
802-388-4362
TTY/Voice 802-388-6688

Intervale Foundation
128 Intervale Road
Burlington, VT 05401
802-660-3508

Keeping Track
P. O. Box 848
Richmond, VT 05477
802-434-7000

Lake Champlain Basin Program
54 West Shore Road
Grand Isle, VT 05458
802-372-3213

Lake Champlain Islands Chamber of
Commerce
Route 2
North Hero, VT 05474
802-372-5683

Lake Champlain Maritime Museum
Basin Harbor Road
Ferrisburg, VT 05456
802-475-2022

Lake Champlain Regional Chamber
of Commerce
60 Main Street
Burlington, VT 05401
802-863-3489

Mad River Path Association
P. O. Box 683
Waitsfield, VT 05673
802-496-PATH (7284)

Middlebury Area Land Trust
Route 7 South
Middlebury, VT 05753
802-388-1007

Missisquoi National Wildlife Refuge
P. O. Box 163
Swanton, VT 05488-0163
802-868-4781

City of Montpelier
Park Commission
39 Main Street
Montpelier, VT 05602
802-223-5141

Moosalamoo Partnership
c/o Brandon Area Chamber of
Commerce
P. O. Box 267
Brandon, VT 05733
802-247-6401

Mount Independence State Historic
Site
Orwell, VT 05760
802-759-2412

The Nature Conservancy-
Vermont Chapter
27 State Street
Montpelier, VT 05602
802-229-4425

Perkins Museum of Geology
University of Vermont
Colchester Avenue
Burlington, VT 05401
802-656-8694

Rock of Ages Corporation
P. O. Box 482
Barre, VT 05641
802-476-3119

Town of Shelburne
Parks & Recreation Department
P. O. Box 88
Shelburne, VT 05482
802-985-9551

Shelburne Farms
Harbor Road
Shelburne, VT 05482
802-985-8686

Sterling Falls Gorge Natural Area
91 Sterling Gorge Road
Stowe, VT 05672
802-253-9035
e-mail: gander07@realtor.com

Stowe Mountain Resort
5781 Mountain Road (Route 108)
Stowe, VT 05672
802-253-3000
http://www.stowe.com/smr

University of Vermont
Environmental Program
155 South Prospect Street
Burlington, VT 05401
802-656-4055

Vermont Department of
Fish and Wildlife
111 West Street
Essex Junction, VT 05452
802-878-1564; 800-640-3714

Vermont Department of Fish and
Wildlife
Nongame and Natural Heritage
Program
103 South Main Street
Waterbury, VT 05672
802-241-3700

Vermont Department of Forests,
Parks, and Recreation
Vermont Agency of Natural
Resources
103 South Main Street, 10 South
Waterbury, VT 05671-0603
802-241-3655
http://www.state.vt.us./anr/fpr/parks

Vermont Division for Historic
Preservation
135 State Street
Montpelier, VT 05633-1201
802-828-3051

Vermont Folklife Center
2 Court Street
Middlebury, VT 05753
802-388-4964

Vermont Historical Society
Pavilion Building
109 State Street
Montpelier, VT 05602
802-828-2291

Vermont Institute of Natural Science
(VINS)
R.R. 2, Box 532
Church Hill Road
Woodstock, VT 05091
802-457-2779

VINS-Montpelier
North Branch Nature Center
713 Elm Street, Route 12
Montpelier, VT 05602
802-229-6206

Vermont Youth Conservation Corps
92 South Main Street
P. O. Box 482
Waterbury, VT 05676
802-241-3699

Town of Williston
Department of Public Works
Town Hall
722 Williston Road
Williston, VT 05495
802-878-1239

Winooski Valley Park District
Ethan Allen Homestead
Burlington, VT 05401
802-863-5744

New York

Adirondack Nature Conservancy
& Adirondack Land Trust
P. O. Box 65
Keene Valley, NY 12943
518-576-2082

Ausable Chasm and Company
P. O. Box 390, Route 9
Ausable Chasm, NY 12911
518-834-7454
800-537-1211
Champlain Shores in the Adirondacks

Visitors and Convention Bureau
P. O. Box 310
101 West Bay Plaza
Plattsburgh, NY 12901-0310
518-563-1000

New York State Office of Parks,
Recreation and Historic Preservation
Point au Roche State Park
19 Camp Red Cloud Road
Plattsburgh, NY 12901
518-563-6444

New York State Office of Parks,
Recreation and Historic Preservation
Thousand Islands Region
P. O. Box 247
Keewaydin State Park
Alexandria Bay, NY 13607
315-482-2593

Bibliography

Bentley, W. A., and W. J. Humphreys. *Snow Crystals*. New York: Dover Publications, 1962.

Burns, G. P., and C. H. Otis. *The Handbook of Vermont Trees*. Rutland, Vermont: Charles E. Tuttle Company, 1979.

Cobb, Boughton. *A Field Guide to the Ferns*. Boston: Houghton Mifflin, 1975.

Day Hiker's Guide to Vermont. 3d ed.. Montpelier, Vermont: Green Mountain Club, 1989.

DiCesare, Laurie. *A Guide to Colchester's Parks and Natural Areas*. Colchester, Vermont: Colchester Parks and Recreation Department and Paw Prints Press, 1993.

Dodge, Harry W., Jr. *The Geology of D.A.R. State Park, Mt. Philo State Forest Park, Sand Bar State Park*. Montpelier, Vermont: Department of Water Resources, 1969.

Exploring Lake Champlain and Its Highlands. Burlington, Vermont: Lake Champlain Committee, 1981.

Gange, Jared. *Hiker's Guide to the Mountains of Vermont*. Huntington, Vermont: Huntington Graphics, 1994.

Gibbons, Euell. *Stalking the Wild Asparagus*. New York: David McKay Company, 1972.

Higbee, William Wallace. *Around the Mountains*. Charlotte, Vermont: Charlotte Historical Society, 1991.

Lawrence, Gale. *A Field Guide to the Familiar*. Englewood Cliffs, New Jersey: Prentice-Hall, 1984.

Lindemann, Bob, Mary Deaett, and the Green Mountain Club. *Fifty Hikes in Vermont*. 4th ed. Woodstock, Vermont: Backcountry Publications, 1997.

Lingelbach, Jenepher. *Hands-On Nature*. Woodstock, Vermont: Vermont Institute of Natural Science, 1988.

Long Trail Guide. 24th ed. Waterbury Center, Vermont: Green Mountain Club, 1996.

Ludlum, David M. *The Vermont Weather Book*. Montpelier, Vermont: Vermont Historical Society, 1985.

Mikolas, Mark. *Nature Walks in Southern Vermont*. Boston: Appalachian Mountain Club Books, 1995.

Miller, Dorcas. *Berry Finder: A Guide to Native Plants with Fleshy Fruits*. Berkeley, California: Nature Study Guild, 1986.

————*Track Finder: A Guide to Mammal Tracks of Eastern North America*. Berkeley, California: Nature Study Guild, 1981.

Natural Communities of Vermont: Uplands and Wetlands. Montpelier, Vermont: Vermont Agency of Natural Resources, 1996.

Petrides, George A. *Field Guide to Trees and Shrubs*. 2d ed. Boston: Houghton Mifflin, 1972.

Stewart, David P., and Paul MacClintock. *The Surficial Geology and Pleistocene History of Vermont*. Bulletin No. 31. Montpelier, Vermont: Department of Water Resources, 1969.

Stout, Marilyn. *Vermont Walks: Village and Countryside: Walking Tours of Forty-Three Vermont Villages and Their Surroundings*. Montpelier, Vermont: Vermont Life, 1995.

Van Diver, Bradford B. *Roadside Geology of Vermont and New Hampshire*. Missoula, Montana: Mountain Press Publishing, 1987.

Vermont Atlas and Gazetteer. 9th ed. Freeport, Maine: DeLorme, 1996.

Wessels, Tom. *Reading the Forested Landscape*. Woodstock, Vermont: Countryman Press, 1997.

About the Author

Elizabeth Bassett is a graduate of Wellesley College and holds a Master's degree from Tufts University. After more than a decade of city living in Boston, San Francisco, and New York, and Jeddah, Saudi Arabia, she and her family settled in Vermont's Champlain Valley.

Bassett's writing has appeared in *Vermont Life*, *National Gardening* magazine, *AMC Outdoors*, and *Wellesley* magazine, among other publications. Additionally, she is a regular contributor to *The Charlotte News*. She established the Vermont Institute of Natural Science's ELF Program (Environmental Learning for the Future), a hands-on nature program for young students, at the local elementary school. An EMT for many years, she served on Vermont's District #3 Emergency Medical Services Board and is active in many local organizations.

An avid runner, hiker, and skier, Bassett lives in Charlotte, Vermont where she savors the outdoors with her husband and their two children.

About the AMC

THE APPALACHIAN MOUNTAIN CLUB pursues an active conservation agenda while encouraging responsible recreation. Our philosophy is that successful, long-term conservation depends on firsthand experience of the natural environment. AMC's members pursue interests in hiking, canoeing, skiing, walking, rock climbing, bicycling, camping, kayaking, and backpacking, and—at the same time—help safeguard the environment.

Founded in 1876, the club has been at the forefront of the environmental protection movement. As cofounder of several leading New England environmental organizations, and as an active member working in coalition with these and many other groups, the AMC has successfully influenced legislation and public opinion.

Conservation

The most recent efforts in the AMC conservation program include river protection, Northern Forest Lands policy, Sterling Forest (NY) preservation, and support for the Clean Air Act. The AMC depends upon its active members and grassroots supporters to promote this conservation agenda.

Education

The AMC's education department offers members and the general public a wide range of workshops, from introductory camping to intensive Mountain Leadership School taught on the trails of the White Mountains.

In addition, volunteers in each chapter lead hundreds of outdoor activities and excursions and offer introductory instruction in backcountry sports.

Research

The AMC's research department focuses on the forces affecting the ecosystem, including ozone levels, acid rain and fog, climate change, rare flora and habitat protection, and air quality and visibility.

Trails Program

Another facet of the AMC is the trails program, which maintains more than 1,400 miles of trail (including 350 miles of the Appalachian Trail) and more than 50 shelters in the Northeast. Through a coordinated effort of volunteers, seasonal crews, and program staff, the AMC contributes more than 10,000 hours of public service work each summer in the area from Washington, D.C. to Maine.

In addition to supporting our work by becoming an AMC member, hikers can donate time as volunteers. The club offers four unique weekly volunteer base camps in New Hampshire, Maine, Massachusetts, and New York. We also sponsor ten-day service projects throughout the United States, Adopt-a-Trail programs, trails day events, trail skills workshops, and chapter and camp volunteer projects.

The AMC has a longstanding connection to Acadia National Park. Working in cooperation with the National Park Service and Friends of Acadia, the AMC Trails Program provides many opportunities to preserve the park's resources. These include half-day volunteer projects for guests at AMC's Echo Lake Camp, ten-day service projects, weeklong volunteer crews in the fall, and trails day events. For more information on these public service volunteer opportunities, contact the AMC Trails Program, Pinkham Notch Visitor Center, P.O. Box 298, Gorham NH 03581; 603-466-2721.

Alpine Huts

The club operates eight alpine huts in the White Mountains that provide shelter, bunks and blankets, and hearty meals for hikers. Pinkham Notch Visitor Center, at the foot of Mt. Washington, is base camp to the adventurous and the ideal location for individuals and families new to outdoor recreation. Comfortable bunkrooms, mountain hospitality, and home-cooked, family-style meals make Pinkham Notch Visitor Center a fun and affordable choice for lodging. For reservations, call 603-466-2727.

Publications

The AMC main office in Boston and at Pinkham Notch Visitor Center in New Hampshire, the bookstore and information center stock the entire line of AMC publications, as well as other trail and river guides, maps, reference materials, and the latest articles on conservation issues. Guidebooks and other AMC gifts are available by mail order 1-800-262-4455, or by writing AMC, P.O. Box 298, Gorham NH 03581. Also available from the bookstore or by subscription is Appalachia, the country's oldest mountaineering and conservation journal.

Index

Abenakis, 36, 42, 49, 239
Adirondacks, 10, 11, 16, 91, 92,
    131, 156, 183, 196, 248
Alburg Dunes State Park, 24
Alder
    black (winterberry), 67
    speckled, 170–71
Allen, Ethan, 44
Allen, Fanny, 44
Allen, Ira, 49
Allen Brook, 60
Allen Hill Trail, 104
Amphibians, 85–87, 252
Arrowhead (duck potato), 46,
    67–68
Ash
    black, 44
    white, 156
Avery, Samuel Putnam, 129

Baker, Remember, 49
Ball Island, 10
Basswood (linden) trees, 233–34
Beach gravel, 122
Beach pea, 74
Bears, 226, 250, 252
Beaver, 5, 34, 97, 179–80
Beech trees, 143, 152, 181, 250
    American, 172
    blue, 172
Bentley, W. A. "Snowflake," 35
Birches
    blue beech, 172
    paper (canoe/white), 174,
        232
    sweet (black or cherry), 112,
        174, 178, 231
    yellow (gray/silver), 174,
        187–88, 231–32
Bird's-foot trefoil, 76, 78
Birds of Vermont Museum, 164
Bird watching, 135–40, 143

Bitternut hickory, 92, 113
Blackberry, 160
Black Creek Trail, 1–7
Bladderwort, 238
Bloodroot, 84, 118
Blueberries, 214–15
Bluebirds, 6
Blue cohosh, 251
Bog cranberry, 67
Bogs, 47, 62, 65, 69–70
Box elder, 38, 71–72
Bronson Hill volcanic arc, 196
Browns River, 31
Buck Mountain, 120
Buckthorn, European, 110, 149
Burlington Woolen Mill, 50
Butter-and-eggs, 238
Butternut Hill, 93
Butternut trees, 156, 225, 228, 234
Buttonbush, 72–73
Button Point, 130
Buttons, 133

Calkins Farm, 39
Camel's Hump, 92, 127
Cardinal flower, 98
Carney, James, 227
Cedar, white, 125, 229
Cemeteries
    Hope, 197
    Ricker, 229
    Upper, 227
Champlain, Samuel de, 42
Champlain Mill, 51
Champlain Nature Trail, 129–34
Champlain Sea, 57, 114, 121–22,
    133
Charlotte the Whale, 134
Chasm, Ausable, 242–47
Chipmunks, 190
Chittenden, Thomas, 31
Chittenden Mill, 31

Clay Brook, 33
Clay soil, 110
Clintonia (blue-bead lily), 62, 188
Clintonville Pine Barrens, 247
Clossey, William, 227
Club moss, 61, 64, 177
Coach Barn, 92
Cobble beaches, 9, 11, 16, 21
Colchester Merino Mill, 51
Colchester Point, 65–66
Community gardens, 39–40
Conifers, 202–3
Cook's Garden, 39
Corral reef, fossilized, 129–33
Cottonwood, 39, 44, 92

Dalley, Dan, 233
Deer, 240–41
Dogwood, alternate-leaved, 232
Downy hudsonia, 65–66
Duckweed, 96

Eagle Bay, 11–12
Edge, 98
Elderberry, red, 91, 238
Ethan Allen Homestead, 36, 38,
    42–48
Eurasian water milfoil, 29

False hellebore, 33, 234
Farm Barn, 91
Farm Trail, 88–93
Fastie, Christopher, 94
Fens, 47, 48
Ferns
    bracken, 78–79, 172
    Christmas, 119, 152
    cinnamon, 3, 4–5, 62
    identifying, 119, 121
    interrupted, 3, 4
    life cycle of, 6
    maidenhair, 154, 250
    ostrich, 167
    polypody, 102, 119
    royal, 3, 4, 47
    sensitive, 3, 4, 47
    sweet, 79–80, 82
    walking, 154
    wood, 119

Fir, balsam, 189, 203, 213
Fire, role of, 81
Fish hatchery, 25–30
Fish lift, 53
Flowering alpine plants, 214
Fort Ticonderoga, 147, 149, 151
Fort Ticonderoga ferry, 151
Fringed polygala (gaywings), 154
Frost, Robert, 170–75

Geese, 135–36, 143
    Canada, 138
    greater snow, 138–39, 143
Ginger, wild, 225
Glacial erratics, 183, 200, 215,
    219–20
Glacial kame, 119, 158
Goldthread, 34, 62
Goodell, Almeron, 225–26
Goodell, Bert, 225
Gordon-Center House, 27
Gorge, defined, 221
Grand View House, 141
Granite quarry, 193–97
Grapevines, wild, 15
Green City Farm, 38, 39
Green Mountains, 10, 91, 130
Grouse, ruffed, 226

Half Moon Cove, 75
Hare's tail cotton grass, 215
Hawkins Bay, 127
Hawks, 117, 143
Hawley House, 123
Hawthorne trees, 10
Heaths, 215–16
Hemlocks, 12, 33, 58, 108, 125,
    187–88, 220–21
    eastern, 56, 59
Hepatica, 115, 153
Herbert, Patsy, 227
Herbert, Tom, 228
Herb Robert, 184–85
Heron, great blue, 136
Hibernation, 251
Higbee, William Wallace, 111
Hill, David, 225
Hill-Brownell Education Center, 44
Hires, Christine L., 158

Hobblebush (witch-hobble), 172, 177, 186
Hog peanut, 73
Hope Cemetery, 197
Hop hornbeam
    American, 172
    eastern (ironwood), 149
Horsetails, 15, 17
Howe, Frank, 31
Howe, Lucius, 31
Hubbard, John E., 198
Hyde, Jedediah, Jr., 30
Hyde log cabin, 30

Ice Age, 131–33
Indian Brook Reservoir, 82
Indian cucumber root, 221
Indian pipe, 62, 233
Indian pokeweed, 33, 234
Inn at Shelburne Farms, 91
Insects, 23
Interpretive Trail, 55–59
Island Farm Nature Trail, 9–10

Japanese knotweed, 206–7
Jewelweed (touch-me-not), 143, 146
Joe-pye weed, spotted, 207
Johnson farm, 225

Kettle holes, 60, 69
Killdeer, 18
Kill Kare State Park, 13
Knight, John, 14
Knight Point House, 14
Knight Tavern, 14
Krummholz, 214, 238

Labrador tea, 215
Lake Champlain Maritime Museum, 134
Lake Vermont, 114, 121–22, 132, 133
Lampreys, sea, 27, 29
Larch, 118, 203
Laurel
    bog, 67
    sheep, 67, 78

Leather leaf, 67
Lewis Creek, 106
Lichens, 102
Limestone, 104–5, 156–57
    cliffs, 51, 52
Lone Tree Hill, 90, 91
Loons, 127
Lycopodium, 61, 64

MacDonough Point, 123
Maples
    mountain, 231
    red (swamp), 5, 62, 74
    silver, 5, 39, 74, 97
    striped, 58, 177
    sugar, 15, 200
Maple syrup, 159
Maquam Bog, 65
Maquam Creek Trail, 1–7
Marshes, 47
Mayflower (trailing arbutus), 34, 78
Meadowsweet, 173
McCabes Brook, 94, 96, 97
McNeil Electric plant, 39
Meandering river, 169
Middlebury Range, 131
Miskell, David, 92
Moose, 225
Moss, 102
    club, 61, 64, 177
    sphagnum, 67, 69–70
Mountain lion (panther), 248
Mount Defiance, 147, 149
Mount Ellen, 130
Mount Independence, 147–51
Mount Mansfield, 211–16
Mt. Philo, 92, 114, 117–22, 127
Mt. Philo Inn, 117
Mullein, 238–39
Murphy, Jennifer, 55

Nettles
    stinging, 41, 186, 233
    wood, 38, 41, 233

Oak, 120
    black, 79

Oak (*continued*)
    bur, 109
    chestnut, 100, 102
    red, 15–16, 114, 239
    white, 114
Old growth, 109–10
Olmsted, Frederick Law, 99, 92
Otters, 209
Ovenbirds, 225
Oxbow, 169

Partridgeberry, 58, 64
Pease, George, 111
Pease Mountain, 92, 104, 111–16
Perkins, H. E., 55
Pinchot, Gifford, 89
Pines
    Austrian, 203
    pitch, 76, 79, 203, 247
    red, 57, 58, 118, 125, 203
    Scotch, 117–18, 203
    white, 56, 57, 61, 96, 109,
        112, 125, 203, 233
Pitcher plant, 68–69
Pitch pine, 76, 79, 203, 247
Potash Brook, 55, 56–57
Potholes, 53, 187, 219, 246
Praying mantises, 145
Purple loosestrife, 73, 74

Quaker Smith Point, 92
Quartzite, Monkton, 59, 114, 119,
    120

Raptors, 137, 145
Raspberry, 160
Ravens, 213
Red osier dogwood, 74
Redstone Quarry, 59
Red-winged blackbirds, 139–40
Rena Calkins Trail, 36, 38
Rhodora, 67
Ricker, Gideon, 229
Ricker, Joseph, 227
Robertson, Robert H., 90
Rokeby Museum, 128
Rutland and Burlington Railroad,
    111

St. Albans Bay, 9
Salmon, 53
Salmon Hole, 49, 53
Sand dunes, 24, 71–75, 240
Sassafras trees, 96
Schistosity, 220
Sedge
    Bigelow's, 215
    Pennsylvania, 154
    plantain-leaved, 152
Seed dispersal, 145–46
Sensory Trail, 160
Serviceberry trees, 113–14
Shagbark hickories, 15, 143
Sheep's Knoll, 93
Shelburne Bay Park, 94, 100–105
Shelburne Farms, 88–93, 94
Shelburne Point, 88, 94, 100
Shelburne Museum, 90, 93, 94, 96
Ship (Shin) Island, 130
Shorebirds, 38
Skunk cabbage, 46
Snail-like fossils, 131
Snake Mountain, 114, 120, 130,
    137, 141–46
Sparrows, white-throated, 213
Sphagnum moss, 67, 69–70
Spiders, 16–17
Spikenard, 177
Spruces
    black, 171–72, 203
    Norway, 118, 203
    red, 171, 172, 203
Stinging nettles, 41, 186, 233
Sugarbush Range, 130
Sumac, 13
Summit House, 211
Sunderland Brook, 76
Swamps, 47

Tamarack, 118, 203
Thimbleberry, 160
Thorp Brook, 106, 109
Ticonderoga, 96
Tracking, 98–99
Trail Around Middlebury (TAM),
    175

Trees
    identifying, 163
    old, 109–10
    pioneer, 12–13
Trillium
    large-flowered, 123, 125, 191
    painted, 192
    purple, 192
    red and white, 114–15
Trout lilies, 131
Turkey, wild, 116
Turtlehead, 47
Turtles, 21, 144

Vermont Railroad, 106
Virginia creeper, 15, 38
Virginia waterleaf, 185
Virgin's-bower, 208

Walking stick, 145
Water arum (wild calla), 46, 68
Waterbury Center Day-Use Park,
    230, 235
Water skaters (striders), 33, 39
Webb, Derrick, 90, 91
Webb, Electra Havemeyer, 90
Webb, James Watson, 90
Webb, Lila Vanderbilt, 88
Webb, William Seward, 88, 90

Welcher, Amy, 129–30
Wells, 228–29
Wessels, Tom, 81, 156
Wetlands, 47–48
White Mountains, 196
Wild bergamot, 10
Wild cucumber (balsam apple), 38,
    167
Williams, Arthur, 106
Willow, 73, 74
    black (swamp), 39, 44, 47
Winooski One, 51, 52–53
Wintergreen, 57, 78
Winter survival, animals and,
    251–52
Witch hazel, 183
Woodcock, 3, 20, 21–22
Wood nettles, 38, 41, 233
Woodpeckers, 58, 125
Wool mills, 50–51

Yew, American (ground hemlock),
    127

Zebra mussels, 29

Alphabetical Listing of Areas

Abbey Pond Trail, p. 176

Allen Hill, p. 100

Ausable Chasm, p. 242

Burton Island State Park, p. 8

Button Bay State Park, p. 129

Colchester Bog Natural Area, p. 65

Colchester Pond, p. 82

Coon Mountain Preserve, p. 248

Dead Creek Wildlife Management Area, p. 135

Delta Park, p. 71

East Woods Natural Area, p. 55

Ed Weed Fish Culture Station, p. 25

Ethan Allen Homestead, p. 42

Green Mountain Audubon Nature Center, p. 158

Hubbard Park, p. 198

Intervale, p. 36

Kingsland Bay State Park, p. 123

Knight Point State Park, p. 14

LaPlatte River Marsh Natural Area, p. 94

Leicester Hollow and Chandler Ridge, p. 181

Little River State Park, History Trail, p. 223

Little River State Park, Stevenson Brook Nature Trail, p. 231

Mad River Greenway, p. 165

Missisquoi National Wildlife Refuge, p. 1

Mount Independence Historical Site, p. 147

Mt. Philo State Park, p. 117

Mount Mansfield, Tundra Trail, p. 211

Mud Pond Conservation Land, p. 60

North Branch Nature Center and North Branch River Park, p. 204

North Hero State Park, p. 19

Old Mill Park, p. 31

Pease Mountain Natural Area, p. 111

Point au Roche State Park, p. 236

Robert Frost Interpretive Trail, p. 170

Rock of Ages Granite Quarry, p. 193

Shaw Mountain Natural Area, p. 152

Shelburne Farms, p. 88

Snake Mountain Wildlife Management Area, p. 141

Sterling Falls Gorge Natural Area, p. 217

Sunny Hollow, p. 76

Texas Falls, p. 187

Williams Woods Natural Area, p. 106

Winooski Nature Trail, Winooski One, and Salmon Hole, p. 49